Hiking
New Hampshire

Second Edition

Larry Pletcher

**American
Hiking
Society**

Published in Cooperation with the
American Hiking Society

FALCON®

Guilford, Connecticut
An imprint of The Globe Pequot Press

Cover photo of Franconia Ridge Trail / © New England Stock

All black-and-white photos by the author unless otherwise noted.

Library of Congress Cataloging-in-Publication Data is available.

ISBN 1-56044-789-3

♻ Text pages printed on recycled paper.

Manufactured in the United States of America
Second Edition/First Printing

CAUTION
Outdoor recreational activities are by their very nature potentially hazardous. All participants in such activities must assume the responsibility for their own actions and safety. The information contained in this guidebook cannot replace sound judgment and good decision-making skills, which help reduce risk exposure, nor does the scope of this book allow for disclosure of all the potential hazards and risks involved in such activities.

Learn as much as possible about the outdoor recreational activities in which you participate, prepare for the unexpected, and be cautious. The reward will be a safer and more enjoyable experience.

Contents

Acknowledgments vii

Map Legend viii

Overview Map ix

Introduction 1

Fundamentals 4

    Things to Know Before You Go 4

    Weather 5

    Preparation 7

    Bugs and Other Nuisances 7

    Respecting the Land 8

    Wilderness Areas, Forest Protection Areas, and No-Trace Camping 9

    Parking Fees in White Mountain National Forest 10

    Treading Lightly 11

Enjoying the Trail 12

    Hiking with Children 12

    Hiking for the Physically Challenged 13

    Huts, Tent Platforms, and Shelters 14

    Hiker Shuttle 15

    Wildlife 15

    Plants and Trees 17

THE HIKES

The Seacoast

    1 Blue Job Mountain 18

    2 Great Bay Estuarine Reserve 21

    3 Great Bay National Wildlife Refuge 25

    4 Odiorne Point State Park 27

    5 Urban Forestry Center, Brooks Trail 30

Merrimack Valley

    6 Silk Farm Wildlife Sanctuary 33

    7 Bear Brook State Park, Catamount Trail 36

    8 Hyla Brook Nature/Poetry Trail 39

    9 Mine Falls Park, Nashua River Trail 41

   10 Pawtuckaway State Park, Boulder Field Trail 44

   11 Pawtuckaway State Park, South Mountain Loop 47

   12 Uncanoonuc, North Peak 50

Monadnock Region

   13 Crotched Mountain 54

   14 DePierrefeu-Willard Pond Wildlife Sanctuary 57

15 Harris Center for Conservation Education, Harriskat Trail 60
16 Mount Monadnock, Pumpelly Trail 63
17 Mount Monadnock, White Cross Trail 66
18 Pack Monadnock, Wapack Trail 68
19 Pisgah State Park, Kilburn Loop 71
20 Rhododendron State Park 74
21 Sheldrick Forest 76

Dartmouth/Lake Sunapee Region

22 Fox State Forest, Ridge Trail 79
23 John Hay National Wildlife Refuge 82
24 Mount Kearsarge, Rollins Trail 85
25 Mount Kearsarge, Winslow Trail 89
26 Philbrick-Cricenti Bog 90
27 Pillsbury State Park, Monadnock-Sunapee Greenway 94
28 Ragged Mountain 97
29 Mount Sunapee, Andrew Brook Trail 101

Lakes Region

30 Mount Cardigan, West Ridge Trail 104
31 Mount Cardigan, Manning Trail 108
32 Mount Chocorua, Liberty Trail 110
33 The Loon Center at the Markus Wildlife Sanctuary 114
34 Hebron Marsh and Paradise Point 117
35 Mount Major 120
36 Mount Passaconaway, Dicey's Mill Trail 122
37 Squam Lakes Natural Science Center 126
38 Belknap Mountain, Red Trail 128
39 West Rattlesnake 130
40 Three Ponds Trail 133
41 White Lake State Park 136

The White Mountains

Waterville Valley 139
42 Mount Tripyramid, Livermore Road 140
43 Greeley Ponds and Mount Osceola 143
44 Cascade Path 147
45 Sandwich Mountain, Algonquin Trail 149
46 Guinea and Black Mountain Pond Trails 152
47 Mount Tecumseh 156
48 Welch and Dickey Mountains 158

Mount Moosilauke 162
49 Glencliff Trail 163
50 Gorge Brook, Asquam Ridge Loop 165

Franconia Notch 168
51 The Flume 168
52 Cannon Mountain, Kinsman Ridge Trail 171
53 Mount Lafayette/Mount Lincoln, Bridle Path Loop 174
54 Liberty Spring Trail, Mount Liberty/Mount Flume 177
55 Lonesome Lake and Kinsman Peaks 181
56 The Old Man and Profile Lake 184
57 Mount Pemigewasset 186

Crawford Notch 189
58 Arethusa Falls Trail 189
59 Mount Carrigain, Signal Ridge Trail 193
60 Crawford Path, Mizpah Spring Loop 196
61 Nancy Pond Trail 200
62 Rocky Branch, Davis Path, Isolation Trail Loop 204
63 Dry River, Mount Isolation 207
64 Mount Willard 211
65 Webster-Jackson Trail 213

Pemigewasset Wilderness and Zeland Notch 216
66 Ethan Pond Trail 216
67 Gale River and Bondcliff Trails 219
68 Mount Hale, Zealand Loop 223
69 Franconia Brook and Lincoln Brook Trails 227
70 Pemigewasset Traverse 230

Kancamagus Highway 234
71 Mount Chocorua, Champney Brook Trail 234
72 Hancock Notch Trail, Hancock Loop 237
73 Sawyer Pond Trail 240
74 Sabbaday Falls 243

North Conway 245
75 North and South Doublehead, The Old Path and Ski Trail 245
76 Mount Kearsarge North 248
77 Mountain Pond Trail 251
78 North Moat Mountain 254

Presidential Peaks 260
79 Mount Jefferson, Caps Ridge Trail 260
80 Cherry Mountain Trail 264
81 Edmands Path 267
82 King Ravine: The Air Line, Short Line, and King Ravine Trails ... 270
83 Lowe's Path, the Gray Knob Trail, the Randolph Path,
   and Edmands Col 275
84 Mount Madison, Valley Way Trail 279
85 Great Gulf Trail, Spaulding Lake 284
86 Presidential Traverse 289
87 Mount Washington, Ammonoosuc Ravine Trail 294
88 Mount Washington: Boott Spur and Davis Path 298

Carter Range 303
89 Imp Trail Loop 304
90 Carter-Moriah Trail 306
91 Nineteen Mile Brook Trail 309
92 Baldface Circle Trail 312
93 Wild River 317

Pilot Range 320
94 Rogers Ledge and Unknown Pond 320
95 Mount Starr King/Mount Waumbeck 324

The North Country
96   Table Rock, Dixville Notch 326
97   Fourth Connecticut Lake 329
98   Nash Stream, Sugarloaf Mountain Trail 331
99   Phillips Brook Backcountry Recreation Area 334
100 Scotland Brook 337

Appendices
Appendix A: USDA Forest Service Offices 340
Appendix B: Trail Ratings and Equipment 341

Index 343
About the Author 349

Acknowledgments

While doing the playful work of preparing this guide, I've been heartened to discover that the forests, mountains, and wilderness areas that make up this fabulous state are in friendly and caring hands. Field personnel from federal, state, and local agencies, as well as private hiking and conservation organizations, have revealed their knowledge, good humor, and dedication countless times and in multiple ways. I'll never know their names, but my appreciation goes to each of the many people who enthusiastically provided assistance as I wandered the trails of New Hampshire.

A few special thanks are in order. Tim and Barbara for their timely advice, Randall for his welcome encouragement, Peter for the borrowed darkroom, Ted for Hike 75, and especially Dwight, wherever you are, for that first trip on Mount Moosilauke some twenty-odd years ago.

I've learned too, that even enjoyable projects require the abiding love and patience of the people closest to you. This book is dedicated to Carol and Jen, who never wavered in their support.

Map Legend

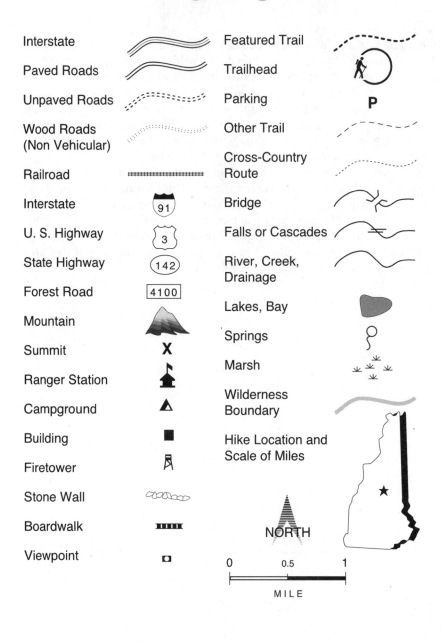

Interstate		Featured Trail	
Paved Roads		Trailhead	
Unpaved Roads		Parking	P
Wood Roads (Non Vehicular)		Other Trail	
Railroad		Cross-Country Route	
Interstate	91	Bridge	
U. S. Highway	3	Falls or Cascades	
State Highway	142	River, Creek, Drainage	
Forest Road	4100	Lakes, Bay	
Mountain		Springs	
Summit	X	Marsh	
Ranger Station		Wilderness Boundary	
Campground		Hike Location and Scale of Miles	
Building			
Firetower			
Stone Wall			
Boardwalk			
Viewpoint			

NORTH

0   0.5   1

MILE

Overview Map

Swinging Bridge carries the Wilderness Trail across the Pemigewasset.

Introduction

From the alpine summit of Mount Washington to the crashing ocean surf at Odiorne Point, New Hampshire was made for hiking. Throughout the state, a boundless assortment of well-marked trails unveils the brilliant spectrum of nature's diversity.

Lace up your boots and sample New Hampshire's variety. Find the secluded headwaters of the Connecticut River among countless acres of North Country forest. Climb the challenging Caps Ridge Trail over White Mountain granite to Presidential Peaks. Disappear for a few mellow days near the shore of Shoal Pond, or admire Thoreau Falls in the heart of the Pemigewasset Wilderness. Explore a notch: Crawford, Sandwich, Dixville, Zealand, or Franconia, where the Old Man lives. Follow Dry River to a mountain named Isolation, or the Davis Path to the Bigelow Lawn. In a state where nature is never far away, trails await that are even closer to home. Watch a blue heron work a riverbank in the urban core of the Merrimack Valley. Walk the shore of a vast saltwater estuary on Adam's Point by Great Bay. Hike with your family to a fire tower overlooking Lake Sunapee, or backpack through a forgotten park full of wildlife in easily accessible central New Hampshire.

The more you explore nature's intricate array, the more you will sense the subtle variations in the fabric of this land.

The view of Hollywood's Golden Pond (what we call Squam Lake) at the end of the West Rattlesnake Trail will feel intimate and peaceful compared to the powerful vista from nearby Mount Major. Set in the soft texture of its surrounding plain, the glacially scoured symmetry of majestic Mount Monadnock will uplift your spirits. Circled by immense White Mountain peaks, awesome, ice-gouged Great Gulf will demand humility. Explore Great Turkey, Willard, Greeley, and Mud Ponds, Pisgah Lake, or Lake Solitude. Distinctive memories will remain, along with a conviction that each was unique.

The wide diversity and subtle variations in New Hampshire's environment are reflected in the trails included in this hiking guide. Whether you are a family day-tripper or long-distance hiker, old hand or novice, you will find in this guide outings suited to every ability and interest in all sections of the state. To capture this diversity, one hundred hikes have been selected throughout seven traditional regions of New Hampshire, with the enriched resource of the White Mountains further divided into ten ranges or zones. Locate trails, if you wish, that carry few footsteps, enthrall your children, accommodate disabilities, or extend the season when winter still grips higher terrain. With abundant maps and trail descriptions designed to convey the feel of each hike, this guide will help you quickly find what you like and plan your adventure.

While exploring this state's natural gifts, you will find that New Hampshire is a curiously civilized place. One hundred and fifty years ago, 80 percent of the state was covered with field and pasture. Today, more than 85 percent is forested. Signs of human habitation from generations past echo in

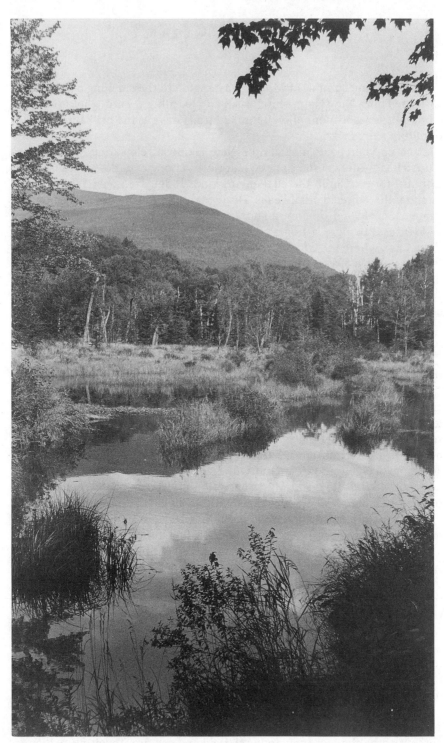

Backcountry views of the Sandwich Range.

the woods along many of the hikes described in this guide. Miles into the forest, high on the side of a hill, stone walls disappear beyond tree trunks, and old foundations hint at human ventures long since decayed. I have included only a taste of the intriguing history of these remains. As for the rest, I ask you to pause on occasion as you walk these trails to hear what insights such artifacts whisper of our relationship to the environment and of the enduring quality of this land.

Though civilized, New Hampshire is anything but tame. The alpine regions of the White Mountains are reputed to have the worst weather in America. First climbed by Europeans 350 years ago, Mount Washington and other New Hampshire peaks still challenge the hiker's stamina—and even the hiker's ability to survive. Read this Introduction and Appendix B of this guide for specific suggestions to prepare for either a safe, properly equipped hike to a rigorous peak or a comfortable outing to a quiet woodland wilderness.

As we travel this fabulous terrain, each of us must do our part so as not to destroy what we came to appreciate. Please walk softly and be considerate of your fellow beings. The introductory sections of this guide explain techniques of low-impact camping now mandated by regulation in portions of White Mountain National Forest. Observe the golden rule of "Pack it in; pack it out," and understand the need to stay on the trail in alpine zones, where even our footsteps must not be left behind if fragile plant species are to survive.

Trails, abandoned roads, and logging paths abound in this state, and rambling through the woods is a local tradition. The one hundred hikes in this guide are merely a sample of these many trails. I could not describe them all; I wouldn't want to. This book is a guide that points the way. Treat the land with respect and be free to discover your own favorite place in the nooks and crannies of a state made for hiking.

Fundamentals

THINGS TO KNOW BEFORE YOU GO

Nature has been unusually kind to New Hampshire, endowing it with inordinate beauty and few inherent dangers that prevent its enjoyment. Specters of grizzly bears do not haunt our trails, and experienced naturalists are hard pressed to find any poisonous snakes that may remain. I suppose it is this lack of notorious concerns that allows many people to blithely venture forth with little understanding of the more commonplace hazards of backcountry travel.

In truth, the greatest danger on New Hampshire trails is the lack of preparation, judgment, and old-fashioned common sense that we humans bring with us. This failing may result from the unique parameters of the natural world we encounter—especially in the White Mountains. Our senses simply resist the notion that hypothermia may await on a friendly looking peak that we observe from below in the warm sun and cool breeze of a mellow summer day.

On most trails, of course, hikers do not encounter such extremes. The **General description, Elevation gain,** and **Difficulty** ratings that appear at the beginning of each hike in this guide serve as quick reference indicators of the trail conditions you will find. While useful, keep in mind that such information can never replace preparation, judgment, and common sense. You still need to know how to evaluate changes in weather, tailor your preparation to the character of the hike, and pass over the land with minimal impact. The following should help you safely get started.

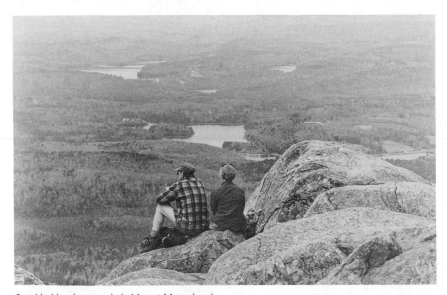

Speckled landscapes circle Mount Monadnock.

WEATHER

New Hampshire is blessed with extended seasons of gorgeous hiking weather. By April, a few mild days make spring walks through woodlands or to small mountain peaks perfect cures for the memory of winter. Summers are warm, even hot at times. Dry polar air limits sultry conditions to a handful of days and cools the nights for comfortable sleeping. Autumn is perfect, a time when the woods blaze with color, and crisp cool air makes everyone a hiker.

Why then, with such wonderful conditions, are some trails posted with signs that warn hikers about the "Worst weather in America?"

The summits of many of New Hampshire's largest mountains virtually inhabit a different part of the world. The climate is arctic, featuring plant species common to Labrador and Greenland. Wind speeds have been clocked at more than 230 miles per hour, and 72 degrees F is the warmest temperature ever recorded on the summit of Mount Washington. A good day will be cool and windy. On my last visit to the Presidential Peaks it was 38 degrees, visibility was less than 100 feet in fog and driving rain, winds were gusting to 45 miles per hour, and possible thunderstorms were in the forecast. It was late July. People have lost their lives to such conditions in August.

Mount Washington weather is often unrelated to conditions found in the rest of the state. It is common to drive two hours under beautiful blue skies only to find this peak obscured by clouds. To complicate matters, it is difficult to obtain accurate predictions for White Mountain weather. The statewide forecast available from the National Weather Service in Concord by calling 603-225-3280 has the best chance of conveying a reliable picture in advance of your trip. Once in the area, the Appalachian Mountain Club (AMC) facility at Pinkham Notch provides dependable reports of current summit conditions, as well as reality checks for prospective hikers dressed in T-shirts and sneakers.

The best method for dealing with harsh weather is to avoid it. Obvious advice, yet hikers invariably make the mistake of pushing on in an effort to bag a peak in the face of deteriorating weather. Higher altitude will only bring colder, wetter, and windier conditions. Problems will be greatly magnified above timberline, where foul weather makes trails difficult to follow.

The hikes described throughout this book stress the fabulous scenery that can be found well below the mountain summits. Neither the hiking experience nor your reputation will be ruined if you don't make it all the way to the top. If conditions cause the least shred of doubt in your mind, turn back from the peak, or stay at lower altitudes. Better yet, use this guide to select a hike in a less mountainous region of the state, where the weather may very well be lovely.

Remember, too, that hypothermia can occur at temperatures well above freezing, that being damp accentuates the hazard, and that it need not be raining for summer hikers to be at risk. A sweaty struggle up a mountain peak, a brush against wet evergreens, and a stiff breeze with temperatures in the 50s can lead to the lowering of core body temperature that defines hypothermia. Preparation and prevention are the best cures. Anticipate cold

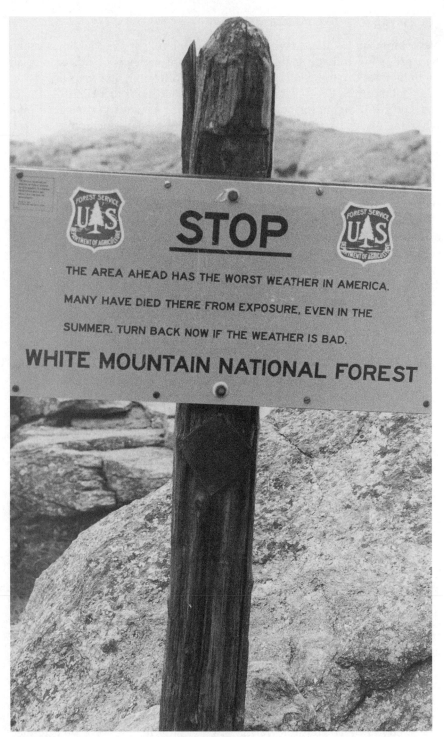

A high peak reminder of the need for common sense.

temperatures at high altitude, layer your clothing, always pack rain gear, and turn back when you sense you are pushing your limits.

Lightning is a concern, yet if common sense prevails, it is possible to quickly descend and readily avoid danger on most New Hampshire trails. There are always exceptions. A weather eye and sober consideration are required before venturing onto the knife-edge portion of Franconia Ridge or traversing the Presidential Peaks, where miles of exposed trail offer no escape and no protection. There is simply no excuse for being in such regions if storms are in the offing.

Especially in the high peaks, if the weather turns bad, thunderstorms threaten, or you are cold and wet and tired, get off the mountain as soon as possible, or seek shelter in any nearby hut. In extreme conditions, it is often better to immediately lose elevation rather than delay relief by trying to complete a preplanned route. Before setting out into areas prone to severe weather, experienced hikers anticipate the worst by locating escape routes that quickly lead below timberline to reliable protection. When preparation, good judgment, and experience fail, knowledge of such trails is a comforting backup.

PREPARATION

You don't need experience or specialized training to happily explore trails in New Hampshire, but your clothing and equipment must meet the demands of any conditions that could likely arise. Thoughtful preparation is the cornerstone of safe hiking. Some trails in this state can be walked in T-shirts and sneakers. On others, such attire may endanger your life. Hikers need to know the difference and prepare accordingly.

Remember, too, that cell phones and global positioning systems won't keep you warm and don't offer protection. Communication with the outside world is no replacement for self-reliance. Especially in the White Mountains, hikers who lack proper gear can easily die of exposure before rescue teams arrive. To stem an epidemic of avoidable emergencies, the New Hampshire Fish and Game Department now reminds hikers that they will be charged with substantial costs if their reckless or negligent actions necessitate a search and rescue.

Read Appendix B for information on trail ratings and specific details on what your pack should contain for easy, moderate, difficult, or extended hikes. Then check the trail information listed at the beginning of each hike for help in deciding what gear you'll want to carry on any trail you'd like to try.

BUGS AND OTHER NUISANCES

Black flies top this category hands down. These tiny bite-till-you-bleed monsters are the bane of New England. Luckily for us, they don't live very long. The first hatch appears in southern New Hampshire early in May before sweeping northward to pester the White Mountains late into June. Everything from foul-smelling home-brews to a well-known women's skin softener is employed to repel these creatures. I stick with any good commercial product with DEET because it also repels mosquitoes that come later. Altitude and strong breezes help to discourage both of these pests, which are naturally past their peak by mid-July.

Deer ticks *(Ixodes dammini)* may carry Lyme disease. The flu-like symptoms of this illness include fever, chills, fatigue, and body aches; a distinctive bull's-eye rash may appear. Severe, long-term complications can result if left untreated. Although present in New Hampshire to only a limited degree, exposure should be considered a possibility in those parts of the state outside the high mountains. Covering your legs with long pants and spraying with a repellent containing DEET are recommended precautions. The good news is that the insect must be on your body many hours before the disease is transmitted. Do an inspection, and if the pinhead-sized tick is found on your skin, simply remove with tweezers as soon as you can. Contrary to conventional wisdom and for reasons that do not bear repeating, you should try not to kill or maim the critter until after you succeed in removing it from your body.

Giardia lamblia is a water-borne intestinal parasite that may be present in any surface water. To avoid debilitating diarrhea and cramps that require medical treatment, do not drink from streams, lakes, or rivers without first either purifying the water with a commercial filter fine enough to remove the Giardia, boiling the water for five minutes, or treating the water with iodine tablets in accordance with the tablets' instructions.

I hesitate to place beloved mammals into the same category as the scourges above, but black bears and moose can be a nuisance or worse. Black bears are not normally aggressive unless they have become habituated to raiding camp food or sense that you may endanger their young (a highly subjective bearish decision). Moose are fun to watch and often don't mind the attention. However, nearsighted males, never a jovial lot, become even less personable during rutting season. The rules are simple. Always hang your food pack overnight. Keep a respectful distance. Do not antagonize wildlife. A call to the nearest USDA Forest Service headquarters can help you avoid campsites where bears have been a problem.

RESPECTING THE LAND

I have often tried to figure out why some hikers continue to pollute their wilderness environment. Is it just inadvertence, or some insidious black hole of respect and awareness that only occurs in fresh mountain air? What else explains why people who would not dream of throwing food scraps out their kitchen window calmly toss such items about a campsite or trail?

Garbage does not change its character in a wilderness setting. My personal pet peeve, the orange peel, is routinely jettisoned as harmless "organic" litter but resists disintegration as a long-term survivor beside an alpine trail. Remember that "Pack it in; pack it out" is the golden rule of responsible hiking. Remember, too, that disposable juice containers are not disposable in backcountry campfires, and cigarette butts and candy wrappers seem to never disappear.

The obligation to respect and protect the trailside environment does not fall on backcountry campers alone. The numbers of people visiting our forests are simply so great that all of us must do our part to ensure that the terrain we travel retains no record of our visit. No candy wrappers, no orange peels, no charred bits of aluminum. Carry a small trash bag in your pack, and please consider taking the extra step of leaving the woodlands even cleaner than they were before you began.

WILDERNESS AREAS, FOREST PROTECTION AREAS, AND NO-TRACE CAMPING

Additional demands are made on overnight guests. Nearly 800,000 acres of White Mountain National Forest contain ample backpacking opportunities. The area is so large that a confusing assortment of regulations applies to various portions of these federal lands. Four wilderness areas carry the most stringent restrictions, prohibiting motorized and mechanical equipment (no mountain bikes!) and limiting hiking and camping groups to a maximum of ten.

Throughout the White Mountain National Forest, additional Forest Protection Areas (FPAs), (formerly called Restricted Use Areas, or RUAs) have also been established that prevent camping completely in some areas, within a quarter-mile of various shelters, roads, trails, and streams, and within 200 feet of certain heavily used trails. Except in the winter, no camping is permitted above timberline, defined as areas where trees are less than 8 feet tall.

Presently, outside of the Great Gulf Wilderness, clear maps of Forest Protection Areas are not available except as you find them posted at trailheads

Liberty Cabin on Mount Chocorua.

and on affected routes. Signs inform hikers when they enter or leave an FPA, but you need to obtain the written regulations in advance and read them carefully to plan an overnight trip into the backcountry. Ask for the "White Mountain National Forest Backcountry Camping Rules" at any of the USDA Forest Service offices listed in Appendix A.

The reality in New Hampshire is that limited backcountry camping is available outside of the White Mountain National Forest. State facilities permit camping and open fires only at designated campsites, and use of private land is subject to owner's permission and local regulation of open fires. If you do find a chance to camp elsewhere, protect the ecology by following the "No-Trace" rules promulgated by the USDA Forest Service, even in areas where those rules do not technically apply.

Outside of defined FPAs and wilderness areas, these rules of No-Trace camping are imposed only by your conscience. Please don't let the rest of us down. Select a campsite at least 200 feet from trails, lakes, and other water sources, limit the size of your group to ten or less, and attend to washing and sanitation at least the same 200 feet from campsites and sources of water.

If they ever truly existed, the days of trenching your tent, cutting boughs for bedding, and hacking up the forest for firewood are long since gone. Backcountry campfires are next on my list of outmoded practices that should eventually disappear. A backpacker's stove is more convenient for cooking and far kinder to the environment. If you really need the ambiance of an open fire, consider the use of shelters, designated campsites, and tent platforms that are widely scattered throughout the national forest. Most of these sites have fire rings and are a good way to accommodate backcountry use while limiting the impact on the woodland environment.

PARKING FEES IN WHITE MOUNTAIN NATIONAL FOREST

Since 1997, the White Mountain National Forest has participated in the Recreation Fee Demonstration Program, which imposes a new fee for parking in the national forest. While many hikers and residents are less than pleased by the new program, proceeds are meant to care for existing recreational facilities or to fund forest improvements. Details of the program have changed since its inception, and a grace period no longer applies. The bottom line for hikers is that all unattended vehicles in the White Mountain National Forest must display a parking sticker. If you don't have a sticker, you'll get a $50 fine.

As of this writing, seven-day stickers cost $5, annual stickers cost $20, and individual households can include a second vehicle for an additional $5 ($25 annual fee). A few trailheads have iron rangers where a day-pass for that location only can be purchased for $3 (if you have exact change).

Parking stickers are available at all Forest Service offices and from about fifty vendor locations in the vicinity of the national forest. Unfortunately, the locations of vendor outlets are subject to frequent change. Hikers are encouraged to call any Forest Service office (see Appendix A) for a current list of vendors where stickers can be obtained.

TREADING LIGHTLY

You may be surprised to discover how much effort is invested in maintaining routes for ease of climbing and erosion control. Walking outside the scope of established trails is generally unnecessary and hinders these efforts. Please stay on the trail.

Above timberline, the need to be wary of our own footsteps is even more critical. In some instances, endangered plant species lie perilously close to the trail, unremarkable to most hikers who pass them by. Whether endangered or not, plants in the alpine environment share thin soils, slow growth rates, and a delicacy that belies their harsh environment. These species do not recover rapidly from the tread of human footsteps. Some do not recover at all. They are part and parcel of the intricate beauty of high mountain summits that are very special destinations for New Hampshire hikers. Pass carefully and respect their right to survive in regions where thoughtless steps exact a heavy toll.

Enjoying the Trail

Above all else, hiking in New Hampshire is meant to be fun. Whether your interests include photography, botany, bird watching, human history, or the simple joy of warm sun on your face and a trail that leads somewhere new, you can draw pleasure from any facet of this sport that you happen to find appealing. For hikers of any age, experience, ability, or interest, the following information may add to your enjoyment of New Hampshire's trails.

HIKING WITH CHILDREN

Kids and trails are a natural combination. Including youngsters in this sport at the earliest age possible will increase the pleasure of both parents and

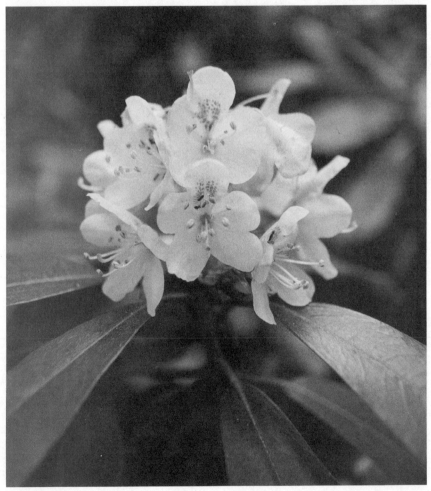

Rhododendron.

children. Even if toddlers just ride on your back, they are becoming attuned to the experience of hiking. In time, they will graduate to more grown-up efforts, and be off on their own with self-confidence and awareness that may last a lifetime.

Several trails in this hiker's guide indulge the very special interests of younger children. The Seacoast Science Center at Odiorne Point, featuring hands-on contact with ocean inhabitants, and the Squam Lakes Natural Science Center, with resident black bears, foxes, and otters, will be huge hits both with younger kids and their hiking companions of any age.

As children grow older, they can join in on wonderful family hikes found throughout New Hampshire. Try the Red Trail to Belknap Mountain, the easy walk from Rollins State Park to the top of Mount Kearsarge, or Waterville Valley's engaging Cascade Path. Consult the "General description" at the beginning of each hike in this guide to key yourself in to many more family outings and child-friendly trails that abound in this state.

Once families become seasoned New Hampshire hikers, children can be included on many of the "adult" trails described in this guide. Kids will be outright eager to carry their own small-sized pack, and are sure to be happy scrambling about summits like Mount Monadnock, or splashing in the waters of Greeley Ponds. Just be certain not to discourage kids with overly ambitious plans. Take extra time for frequent stops, and fuel them up often with juice and snacks. Also remember that in their own small-sized way, children need to be as well prepared as adults. On extended hikes, make sure that they carry at a minimum rain gear, wool hats, mittens, and extra clothing comparable to yours.

On longer trails, kids more amiably accept the challenges of hiking if they share the companionship of other children. Team up with other parents, or check with your local YMCA, school, or various hiking clubs that sponsor group trips throughout the state. Another alternative is to investigate trails associated with science centers, conservation groups, or the Audubon Society. Organizations like these frequently schedule family walks that cater to children's interests as part of their regular program of environmental education.

HIKES FOR THE PHYSICALLY CHALLENGED

Several locations provide special facilities to accommodate physically challenged persons who wish to enjoy the natural beauty of this state. Beaches and picnic grounds at Bear Brook and White Lake are fully barrier free, as are designated campsites at several campgrounds in the White Mountains. In the Seacoast Region, the Urban Forestry Center maintains a barrier-free "Garden for the Senses" that may also be enjoyed by the visually impaired, and a barrier-free trail in the Great Bay National Wildlife Refuge allows easy access to the peaceful shore of a freshwater pond.

Most people with disabilities will encounter little or no difficulty on many trails or at associated facilities included in this guide. Odiorne Point, Pawtuckaway Park, Mine Falls Park, Franconia Notch, and Paradise Point Nature Center are included within the list of appealing attractions available to the majority of the physically challenged. In other cases, although the hike itself may be inaccessible to most people with disabilities, picnic and view areas may be readily enjoyed. The vistas from Pack Monadnock and Mount Kearsarge are among the destinations that all people can fully appreciate. Refer to the "General description" listing at the beginning of each hike to find locations with special facilities for the physically challenged, and check hike descriptions for trails that may otherwise be suitable for persons with certain limited types of disabilities.

HUTS, TENT PLATFORMS, AND SHELTERS

Aside from a designated campsite or a favorite wilderness nook, backcountry visitors to the White Mountains can select their level of overnight comfort from an unusual list of attractive options. Pitch your tent on a wooden platform with long-distance views, share a bunkroom and warm meals in a picturesque hut, or strike a happy medium in a rustic shelter or cabin—the choice is up to you.

For the most indulgent option, reserve space in one of the eight Appalachian Mountain Club (AMC) huts linked by trails in the heart of the White Mountains. Seasons vary widely, but all huts provide bunkroom sleeping with breakfasts and family-style suppers served in large dining/common rooms with impressive wilderness views. Huts are often cool and damp depending on weather. It's not the Ritz, but it is the only realistic way for many people to have an overnight experience in the world above timberline, where Forest Protection Areas prevent independent camping. Several

Lakes of the Clouds Hut living up to its name.

trails described in this guide also access an AMC hut. Further information and hut reservations are available from the AMC at (603) 466-2727.

More solitary types will appreciate the convenience of the tent platforms that are scattered throughout the White Mountain National Forest. In popular areas, platforms reduce campers' impact on the environment, and on trails like the Valley Way, they provide level sites and beautiful views that otherwise would not be possible. Hike descriptions in this guide will let you know if platforms are available along a particular route. Information for all areas can also be obtained from any local USDA Forest Service office.

My favorite alternatives are the Adirondack-style shelters that still exist in several locations, but a few cautions are in order if you intend to stay in any of these rustic, three-sided log structures. Regulations preclude this type of improvement in designated wilderness areas, and many of the structures are showing their age. Check in advance with a USDA Forest Service office to make sure that the shelter you plan to visit has not been removed.

Shelters typically hold six to eight people, obviate the need to carry a tent, and are generally surrounded by a Forest Protection Area that restricts camping within the vicinity. With or without a tent, however, you may find yourself stranded if you breeze into a full shelter just before dusk. Arrive early and be prepared to camp elsewhere, especially on weekends.

HIKER SHUTTLE

The peak-season Hiker Shuttle operated by the AMC is probably the most under-utilized convenience in the White Mountains. Four shuttle routes connect Franconia, Crawford, and Pinkham Notches in loops that pass north of the Pemigewasset Wilderness and encircle the entire Mount Washington Range. With a little advance planning and for a reasonable fee, the shuttle enables hikers to plan extended traverses through the Franconia Ridge, Pemigewasset, Crawford Notch, and Presidential Peak areas without the necessity of leaving or shuttling a vehicle. Reservations, routes, and schedules are available from the AMC reservation number, (603) 466-2727.

WILDLIFE

Wildlife is bountiful in New Hampshire, but don't be surprised to observe relatively little on high-altitude White Mountain trails. As if to balance the spectacular scenery, most wildlife will be seen at lower elevations and especially on some of the lesser-known hikes in the southern half of the state.

In northern New Hampshire, ravens, spruce grouse, and Canada jays are commonly seen birds that are each bemused by humans in their own distinctive way. Deer and bears are spotted only rarely, usually in passing glances as they merge into the woods. Moose are popular roadside attractions, particularly at dawn and dusk along the Kancamagus Highway. The coloration of moose makes them difficult to see in dim light, and they have a bad habit of veering into the path of oncoming traffic. The result is often fatal for both moose and human. Be alert and slow down if you see these large animals by the side of the road.

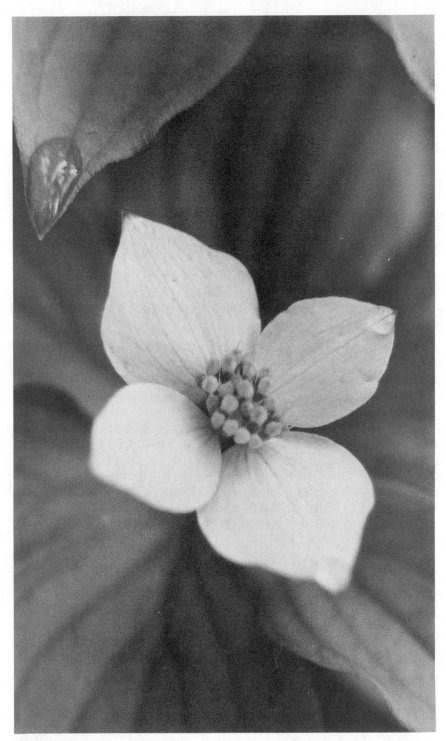

Bunchberry brightens the forest floor.

In southern New Hampshire, Hebron Marsh, Willard Pond, Pillsbury State Park, Fox State Forest, and Great Bay are a few of the places where chances to view the diversity of wildlife are at their peak. Loons, hawks, waterfowl, songbirds, bears, deer, moose, beavers, and foxes can be observed by patient hikers who take the initiative to explore areas of the state where mountain scenery is less ostentatious. My favorite hikes in these out-of-the-way corners are well represented in this guide. They are heartily recommended for wildlife viewing and superb recreation during extended hiking seasons.

PLANTS AND TREES

Knowledgeable visitors are drawn to the stunning high peaks of the White Mountains by unique mosses, lichens, and miniaturized plants from alpine azalea to mountain cranberry. Informed hikers also appreciate the evolved varieties that inhabit marshes at more commonplace locations like Pisgah State Park and Mud Pond. Happily for most of us, though, ordinary people with no training at all can thoroughly enjoy the trillium, bunchberry, and extravagance of wildflowers that line most New Hampshire trails in the spring of each year.

The familiar white pine, hemlock, maple, oak, beech, and birch that dominate New Hampshire's landscape are responsible for the largest annual influx of hikers into this region. In the fall, when the black flies and mosquitoes are long gone, some inexplicable mix of soil chemistry and water produces in New England's vast hardwood forests a brilliance and intensity of color that is simply unequaled. As the wave of peak color sweeps from north to south from early September to the middle of October, vivid foliage and invigorating weather create ideal conditions for a New Hampshire hike. If you haven't done so by then, autumn is the perfect time to select a trail and come join the fun.

The Seacoast

With a pinch of salt, the Seacoast Region adds its perfect dash of seasoning to New Hampshire's outdoor flavor. Wedged between the borders of Maine and Massachusetts, 18 miles of ocean coastline frame the state's first window on the world and fascinate us with remnants of our early colonial history.

There are beaches here, of course, and ocean waves breaking on rocky shores, with tide pools and sand flats that draw visitors to Odiorne Point. But the heart of this delicate region is found back from the immediate coast, where sinuous fingers of tidal estuaries probe pastures of long-ago farms. The enduring beauty of this coastal plain evokes memorable images of a pastoral land interrupted by salt marshes and visions of small boats abandoned by a falling tide.

The ultimate estuary is Great Bay, where upland fields, forest, and freshwater rivers meet mud flats and coastal tides in a melding transition from mountain to sea, symbolic of the entire region. The result of this meeting is a critical environment that nurtures an assortment of wildlife more diverse than can be found anywhere else in the state. Fish, oysters, horseshoe crabs, deer, bald eagles, migratory birds, and waterfowl attract anglers, hikers, and patient observers throughout each season of the year.

1 Blue Job Mountain

General description:	A short family walk to the best mountain views in the Seacoast Region.
General location:	About 8 miles northwest of Rochester, in the town of Strafford.
Length:	1.1 miles round trip.
Difficulty:	Easy.
Elevation gain:	350 feet.
Special attractions:	A mountaintop fire tower with spectacular views and surrounding lawns for picnicking. Easily accessible by families, even with very young children.
Maps:	USGS Baxter Lake quad.
For more information:	None available. Officially, this is a working trail for access to the fire tower.

Key points:
  0.55 Summit fire tower.

Finding the trailhead: From the Spaulding Turnpike, take exit 13 onto U.S. Highway 202 south and turn right after 2.9 miles onto Pond Hill Road. Bear right,

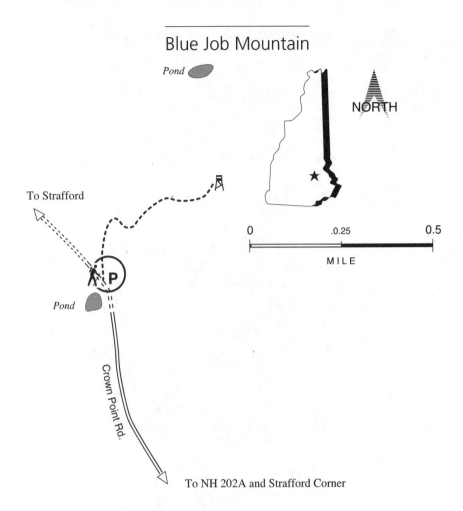

Blue Job Mountain

Pond

NORTH

To Strafford

P

Pond

Crown Point Rd.

0   .0.25   0.5

MILE

To NH 202A and Strafford Corner

staying on Pond Hill Road where the second Crown Point Road diverges, and continue another 1.6 miles to the intersection with New Hampshire Route 202A. Drive straight across this intersection onto the first Crown Point Road. Blue Job Mountain and the Blue Hills Range will soon appear ahead at a sharp bend atop a hill.

After descending from the viewpoint, look for a stop sign with a grange hall and marsh on the left. Turn left at this unmarked intersection onto Crown Point Road and continue past a church and historic section of colonial homes. At 3.3 miles from the grange hall across from a farmhouse sitting very close to the road, look for a small parking area on the right partially bordered by boulders that hide the head of the trail.

The hike: Astonishing vistas that sweep the state from the snow-clad summit of Mount Washington to the Atlantic's white-capped surf make this easy family hike a fitting introduction to New Hampshire. At a height of only 1,356 feet, Blue Job Mountain is nevertheless the dominant peak in the rolling plain of coastal southeastern New Hampshire and boasts superlative

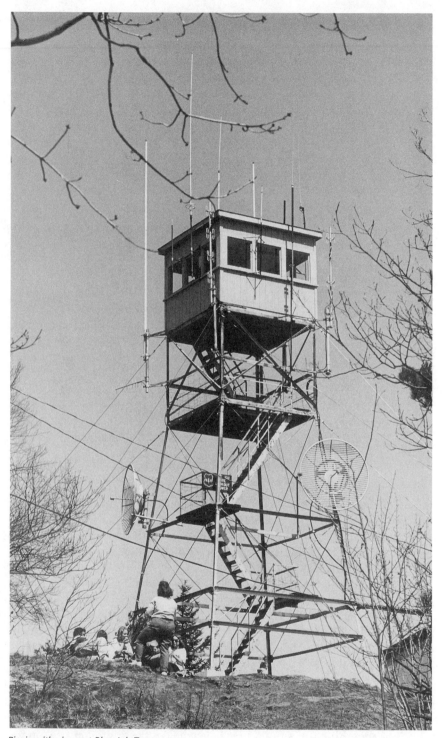

Picnic with views at Blue Job Tower.

views. To the west, unobstructed vistas extend from Mount Monadnock to Sunapee, Kearsarge, and Cardigan Mountains along New Hampshire's serrated spine. Turning 90 degrees right, the view includes the low-lying Lakes Region to the Squam Mountains, the Sandwich Range, and the impressive White Mountains that rise in tiers to the north.

Although unmarked, the well-worn path to the top of Blue Job Mountain is easily recognized as it leaves the parking area through a badly overgrown field. While the trail rises gradually out of the sprout wood, a power line that runs to the unseen fire tower is barely visible on the left, but views almost immediately begin to open behind your back. Come prepared for a lusty wind that often increases with the view.

This is an easy climb up a southerly slope covered with scattered large trees, blueberries, wildflowers, moss, and juniper. Experienced hikers will just be warming up when the trail levels out on the upper ledges leading to the peak. Besides the view and easy walk, children will enjoy the fire tower and the grassy open summit that's a favorite picnic spot. Several structures huddle at the top, amid lawns terraced by stone walls. Even in a stiff breeze, it's easy to find a sunny, protected place to relax, refresh, and appreciate the view.

Summer haze may limit your enjoyment of Blue Job. The town history speaks of watching clipper ships sailing off the Isles of Shoals, but I confess that even on a clear spring afternoon, my gaze wasn't able to penetrate the smog that blanketed Boston and the coastline to the south. For best results, visit in spring or fall, or coordinate your hike with the arrival of one of those high-pressure fronts that cleanse our summer air.

2 Great Bay Estuarine Reserve

General description:	A short loop along the shore of New Hampshire's largest saltwater bay.
General location:	About 5 miles from Portsmouth on the western shore of Great Bay.
Length:	A little less than 1 mile.
Difficulty:	Easy.
Elevation gain:	Less than 100 feet.
Special attractions:	A full spectrum of unique estuarine environments, including upland fields and forests, salt marshes, mud flats, and a tidal creek.
Maps:	Maps and trail guides are available at the trailhead or from the address below; also USGS Portsmouth quad.
For more information:	Reserve Manager, National Estuarine Research Reserve, NH Fish and Game Department, 225 Main Street, Durham, NH 03824, (603) 868-1095.

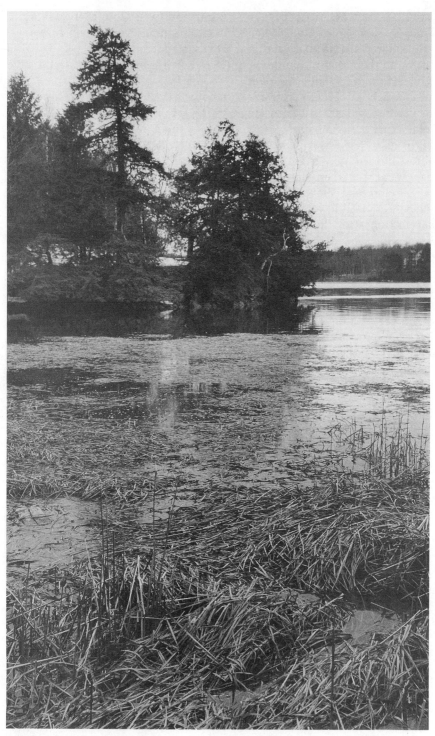

Salt marsh habitat on Great Bay.

Great Bay Estuarine Reserve

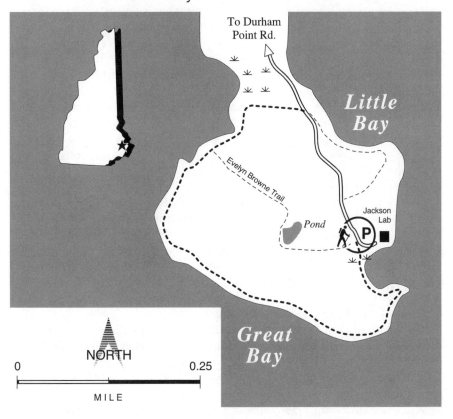

Key points:
    0.15 Tidal shore.
    0.7   Salt marsh.

Finding the trailhead: Take U.S. Highway 4 east from Concord, or west from Portsmouth, to the well-marked intersection with New Hampshire Route 108 in Durham. Follow Route 108 south through the outskirts of downtown Durham as it turns sharply left and passes the police station and town offices. One mile from US 4,

turn left again onto Durham Point Road, which continues through a remote residential area of interesting marshes and woodlands. To enter the estuarine reserve at Adams Point, turn left onto a paved one-lane road 3.7 miles from Route 108, and 0.3 mile after the intersection with Dame Road. It is easily missed. The only marker is a section of chainlink fence with a brown sign noting that the area is closed from 10 P.M. to 4 A.M. Parking is available at a boat launch and next to an overlook platform across from the Jackson Research Lab near the end of the access road. The trailhead is across the access road from the lab parking lot.

The hike: Great Bay is a critical natural environment where three freshwater rivers empty into the tidal salt water of a vast inland bay. Located on the Atlantic Flyway, the nutrient-rich waters, marshes, and surrounding forests provide habitat for an incredibly diverse array of wildlife from bald eagles to horseshoe crabs.

The trail circles Adams Point, once an island, now a peninsula separating Great Bay from Little Bay to the north. At high tide, sections of the trail through upland fields and forests give the impression of a stroll along the shores of any large New England lake. Hemlock, oak, white pine, blueberries, and, sad to say, poison ivy are much in evidence along the rocky shore. Then again, lobster pots, mooring buoys, and oyster boats don't fit the freshwater mold. At low tide, with the tangy smell of the sea, there is no such confusion, and hikers are free to explore the tidal mud flats and rocky beaches that border much of the route.

From the parking area near the overlook platform, pass the trailhead for the Evelyn Browne Trail that cuts across a field and largely avoids the shore. Instead, walk a few paces down the road in the direction of the research lab where a better trail passes through a gate on the right and drops to a cattail marsh before rising into the upland field that covers one-third of the point. The path follows the edge of the field along the tidal shore, but hikers are free to wander to viewpoints over the bay or to comfortable picnic spots at a height of land with panoramic views.

The trail is not marked, but the stony course through the woods is obvious as it moderately rises and falls past a shorefront studded with vertical drops to water level. As the trail circles back toward the access road, it reveals the inlet of a tidal creek, a large salt marsh, and mud flats at low tide. Look in this area for a large variety of sea birds, ducks, hawks, and waterfowl.

The woodland path terminates at the access road 0.2 mile north of the parking area. Turn right to return to your car. As a final diversion, though, follow the conclusion of the Evelyn Browne Trail that enters the woods across the road, affords a view of Little Bay, and returns to the road near stone pillars just before the parking area.

For further exploration of Great Bay, especially for those with botanical interests, the Sandy Point portion of the reserve offers a short trail and boardwalk across a tidal marsh. This newly constructed, barrier-free path complements a very attractive discovery center. The Sandy Point section is reached from Depot Road off state Route 33 (formerly Route 101), 5.5 miles west of Interstate 95. Contact the center at (603) 778-0015.

3 Great Bay National Wildlife Refuge

General description:	Two easy nature walks in a nearly new wildlife refuge.
General location:	About 5 miles west of Portsmouth on the eastern shore of Great Bay.
Length:	Choice of 0.5-mile or 2-mile walks.
Difficulty:	Easy.
Elevation gain:	Negligible.
Special attractions:	Wildlife viewing near Great Bay, and a wheelchair-accessible trail to the shore of a peaceful pond.
Maps:	Maps and brochures are available from the information kiosk at the trailhead.
For more information:	Refuge Manager, Great Bay National Wildlife Refuge, 336 Nimble Hill Road, Newington, NH 03801, (603) 431-7511.

Key points:
0.55 Trail junction in field.
0.95 Great Bay overlook.

Finding the trailhead: From exit 1 of the Spaulding Turnpike (also signed as U.S. Highway 4 and New Hampshire Route 16 in the Portsmouth region), drive west on Pease Boulevard following signs for the Pease International Tradeport. After several lights, turn right at a stop sign onto Arboretum Road (an intersection that is also marked with a sign for the Great Bay Wildlife Refuge). Follow this winding road 3.1 miles as it passes the end of a runway, enters the refuge gate, and reaches a large parking lot on the left that comes complete with an information kiosk and modern restrooms.

The hike: Hikers who explored this saltwater shoreline 15 years ago would have found themselves in trouble. Once part of the Pease Air Force Base where high-security nuclear bombers lumbered into the sky, this 1,000-acre tract has now been converted into a national wildlife refuge. Even though an active runway still accommodates commercial aircraft, the upland forests and wetlands that border the Great Bay estuary continue to provide a quiet corner for abundant wildlife. Two easy trails now allow hikers to meander through habitats that are critical for migrating raptors and waterfowl and provide a home for a wide array of year-round residents from river otters to foxes and turtles.

Peverly Pond Trail: An easy 0.5-mile loop that is wheelchair accessible, the path to Upper Peverly Pond is also one of the most soothing trails in the state. Beginning at the corner of the parking lot to the left of the information

Great Bay National Wildlife Refuge

kiosk, the broad and slightly sandy Peverly Pond Trail winds through a forest of young maple trees and skims over damp terrain on wide wooden walkways. The destination of this short loop is a shady grove of pine trees where convenient benches sit on a bed of soft pine-needle duff. Overlooking a freshwater pool edged on the far shore by a cattail marsh aflutter with bird life, the grove is a cool, restful spot to watch the comings and goings of airborne wildlife and to check out the few stumps and trees that testify to the energy of the local beaver clan.

Ferry Way Trail: A gentle 2.0-mile excursion to the wooded shore of Great Bay, the Ferry Way Trail begins across the road from the parking lot next to a chainlink fence that surrounds a former weapons storage area. After crossing the road, follow the fenceline to your right for about a quarter of a mile. While dragonflies and swallows swoop above your head, you'll have time to consider how this stark enclosure designed for military use has become part of a peaceful preserve for wildlife conservation and is being transformed into habitat for endangered upland birds.

At the northwest corner of the fenced enclosure, turn left onto a gravel road that enters a patch of woods, curls past a beaver pond, and tops a rise at the end of a large field within the next 0.3 mile. Skirting an abandoned apple orchard that edges the top of the field, the trail soon splits to form a loop. Follow the grassy swath straight ahead, pass beneath a stately row of shagbark hickory trees, and enter a dense thicket of upland forest that lines the shore of Great Bay.

Near the spot where the trail turns north on top of the bank above the shore, a wooden bench affords a view of Adams Point (see Hike 2) directly across the narrow gap of water that separates Great Bay from Little Bay. To explore at water level, you'll need to drive to Adams Point. Here, in the quieter confines of a national wildlife refuge, warning signs and a post-and-rail fence force hikers to stay on a trail that remains on top of a high embankment but provides a better chance of spotting wildlife. Look for black ducks, osprey, or upland forest mammals as you wander north through waterfront woods for about 300 yards and then curl east through a sundappled grove of coastal beech and birch. Try to spot egrets or herons lurking in a saltwater marsh to the left just before the path turns right to traverse the length of the field; complete the trail-end loop by returning to the top of the rise near the abandoned apple orchard.

4 Odiorne Point State Park

General description: A short coastal walk along the stony shores of Little Harbor and the Atlantic Ocean. Special features for children.

General location: On the seacoast, just south of Portsmouth in the town of Rye.

Length: 2.0 miles round trip.

Difficulty: Easy.

Elevation gain: Nominal.

Special attractions: Ocean frontage, tide pools, fresh- and saltwater marshes, and a science center especially for children.

Maps: Maps are available at the science center or from the address below. Also USGS Kittery quad.

For more information: Seacoast Science Center, 570 Ocean Blvd., Rye, NH 03870, (603) 436-8043.

Key points:
0.75 Frost Point breakwater.
1.3 Junction with north/south artery.
2.0 Return to trailhead.

Finding the trailhead: Interstate 95 (exit 5) and U.S. Highways 1 and 4 converge at the Portsmouth circle. Drive onto the circle and follow the sign for US 1 Bypass to "Beaches and Hampton." Drive south 1.9 miles, past Yokens restaurant on the right, and turn left at the stoplights onto Elwyn Road. For future reference, note the location of the Urban Forestry Center (Hike 5) and continue about 1.5 miles to stop signs at the Foyes Corner intersection at New Hampshire Route 1A. Take Route 1A south (again following signs for beaches) 1.1 miles to the

Odiorne Point State Park

boat launch and north parking area for Odiorne Point State Park. The science center and main entrance are an additional 0.7 mile south on Route 1A.

The hike: Ocean waves crashing on a pebble beach, the salty smell of the sea, bell buoys and horns with the fog rolling in, and gulls keeping watch over foaming surf. Perhaps not the first images that come to mind when you think about hiking in New Hampshire, but Odiorne Point is just the ticket for a substantial change of pace. Add to this a brand new science center, and you have a perfect day hike designed for the entire family.

Located at the main entrance, the Seacoast Science Center is a logical introduction to the park and an absolute must if you're hiking with children.

The center offers a variety of family-oriented discovery programs on weekends and throughout the summer. An interpretive exhibit provides an up-close introduction to starfish, crabs, mussels, and other small seacoast inhabitants. Don't miss the "please touch" tide pool where younger children are encouraged to roll up their sleeves and gently handle living tide pool creatures. Trail maps and complete program schedules are available at the information desk.

To begin the hike, avoid the picnic-ground atmosphere at the southern end of the park and return to the north boat launch parking area. The trail begins on the opposite side of a small stone wall separating the salt marsh from the woodlands. The trail leads to the rocky shore of Little Harbor where the established path soon ends. Just as well. Wander along the stony beach among the mussel and crab shells, seaweed, and assorted curiosities washed up by the sea. As you approach the breakwater, walk the sandy bank above the beach and discover ancient apple trees from the land's farmstead days and the huge oak that dominates Frost Point.

From the breakwater, an inland path leads to a rather natural-looking hill. A detour to the top of what is actually a manmade hummock discloses the remains of one of several World War II military bunkers. The view illustrates Odiorne's strategic location on the southern flank of Portsmouth harbor and explains why early explorers like Verrazano and Champlain were drawn to these waters.

The rocky coast of Odiorne Point.

South of Frost Point, hikers are on their own again without an established trail. Following the rocky shore leads to a strip of beach with Atlantic Ocean breakers on one side and a freshwater marsh on the other. Past the marsh, the established path can be relocated by walking near the top of the stone embankment that fringes the gravel beach. This path quickly connects in turn to the park's central north/south artery. A left turn along the shore leads to the science center via the alternate trail. Turn right for the trail that wends its way back to the northerly parking area through the dense woodlands that blanket the inland portion of the park.

Those who wish to begin their hike at the science center can use the alternate trail to link with the main loop. It originates at the staff access road on the north side of the center.

5 Urban Forestry Center, Brooks Trail

General description: A short woodland walk to a salt marsh and tidal creek, passing a barrier-free "Garden for the Senses."
General location: Near the seacoast in the city of Portsmouth.
Length: 2.0 miles round trip.
Difficulty: Easy.
Elevation gain: Nominal.
Special attractions: Flowers, herbs, a historic residence, a 60-acre salt marsh, and a pebble beach on Sagamore Creek.
Maps: Maps are located in the mailbox at the trailhead. Also USGS Portsmouth quad.
For more information: Urban Forestry Center, 45 Elwyn Road, Portsmouth, NH 03801, (603) 431-6774.

Key points:
0.4 Trail fork, intermediate loop.
1.0 Pebble beach on Sagamore Creek.
2.0 Return to trailhead.

Finding the trailhead: See directions for Hike 4. The Urban Forestry Center is on the north side of Elwyn Road, 0.15 mile east of the intersection of Elwyn Road and U.S. Highway 1.

The hike: Enter the 180 acres of the Urban Forestry Center and you swiftly escape the commercial hubbub of metropolitan Portsmouth. Demonstration forest plantations and ecological study areas permanently buffer important wetlands from urban encroachment and offer idyllic interludes in a peaceful, natural environment. With one exception, minimal preparation is needed to embark on this gentle stroll. The mosquitoes that thrive in this salt-marsh habitat relish summer visitors. Insect repellent is a seasonal prerequisite.

Significant features of this preserve can be enjoyed by those who are physically challenged or visually impaired. A curving brick walkway edged with handrails leaves the parking area on a looping course to the entrance of a beautiful 1800s Cape-style home. This colorful herb- and flower-lined path, a "Garden for the Senses," is designed not only for its visual appeal, but also to elicit response to its tantalizing aromas, sounds, and textures.

Early portions of the Brooks Trail may also be suitable for persons with certain types of physical disabilities. The path proceeds along a smooth, lilac-bordered lane, past the meeting barn at the edge of a lawn, and into woods filled with oak, blackberries, and wild tansy. After converging with a woods road, the composition of the trail becomes less reliable for the physically challenged and eventually problematic where the woods road and trail again diverge.

Before the path narrows, gaps in the forest cover allow inspection of the salt marsh a few steps to the left. A distant church steeple rising beyond the expanse of marsh hay and cord grass suggests how unscathed these wetlands have remained over many generations.

The trail soon divides to form an intermediate loop. Turn left (staying close to the marsh) onto the lower path that crosses a small brook on a plank bridge. The route ascends through a stand of pine, a maple grove, and a

31

congregation of oaks on the high ground overlooking the marsh. Wander off the path among the well-spaced trees to any one of several wetland overviews, and return to the trail that skirts the marsh, passes below a utility line, and soon reconnects with the upper segment of the loop.

Turn left again to reach trail's end, a small, circular turnaround path. Either fork leads to a low embankment above a pebble beach on the open salt waters of Sagamore Creek. These tidal waters bring with them the smell of the sea, sand flats, seaweed, and an enhanced sense of remoteness in New Hampshire's busy seacoast corner. Engage in some bird watching and savor the privacy before making your return.

The upper segment of the intermediate loop is thickly bordered by poplar, sumac, and wild roses. This alternate path is far less scenic, but passes a small pond obscured by underbrush. A shy blue heron that lurks in the area may be reason enough to return by this less attractive route.

Merrimack Valley

At the southern end of the giant watershed that drains much of central New Hampshire, the Merrimack River passes the cities of Franklin, Concord, Manchester, and Nashua on its twisting way to the sea. Destined to house the bulk of a burgeoning population, the Merrimack Valley has seen dramatic changes with the passage of three hundred years. Food source, access route, power supply, waste receptacle, and path for an interstate highway to penetrate rolling hills, the function of the river has shifted with the surges of the human tide.

Happily, the fortunes of the river have turned yet again, cleaned, revived, and appreciated as the natural gift that it is. The Merrimack Valley long ago ceased being hospitable to extended backpacking trips, but with care and planning you can still escape the proximity of urban terrain and envision days when nomadic peoples camped on the fruitful river or hunted game in the vast forests of Bear Brook and Pawtuckaway Parks.

Other hikes in the region recall the diversity of its human history. The farmstead at Hyla Brook, the mills at Mine Falls Park, and the woodland walk at Silk Farm Sanctuary reflect distinct interpretations of humankind's effort to tame the land. Yet these areas still provide modern hikers with a natural means of escape from the demands of urban life.

6 Silk Farm Wildlife Sanctuary

General description:	A short woodland walk to a secluded pond in New Hampshire's capital city.
General location:	In the city of Concord.
Length:	About 0.8 mile.
Difficulty:	Easy.
Elevation gain:	Less than 100 feet.
Special attractions:	Wildflowers in spring, birding in varied habitats, and the boardwalk at Great Turkey Pond.
Maps:	Map and brochure are available at the Audubon nature store near the trailhead. Also USGS Concord quad.
For more information:	Audubon Society of New Hampshire, 3 Silk Farm Road, Concord, NH 03301-8200, (603) 224-9909.

Key points:
- 0.4 Boardwalk on Great Turkey Pond.
- 0.8 Return to trailhead on Forest Floor Trail.

Finding the trailhead: Depart Interstate 89 at exit 2, and turn west on Clinton Street, away from downtown

Silk Farm Wildlife Sanctuary

Concord. Continue 0.1 mile to the intersection with Silk Farm Road and turn right, following signs for the "NH Audubon Center". The driveway for New Hampshire Audubon headquarters, the nature store, and trailhead parking is less than two-tenths of a mile on the left.

The hike: Arriving on Interstate 89, visitors may not realize that this small natural enclave is nestled within 3 miles of the state capitol's golden dome. By far the most rural of the urban walks in this hiker's guide, the Audubon Society's Silk Farm Wildlife Sanctuary provides safe refuge for animals and humans alike. The short trails and convenient location make Silk Farm perfectly suited for a refreshing walk at either end of a busy working day.

A woodchip-covered path near a large, flat boulder on the south side of the parking area designates the start of the Forest Floor and Great Turkey Pond Trails. For a roundabout hike that combines the majority of both routes, follow the yellow markers of the Great Turkey Pond Trail as it loops under white pines behind the parking area. Beginning its counter-clockwise circle, the path makes two right turns before bearing left at a gap in a stone wall that marks the start of the Old Orchard Trail.

Beyond an old pasture filled with small pines and berries, the Old Orchard Trail peeks into a cornfield and provides a longer, optional route to the shore of Great Turkey Pond. The intervening pasture of pine may be worth a short digression, though, if only to eavesdrop on the lively chickadee conversation that flourishes overhead.

The Great Turkey Pond Trail continues along a rudimentary stone wall, easily descending off a knoll as the forest slowly changes into mixed hardwoods with only a smattering of pine. It's quiet enough to hear the amorous drumming of a partridge somewhere in the underbrush, and soon the gleam of sun on water backlights the trunks of the trees ahead. Twenty yards from Great Turkey Pond, the trail swings left and runs parallel to shore for 800 feet or more, passing frequent openings through thickets that are perfect for observing life on the quiet pond.

A wooden post marks the turnaround point at the far end of the Turkey Pond loop. On the right, planks lead over the marsh to a boardwalk that gently noses into open water. Pause here for a while to appreciate this window on the world of migratory and breeding waterfowl that often frequent the area.

Returning to the wooden post, the trail turns sharply left, doubling back on itself, as it crosses seasonal wet areas that house a variety of amphibians. The path angles indirectly up the hill and weaves through a boulder patch before meeting the short connecting link to the Forest Floor Trail at the top of the ridge.

The red tree markers of the Forest Floor Trail lead through open woods of evergreen. A high canopy and thick pine-needle duff discourage brushy undergrowth but foster colorful carpets of wildflowers, as lady's slippers punctuate ground covered by wintergreen and partridge berry. Knowledgeable hikers may also spot homes of ground-nesting birds as the path skirts the margins of the sanctuary and circles back to the trailhead.

7 Bear Brook State Park, Catamount Trail

General description:	A family walk to a low summit in a state park with many amenities. Beach and picnic areas are barrier free.
General location:	East of the Merrimack River, about midway between Manchester and Concord.
Length:	2.6 miles round trip to Catamount Hill; 4.3 miles for the complete loop via Cascade Trail (includes 0.5-mile spur to summit).
Difficulty:	Moderate, but fairly easy between the trailhead and Catamount Hill.
Elevation gain:	400 feet.
Special attractions:	Beach and picnic grounds, a cascading brook, and a child-friendly trail to a summit with local views.
Maps:	A map of hiking trails in Bear Brook State Park is available in season at the park. Also USGS Suncook quad.
For more information:	Manager, Bear Brook State Park, RR1, Box 507, Allenstown, NH 03275, (603) 485-9874.

Key points:
- 1.2 False summit, Catamount Hill.
- 2.3 T intersection by Catamount Brook.
- 2.7 Junction, Cascade and Bear Brook Trails.
- 3.8 Return to trailhead.

Finding the trailhead: The access road to Bear Brook State Park is off New Hampshire Route 28, 5.6 miles south of the Epsom traffic circle, or 3.0 miles north of the junction of Route 28 and U.S. Highway 3. A large state park sign marks the turn onto the Allenstown-Deerfield Road, a public highway that runs through the park. The park tollbooth is a little less than a mile east of Route 28 at a turnout on the right-hand side of the road. A large parking area for picnic and beach facilities is on the left, immediately past the tollbooth. The trail begins within a grove of trees just to the right of the driveway as you enter the beach parking lot.

The hike: Between the close of winter and the arrival of spring, avid hikers suffer malaise when snows melt and warmer weather softens the waterlogged earth. We call it Mud Season, a time when suitable trails are hard to find.

36

Bear Brook State Park, Catamount Trail

Although Bear Brook State Park contains nearly 10,000 acres and miles of worthy trails, this adaptable hike is the best alternative to alleviate early season blues, weeks before most other paths are generally accessible.

With picnic grounds, a beach house under towering pines, and a route that can be adjusted to suit a broad range of abilities, this hike is also quite useful during the peak of the summer season. Adjacent to the trailhead, the picnic grounds and beach are barrier free, featuring paved walkways and a designated picnic site directly on the water. Families with very young children will find the simple round trip to the top of Catamount Hill to be the most appealing alternative, while more adventurous types can pass beyond the summit on a longer loop exploring Bear Brook and the Catamount Brook cascades. Please note, though, that even if you think that pets are part of your family, they are not allowed to accompany you on Bear Brook State Park trails.

From a picnic area near the driveway, the yellow-blazed trail passes over a footbridge south of the beach house, crosses the highway, and edges a second picnic area on an embankment above Bear Brook. The real hike begins just after the trail re-crosses the brook on a larger wooden bridge on the far side of a baseball field. Look for signs for the Catamount Hill Trail, short and long loops.

A wide path rises gradually through mixed pine and hardwoods and soon meets a small dirt road. Turn left on the road for about 30 yards to another signpost that signals a right turn to Catamount summit and beyond. The trail steepens, but the most challenging grades extend for only 150 yards. The path remains broad and smooth for easy walking and levels off near the summit as it swings left to avoid a jumble of boulders encrusted with moss and ferns. Families with younger children may wish to stop on the flat top above these boulders to allow the kids to enjoy their accomplishment, together with the view of Mount Kearsarge and smaller hills nearby. Only those who proceed over the level knoll and descend 0.1 mile down the other side learn that they've crossed a false summit. The true height of land is reached by a 0.5-mile side trail that strictly appeals to purists, since its views are largely obscured.

Beyond the summit, the trail reverts to a more traditional woodland path, a little rougher, a little steeper, and showing signs of much less use. Descending the southeast side of Catamount Hill through airy woods, shading ferns, and spring wildflowers, the route soon passes a junction with a shortcut trail that returns to the picnic grounds. I prefer to bear right, descending farther into thicker woods and crossing a small stream before swinging right again to rise to the top of another hill. On the way down this second slope,

Beach house at Bear Brook State Park.

look carefully for yellow trail markers when crossing an old woods road, and listen for the rushing swoosh of a swollen brook at the bottom of a sharp decline.

The T intersection with the Cascade Trail appears on the opposite bank of Catamount Brook, a roaring jumble of whitewater careening down from Hayes Marsh. Turn left for an extended walk that parallels the beauty of these cascades on a 0.4-mile journey to rendezvous with Bear Brook. During spring runoff, this rolling stretch of trail is the highlight of the hike, as it variously visits the edge of the stream and rises high on an embankment above the noisy flow.

The Cascade Trail ends at the junction with Bear Brook Trail near a dirt road 1.1 miles from the parking area. Turn left on a meandering path that leads northwest between Bear Brook and the road, coming full circle to the wooden bridge that crosses the stream by the baseball field.

8 Hyla Brook Nature/Poetry Trail

General description:	A brief walking introduction to the natural history and poetry associated with the homestead farm of Robert Frost.
General location:	About 13 miles southeast of Manchester in the town of Derry.
Length:	0.5 mile.
Difficulty:	Easy.
Elevation gain:	Nominal.
Special attractions:	The poems and observations of a backyard naturalist in the context of his rural environment. A separate tour of Frost's house and barn is also seasonally available.
Maps:	USGS Windham quad.
For more information:	Manager, Robert Frost Farm, P.O. Box 1075, Derry, NH 03038, (603) 432-3091.

Key points:
- 0.1 Farm field.
- 0.2 Old South Road.
- 0.3 Mending wall.
- 0.5 Return to farmhouse.

Finding the trailhead: Depart Interstate 93 at exit 4 and follow New Hampshire Route 102 east 2 miles through the town of Derry to the Derry traffic circle. Take the first right off the circle onto Route 28 Bypass south. This road becomes Route 28 south as it continues straight through the stoplights 1 mile from the traffic circle. The driveway for the Robert Frost Farm is on the left, 0.6 mile south of the stoplights.

39

Hyla Brook Nature/Poetry Trail

The hike: The Hyla Brook Nature/Poetry Trail is certainly the shortest walk in this hiker's guide, an abbreviated amble barely straying from the meadow that interrupts the woods behind the Robert Frost homestead. It's a simple stroll, spare and unadorned, like the poetry inspired by the hard realities of life encountered on this farm. Should you arrive, however, with the necessary resource of an inquiring mind, your journey here will expand well beyond the confines of the trail.

Passing familiarity with the works of the renowned literary figure, along with the small trail guide provided by the New Hampshire Division of Parks and Recreation, will be invaluable to a full enjoyment of the Robert Frost Farm. The brochure is keyed to numbered signposts along the trail with excerpts of poetry and interpretive insights into the human and natural history of the land. Be sure to pick up a copy before beginning this leisurely stroll.

It would be a mistake merely to walk this trail. Most people tarry and pause at stop 5 to imagine the whisper of the poet's scythe in the meadow grass, or at stop 15 to absorb nuances attached to the famous mending wall, repair of which made good neighbors of Robert Frost and Napoleon Guay. If poetry is not your interest, other stops inform walkers on subjects as diverse as sweetfern tea, the agricultural decline of the second half of the nineteenth century, or the nexus between Druids and oak trees. Most people seem to find something that piques their curiosity.

The walk begins near the parking area behind the barn, and traverses the long side of the meadow, ducking under oak branches encroaching the old stone wall. The trail passes through a bar gap at the end of the field and turns right onto Old South Road, the limiting stone walls among the trees hinting at its former significance. Bearing right again near the seasonal Hyla Brook, named by Frost after the spring peepers that thrive here, the route continues along the sparse ribbon of the mending wall that now separates only the trees. Step through the wall and into the pine woods. The trail re-crosses the brook and quickly ends as it emerges back into sunlight, near the apple trees on the opposite side of the barn.

The Hyla Brook Trail is always available for walking, but the farmhouse is open only for limited hours during a season that seems to vary. Hikers will be disappointed without the trail guide that's available inside the building. Unless you obtain the brochure in advance or happen to pick one up from a basket outside the door, it's probably best to call ahead and visit when the house is open.

9 Mine Falls Park, Nashua River Trail

General description:	A leisurely urban walk along the wooded banks of the Nashua River.
General location:	Within the city of Nashua at exit 5 of the F. E. Everett Turnpike (U.S. Highway 3).
Length:	2.4 miles.
Difficulty:	Easy.
Elevation gain:	Less than 30 feet.
Special attractions:	Canal and river frontage, gatehouse and dam, tall pines and wildlife, near the center of the state's second largest city.
Maps:	Brochure with map and general information is available from the address below. Also USGS Nashua North, Nashua South, Pepperell, Mass., and South Merrimack quads.
For more information:	City of Nashua, Park-Recreation Department, Greeley Park, 100 Concord Street, Nashua, NH 03064-1704, (603) 594-3346.

Key points:
- 0.1   Highway bridge.
- 0.2   Nashua River.
- 1.1   Dam and mill pond.

Mine Falls Park, Nashua River Trail

Finding the trailhead: Follow these directions carefully; this is a confusing area with very heavy traffic. From the north, take exit 5E from the F. E. Everett Turnpike (U.S. Highway 3) and follow signs for downtown Nashua, crossing over the turnpike on New Hampshire Route 111 east. Keep to the left. Immediately after the interchange, take the first left onto New Dunstable Road, travel 3 blocks to a stop sign, and turn left on Liberty Street. Proceed 1 block on Liberty Street, and then turn left again onto West Hollis Street. As soon as you make this turn, you'll see a set of traffic lights where you'll turn right onto Simon Street. Follow Simon Street 0.45 mile through an industrial area to the Whipple Street intersection. Turn left onto Whipple Street, which deadends at the parking area, park entrance, and trailhead.

From the south, it's very easy. Take exit 5A (Simon Street), an alternate exit a little north of 5E, which leads directly to a stop sign. Turn left on Simon Street, drive 0.3 mile, and turn left again on Whipple Street, which deadends at the trailhead.

The hike: This country has been late in catching on to the European tradition of the urban greenway, where residents can stroll amiably for daily exercise or the occasional break from city living. Thanks are due to the citizens of Nashua for preserving Mine Falls Park as a hidden oasis in the heart of this city. Hikers, bikers, joggers, and casual walkers will find respite in this 325-acre natural environment, Nashua's urban greenway.

Most of Mine Falls Park is located between the Nashua River and a canal that once provided waterpower to several of the mills at the eastern end of the park. The banks of the canal are about 25 feet above the level of the river, and the land mass in between is covered by tall white pines and mixed birch, maple, oak, and ash. Trails on the riverbank and woodland level tend to be wide gravel paths under a cool forest canopy, while the upper trail is often a sunny walk on a flat, grassy shoulder that parallels the canal.

From the parking area, follow the paved path over the footbridge across the canal. A variety of trails depart from this point, but bear left and pass under a highway bridge to a junction where all paths to the west diverge. The route described here loops back to this point, so hikers may choose to either bear left to continue following the bank of the canal, or right for the wooded walk along the river. Either choice carries you quickly away from highway noise into a quiet, natural setting.

This is my favorite Mine Falls hike because it's the most peaceful and remote. The path by the river rolls gradually through the woods, past small pools and washes offering extensive cover for a variety of ducks and songbirds. Great blue herons silently work the bank of the river. Along the canal, the path curves gently with the twists and turns of the water course, while small dams and inlets provide visual variety.

At the midpoint of this loop are a millpond, historic gatehouse, and dam on the Nashua River. A side path leads to a mesmerizing view of a whitewater outflow gushing from the dam, but it also approaches unprotected drops into roiling water. Children should be kept on the established trail.

There are over 6 miles of other walks in Mine Falls Park. Naturalists may wish to try the loop to the cove and mill yard at the opposite end as shown on the map. The hike to the east comes very close to city streets and is not well marked in the mill yard area. Nevertheless, this alternate route circles a cove and extensive marshland inhabited by songbirds, ducks, and beavers, apparently oblivious to the proximity of downtown Nashua.

10 Pawtuckaway State Park, Boulder Field Trail

General description:	An afternoon walk in the woods to a jumble of ice-age boulders.
General location:	Southeastern New Hampshire, about midway between Manchester and Portsmouth.
Length:	2.2 miles round trip.
Difficulty:	Easy.
Elevation gain:	400 feet, including a visit to Devil's Den.
Special attractions:	Barn-sized boulders lining a brook, marshes, open ledges, and the caves of Devil's Den.
Maps:	USGS Mount Pawtuckaway quad.
For more information:	Manager, Pawtuckaway State Park, 128 Mountain Road, Nottingham, NH 03290, (603) 895-3031.

Key points:
- 0.6 Boulder field.
- 1.1 Devil's Den.

Finding the trailhead: Reservation Road runs east from New Hampshire Route 107, 4.2 miles south of the intersection of Route 107 with Route 43 North, and 3.1 miles north of the intersection of Route 107 with Route 27. Follow Reservation Road 1.2 miles east, bear right at a fork, and then turn left onto Round Pond Trail 2.3 miles from Route 107. This narrow, unmarked gravel road tracks through deep woods and skirts backcountry marshes for 1.3 miles before turning left at a fork and ending 1.1 miles later at the shore of Round Pond where parking is available. Round Pond Trail is a rough backwoods road that is best left to an SUV or other high-clearance vehicle.

Note: Because of limited parking, park personnel now discourage access from a dirt road that departs Nottingham Road 3.4 miles southeast of Deerfield Parade as described in an earlier edition of this hiker's guide. A metal gate now stops vehicles at the park boundary, No Parking signs line the road, and this once popular trail no longer hosts as many hikers.

The hike: The Boulder Field hike is perfect for one of those lazy afternoons when you feel like poking around outside, but would just as soon avoid strenuous exertion. As it happens, a portion of this walk may be most satisfactory for those who might prefer to amble through quiet woods and watch others expend their energy.

At times of high water, Round Pond is likely to flood a portion of the access road. Just beyond the normal limits of the water, on the opposite side of the road, look for white rectangles marking a trail that crosses the outlet of a marsh and turns north, running between the shore of the marsh and a

Pawtuckaway State Park, Boulder Field Trail

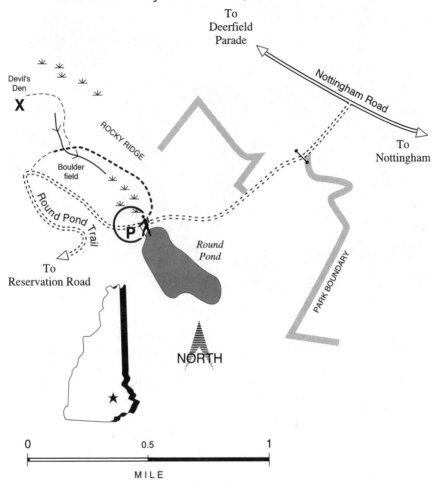

70-foot granite ridge. The exposed face of this outcropping is a favorite hang-out of technical climbers. From this narrowly channeled trail, then, you confront an amusing choice: humans dangling from ropes on one side, or geese paddling on the other.

Pushing on to the far end of the marsh the trail approaches Boulder Field. It's not really a field, of course, but an assortment of massive glacial erratics scattered about the woodlands by the giant sheet of ice that carried them here. This is your chance to wander off the trail, generally snooping around and about these barn-sized chunks of granite. Note how sculptured many of them look, and how they came to rest along the bottom of a shallow wash that rises to low ridges on either side. You won't get lost. The wet bottom-land of the wash leads back to the trail near the edge of the marsh, where the brook seems to disappear beneath a large boulder.

For those with the energy and inclination for further exploration, an-other trail diverges north about 50 yards before the first large boulder by

Round Pond, near the Boulder Field Trailhead.

the brook. A trail sign is posted well above head high, but it's easy to miss while you're ogling the rocks. In about half a mile, this path gradually climbs to the top of a ridge and circles behind an immense 150-foot core of granite boulders. A short scramble of moderate difficulty is required to reach intriguing Devil's Den, two small caves at the base of the soaring tower overlooking another marsh.

11 Pawtuckaway State Park, South Mountain Loop

General description: An extended day hike through woodlands, marshes, and rolling hills typical of southern New Hampshire.

General location: Southeastern New Hampshire about midway between Manchester and Portsmouth.

Length: 4.9 miles round trip.

Difficulty: Moderate.

Elevation gain: 600 feet.

Special attractions: Secluded marshes, beaver ponds, and wooded hillsides, with fire-tower views to Boston and the White Mountains.

Maps: USGS Mount Pawtuckaway quad.

For more information: Manager, Pawtuckaway State Park, 128 Mountain Road, Nottingham, NH 03290, (603) 895-3031.

Key points:
1.4 Junction with South Ridge Trail.
2.1 Spur to viewpoint ledges.
2.2 Fire tower on South Mountain.
3.4 Return to junction with South Ridge Trail via northerly end of South Mountain.

Finding the trailhead: From New Hampshire Route 101, exit 5, follow signs for Route 156 north. You'll quickly come to a T intersection at the second of two sets of traffic lights. Turn left at the T and almost immediately turn right onto Route 156. Follow this highway 1.4 miles north and turn left onto Mountain Road. The park entrance is 2 miles on the left. All turns are well marked with directory signs for Pawtuckaway State Park.

The trailhead is on the left side of the main park road about a quarter of a mile beyond a tollbooth, at the bottom of a hill on the far side of Mountain Pond. Look for a broad path with brown posts, a chain that prevents vehicular access, and an old sign that bears the number 2. Early- or late-season hikers may find the park closed to all but pedestrian traffic. In that event, park at the far end of the administration building parking lot and walk past the closed tollbooth to the trailhead.

The hike: Enveloped in a rolling mix of woodlands typical of southeastern New Hampshire, the popular trail to South Mountain passes marshes, brooks,

Pawtuckaway State Park, South Mountain Loop

Middle Mountain

Shaw Trail

NORTH

South Ridge Trail

0   0.5   1

MILE

Mountain Trail

Park Rd.

Mountain Pond

Pawtuckaway Pond

Toll booth ■**P**

Mountain Rd.

To Raymond

ponds, and pools. High on my list of early-season walks, this route is especially delightful on warm April days before blackflies and mosquitoes have emerged. At the height of the summer, the Mountain Trail receives heavy foot traffic as far as the summit fire tower, but hikers versed in route-finding skills may gain solitude on the back side of the mountain.

A smooth path blazed with white rectangles skirts duck-nesting habitat on the northeastern side of Mountain Pond, then undulates up and down a series of three increasingly higher ridges. In low sections, it crosses a small brook and skirts marshy pools alive with spring peepers. Hikers may glimpse a resident hawk circling on a warm spring breeze. On the hillsides, the path is rockier and narrower, with more abundant glacial erratics. Bear right at a trail junction after 0.6 mile, and try to spot South Mountain's viewpoint ledges that flicker through the treetops as you descend the second ridge.

The junction with the South Ridge Trail is 0.7 mile below the top of South Mountain. Turn right on this path that crosses and re-crosses a stone wall and clambers over a boulder. About half of this climb is a steep scramble over pine duff scattered between massive rocks. Look for a sign for the short spur path that leads to viewpoint ledges. Enjoy the fine Pawtuckaway views before completing the last 0.1 mile of the ascent that rises over gently slanted slabs to the fire tower at the summit.

From the tower, Pawtuckaway Pond spreads close by to the east, while the twin mounds of the Uncanoonuc Mountains rise in the opposite direction. On clear days, those on top may spy a glint of sun on a Boston office tower or turn north to see a snowcap sparkle on a tall White Mountain peak.

My favorite section of this hike extends beyond South Mountain on a faint, grassy path that wends its way between large boulders scattered about the slope. The trail is blazed, but less well used, and definitely not for everyone. Carry a map and compass just in case.

The summit can be a bit confusing since all routes are marked with the same white blaze. The trail for the extended loop leaves the mountaintop at the end opposite from where you arrived. Pass up the route that departs northwest to the left of the fire tower, unless you want to shorten the loop and quickly return to your point of departure.

The longer loop rapidly descends the northerly end of South Mountain, skirting a large marsh in a relatively remote section of the park. Encircling the wetlands are dense forests, berry bushes, and impenetrable jumbles of dead wood—all prime wildlife habitat.

The trail crosses the marsh's outlet brook and intersects the Shaw Trail at the distant turnaround point of the loop. Begin your return by turning left on this snowmobile path and walking to a dirt road in only 0.1 mile. Turn left again on the dirt road, and continue nearly two-tenths of a mile to a point where the road makes a sharp right turn (really the beginning of a distinct S curve). On the left, you'll see the lower end of the route from the fire tower that you passed by at the summit. On the right, the road continues to curve. Split the difference, and proceed straight ahead on a trail that skims the southeastern edge of another marsh reflecting the shadow of Middle Mountain. Within less than four-tenths of a mile the trail returns to the junction with the South Ridge Trail where you began the loop to South Mountain's summit.

12 Uncanoonuc, North Peak

General description:	A two- to three-hour hike to a suburban peak with fine views and a backcountry feel.
General location:	About 6 miles west of Manchester, in the town of Goffstown.
Length:	1.4 miles round trip.
Difficulty:	Moderate.
Elevation gain:	700 feet.
Special attractions:	A sense of remote mountain hiking within sight of the state's largest city. Fine views of Goffstown, the Merrimack Valley, and miles of mountains beyond.
Maps:	USGS Pinardville quad.
For more information:	None available.

Key points:

0.5 Viewpoint slabs.

0.7 North peak summit.

Finding the trailhead: Follow New Hampshire Route 114 (Mast Road) to its intersection with Route 13 at an oblong traffic circle in the town of Goffstown. Drive south on Mountain Road, which leaves the end of this oblong circle next to a gas station, and in 0.3 mile Uncanoonuc North Peak looms ahead. Continue left at a fork at 0.9 mile, where Mountain Road and Lesnyk Road intersect. Almost immediately, both Uncanoonuc peaks will be visible. Drive another 0.55 mile from the Lesnyk Road intersection to a trailhead that is virtually unmarked. Look for a gap in a stone wall, a well-worn path, or perhaps a white rectangular blaze painted on a tree a few feet up the trail. If you're still in doubt, you should be about 275 yards from the last farmhouse, and obvious parking places should be located across the road.

The hike: The Uncanoonucs, North and South, are softly shaped twin mountains prominently visible from Manchester and its immediate suburbs. Allegedly, the name Uncanoonuc derives from a Native American term for what male cartographers traditionally name such alluring double peaks. Whatever the derivation, the natural environment of Uncanoonuc North offers an outstanding hiking experience. Once off the road and into the woods, the backcountry atmosphere of this suburban summit quickly excludes any reminder that you're still within sight of New Hampshire's largest city.

The most difficult part of the hike comes first, as the trail immediately climbs from the road at a moderate grade through a forest of beech, pine, and maple. After 0.2 mile, the pitch eases near a small cave beneath a rocky outcropping, and beyond this ledge the trail curves back and forth up a slope predominantly covered in older-growth white pine. Finally, the path straightens and rises more steeply once again, until glimpses of views are seen through the trees behind you as you climb.

Uncanoonuc, North Peak

To Goffstown

Lesnyk Rd.

Mountain Rd.

NORTH

0   0.5   1

MILE

Farm house

Goffstown
Reservoirs

Mountain Rd.

Mountain
Base Rd.
to Goffstown

Summit, Uncanoonuc
North Peak

*Uncanoonuc
Lake*

Carriage Rd.

X

Summit, Uncanoonuc
South Peak

A cleared area of rocky slabs that is 0.2 mile short of the summit produces the best views on the hike. Someone has even considerately provided a crude bench from which to enjoy the marvelous vista. Spreading below are Goffstown, Glenn Lake on the Piscataquog River, the rolling hills of Dunbarton, and much of central New Hampshire stretching 30 miles to Mount Kearsarge and beyond.

The upper reaches of the trail are quite gradual, encouraging exploration of the mountain's rounded top. Trees on the summit are sparse and low, admitting plenty of sunlight onto grassy fields where scattered rocks provide seating for hikers' picnics. It's a wonderful peak for wandering about, checking views in all directions, or merely sitting a spell and relaxing in the comforting warmth of the sun.

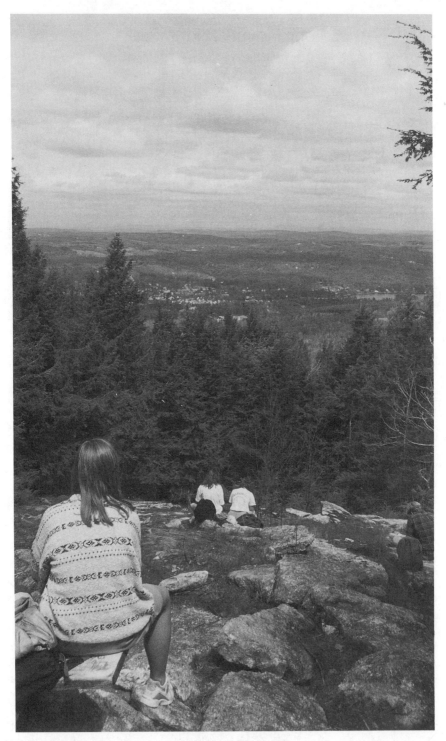

A rest on Uncanoonuc, overlooking views of the Merrimack Valley.

Unfortunately, line-of-sight visibility has been the downfall of Uncanoonuc South. The forest of transmission towers that goes along with the view of the city of Manchester is one of the prices society has paid for instant communication. If you really feel like dealing with high-frequency radio towers, a perimeter road, and a jumble of No Trespassing signs to gain a spectacular urban view, then here's how you reach South Peak. From the oblong traffic circle, return 0.6 mile east on Route 114 to a right turn onto Wallace Road, and in 1.4 miles turn right again onto Mountain Base Road. Go 1.0 mile and park at the nature trail sign across from a tiny beach. Walk along the dirt road, ignoring the Dead End sign, until you see the large Uncanoonuc Nature Trail plaque. The path is much broader and more gradual than the trail to the north peak and it turns right near the top at a signed junction to reach the perimeter road. Follow the road to views at the height of land, and make sure you return the same way you came. A left at the trail junction circles short of the top and down a former cable-car route, which is difficult and definitely not recommended.

Monadnock Region

Visitors to southwestern New Hampshire find themselves in a curiously self-reliant corner of the state. Removed from the vast weekend migrations of tourists ushered north by the interstates, the Monadnock Region preserves a traditionalist's approach to outdoor recreation. This tweedy, wooded landscape scattered with villages, lakes, and ponds still evokes the rural heritage that inspired the play *Our Town* and reminds us that references to Currier and Ives are more than a marketing ploy.

The area's most significant natural feature is the peak that gives the region its name. In geological terms, Mount Monadnock provides the very definition of a resistant mountain of rock above an eroded plain. In this case, the action of a mile-thick glacier thousands of years ago can be seen in the contoured flanks surrounding the mountain's core and in the neatly gouged striations found on rocks along the trails. Fortunately for hiking enthusiasts, Mount Monadnock did not resist alone. Crotched Mountain, Pack Monadnock, and Skatutakee Mountain are among the surviving summits that provide local hikers with marvelous Monadnock views.

Pisgah State Park, Rhododendron State Park, Willard Pond, the Harris Center, and Sheldrick Forest prove that there's much more for hikers to do in these parts than scale predominant peaks. Forest ridges, wild ravines, marshes, brooks, secluded ponds, and small pockets of natural beauty all wait for their discovery in the far-flung corners of this traditional New Hampshire region.

13 Crotched Mountain

General description:	A short family hike to a nubby peak with extensive Monadnock views.
General location:	Midway between Keene and Manchester, near the town of Greenfield.
Length:	3 miles round trip.
Difficulty:	Moderate, but shading strongly toward easy.
Elevation gain:	About 760 feet.
Special attractions:	Panoramic views of Mount Monadnock, Pack Monadnock, and southwestern New Hampshire extending north to Mount Sunapee and beyond.
Maps:	USGS Peterborough North and Greenfield quads.
For more information:	None available.

Crotched Mountain

Key points:
- 0.5 View from knoll.
- 1.4 Summit of Crotched Mountain.
- 1.5 Ledges for scenic views.

Finding the trailhead: Crotched Mountain lies near the middle of a triangle formed by Nashua, Concord, and Keene. Consequently, it can be approached by a variety of routes, all of which must eventually lead either

through the village of Bennington (off U.S. Highway 202), or through the village of Greenfield (at the junction of New Hampshire Routes 31 and 136).

55

Routes 47 and 31 depart US 202 about 8 miles south of the town of Hillsborough. Turn east on these routes, cross a stone bridge into the village of Bennington, and turn right at the stop sign onto Route 31 heading in the direction of Greenfield. Continue south 4.2 miles and turn left onto a town road following signs for the Crotched Mountain Rehabilitation Center.

From Greenfield and the junction of Routes 31 and 136, drive north on Route 31 for 0.8 mile. Turn right, following signs for Crotched Mountain Rehabilitation Center.

From either direction, after turning off Route 31, the town road passes a small pond, climbs quickly uphill, and in 1.4 miles passes the large drive-way to the rehabilitation center on the right. The trailhead is on the left, near the crest of the hill, 0.1 mile past the driveway. Look for a metal gate and a sign that warns against blocking the driveway. Obey the No Trespassing signs and be sure to stay on the trail. There is ample parking on wide shoulders on either side of the road.

The hike: The path to Crotched Mountain provides the finest views for the least effort of any walking trail in the Monadnock Region. This exceptional family outing opens wide-angle vistas of southwestern New Hampshire even to hikers who may choose not to ascend all the way to the summit. Late autumn makes this hike particularly rewarding, when neighboring peaks stand crisp against the dark blue sky, and a coppery cloak covers the tweedy landscape.

As you slip by the gate at the trailhead, take note of the prohibition against camping and fires, and remember that much of the trail crosses private land. A gravel jeep road swings easily uphill to the left through scrubby saplings and passes an open field on the right. Detour a few steps into the edge of the field for an orientation to the notched, ripple-top mountain that waits ahead.

In about a quarter of a mile, the track bends left near camp shelters that look east to the Uncanoonuc summits in Goffstown. Sorry, the shelters are private, but the expansive view can be shared from the edge of the road.

Stay on the jeep path to the next fork above the shelters where the road swings further left, and the trail to the summit continues straight ahead on a second jeep track that is bushier, narrower, and looks much less heavily traveled. Remember this junction, and digress a few extra yards by briefly turning left following the course of the main road. As the trail climbs a steep knoll in the direction of a radio tower, phenomenal views of the Monadnock Region make this short detour well worth the added effort. The arresting outlook to Mount Monadnock and Pack Monadnock is virtually the same as that seen from Crotched Mountain's summit, and this lower vantage actually allows a more northerly view than you'll find on the mountaintop.

Back at the second jeep-track junction, the fork to the summit dips slightly and reveals the mountaintop rising beyond the trees ahead. As the narrow track climbs easily again and commences a hard turn to the left, continue straight on a small footpath that angles into immature woods. When I made this hike, the remnants of a rude cairn still marked this turn for hikers who paused to look.

An easy section of trail crosses former meadows now overgrown with sprout wood, juniper, and occasional blueberries. Bear left at a fork marked with a sign about 20 yards past an opening in a stone wall. The path softly descends, circles, curves, hops a small brook, and rises through gentle slopes of pasture pine to an open ledge with views to the west.

Beyond the ledge overlook, the path turns right through a small, wet area and ascends moderately on a 0.3-mile jaunt to the top of Crotched Mountain. Don't bother with the true summit, which is marred by power lines and the remains of a radio tower. Instead, follow the "Scenic View" sign that leads about 50 yards south to protruding outlook boulders. For best results, descend even farther to a flat lawn on top of a ledge. Kids will enjoy scrambling around the rocky outcrops, and adults will appreciate the view. In the distance, Pack Monadnock dwarfs the hill that holds the rehabilitation center, while symmetrically sloped Mount Monadnock surveys the entire scene. Rising above the colorful valley, the ridge of the Monadnock-Sunapee Greenway (see Hikes 27 and 29) points to Mount Sunapee and a wealth of minor summits to the north. Binoculars would be helpful on this trip. I'm not sure if I was looking at cloud shadows, or if I spotted a sliver of Lake Sunapee on the far side of a distant col.

14 DePierrefeu-Willard Pond Wildlife Sanctuary

General description: A three-hour hike exploring the westerly shore of Willard Pond and the summit of Bald Mountain.

General location: Approximately 15 miles northeast of Keene in the town of Hancock.

Length: 2.25 miles round trip.

Difficulty: Moderate.

Elevation gain: 1,000 feet.

Special attractions: A secluded pond for canoeing, fly fishing, or shoreline exploring, with plentiful wildlife and a summit overview of the major Monadnock peaks.

Maps: Brochure and trail map are available from a mailbox at the trailhead; also USGS Stoddard NH 7.5 x 15.

For more information: Audubon Society of New Hampshire, 3 Silk Farm Road, Concord, NH 03301-8200, (603) 224-9909.

Key points:

0.1 Shore of Willard Pond.
0.5 Base of Bald Mountain at shore of pond.
1.1 Summit.

Finding the trailhead: Two miles east of Dublin on New Hamshire Route 101,

DePierrefeu-Willard Pond Wildlife Sanctuary

turn north at a blinker light onto Route 137. Continue north on Route 137, 6.8 miles to an intersection near the gazebo on the Hancock town common. Turn left onto Route 123, and take careful note of your mileage. Look for a right-hand turn onto a dirt road marked only with a boat ramp sign 3.7 miles past the gazebo. Traveling along the dirt road, bear left at an intersection at 0.4 mile and left again at a fork at 0.6 mile. Look for "NH Audubon Sanctuary" signs before reaching the parking area on the left, 1.5 miles from the highway. The trailhead is about 50 yards beyond a cottage on the far side of the parking area.

From the opposite direction, the left turn from Route 123 onto the dirt road is 3.3 miles south of the intersection of Routes 123 and 9.

The hike: DePierrefeu-Willard Pond Wildlife Sanctuary, the largest preserve of the Audubon Society of New Hampshire, contains more than 900 acres, including the summit of Bald Mountain and about 40 percent of the shore of sequestered Willard Pond. Reposing in quiet surroundings of wooded hillsides, this 100-acre pool grants easy access to canoes and is a favorite fly-fishing hole. For a very unique day, visitors can combine an easy paddle on the placid waters with a shore-side walk or an ascent of the summit that overlooks the pond. Note that spinning rods, motorboats, and the family pet are not welcome at this facility.

The boat launch is so close to the trailhead that few will resist the temptation to first wander to the end of the access road for a clear view down the length of the pond. The water hugs close to the slopes of Bald Mountain rising on the left along the northwestern shore. The hike described here runs about halfway down the length of the pond before curving back on itself to climb the slope at the far end of the mountain.

The Tudor Trail enters the woods about halfway between the cottage and the boat launch. Look for a trail sign, yellow trail markers, and a black mailbox containing maps. The stony path quickly crosses a small brook and returns to the pond amidst a wide assortment of flowering plants, ferns, and blueberries. Occasionally, families of ducks, loons, or mergansers make their way just off the rock-lined shore.

Within a short distance, the Tudor Trail forms a separate loop that departs to the left. Stay on the path close to the water and follow the red markers that

The serenity of Willard Pond.

blaze the Bald Mountain Trail. Continue along the pond, cross a brook, and head into the most intriguing part of the hike, where huge old-growth pine trees match the scale of immense glacial erratics scattered around the hillside. Soon, the trail turns back on itself and begins the often steep climb to the top of Bald Mountain. Catch your breath by pausing to admire the lady's slippers in open glades beside the trail. The ascent includes a set of oversized wooden steps and a quick switchback around granite outcroppings before reaching fine views from ledges covered with blueberries and juniper.

Looking east from the ledges, the vista includes the southern end of Willard Pond and the distinctive profile of Crotched Mountain rising in the distant background. Further southeast, North and South Pack Monadnock share the central view, while unmistakable Grand Monadnock towers in the mists behind.

The trail continues a short distance west to the true summit of Bald Mountain. The easy walk to the flat peak may be worth the extra effort in the off chance of spotting one of several moose that roam here unimpeded by the heavy forest cover and lack of summit views.

15 Harris Center for Conservation Education, Harriskat Trail

General description:	A short afternoon loop on a varied trail connecting two low-lying summits with Mount Monadnock views.
General location:	About 15 miles east of Keene within the town of Hancock.
Length:	4 miles.
Difficulty:	Moderate.
Elevation gain:	700 feet.
Special attractions:	Naturalist programs for young and old, Monadnock views from a formal garden, and one of New Hampshire's most eclectic trails.
Maps:	USGS Marlborough 7.5 x 15, or map available at the Harris Center.
For more information:	Harris Center for Conservation Education, 341 King's Highway, Hancock, NH 03449, (603) 525-3394.

Key points:
    0.25   Junction, Harriskat and Thumbs Down Trails.
    1.5   Summit, Skatutakee Mountain.
    2.5   Junction, Thumbs Up and Thumbs Down Trails.
    3.25   Return to junction, Harriskat and Thumbs Down Trails.

Finding the trailhead: Follow the directions for Hike 14 to the gazebo on the Hancock Town Common. Turn left onto New Hampshire Route 123 and

Harris Center for Conservation Education, Harriskat Trail

continue 2.2 miles north to another left turn at a directional sign for the Harris Center. After traveling 0.45 mile along this road, turn left again onto a dirt road at a second Harris Center sign. Enter the driveway through stone posts 0.65 mile down the dirt road. A parking area is located through a gap in the stone wall to the rear of a large, brown, white-trimmed house. The trailhead is almost directly across from the building on the opposite side of both the driveway and parallel access road. Look for painted paw prints and a sign reading "Briggs Reserve."

From the north, the right-hand turn off Route 123 is 4.9 miles south of the intersection of Routes 9 and 123.

The hike: Upon arrival at the Harris Center, first-time visitors may sense that they're intruding on the grounds of a private estate. The disconcerting feeling intensifies around the front of this spacious home, where lilacs fringe a formal garden, stone benches edge a lawn, and the peaks of Crotched and Pack Monadnock Mountains poke above the manicured shrubbery. No doubt one of the servants will shoo you away as soon as you are spotted.

Rest assured that all are welcome to this 7,000-acre "supersanctuary" situated in the heart of the Monadnock Region. In fact, there is an active attempt to lure people of all ages to the Harris Center through a varied schedule of programs and field trips covering topics as diverse as reptiles and rhododendrons. It's a perfect place to broaden the family's knowledge of nature and enjoy an easy hike, all in the same relaxing day. A full schedule of events is available from the center.

Beyond manicured lawns and naturalist programs, there is plenty of hiking to be done on an extensive network of inviting trails. Short interpretive walks depart into the woods about halfway down the field beyond the formal gardens. Longer hikes penetrate the far corners of the preserve.

The Harriskat Trail is marked with white rectangles and paw prints as it begins a very gradual ascent of Skatutakee Mountain, first stop on an easy loop hike that visits two slopes lying west of the Harris Center. About a third of the way to the summit, continue straight at the first junction with the Thumbs Down Trail, which departs to the right (and will serve as the return leg for completing this loop). The Harriskat Trail weaves easily up a wooded side hill on its way to the broad, flat top of Skatutakee, cleared to provide expansive 180-degree views of Crotched, Pack Monadnock, and Grand Monadnock Mountains.

Thirty yards beyond the Skatutakee summit, bear right onto the Thumbs Up Trail where the Harriskat, Thumbs Up, and Beeline Trails converge. This link between Skatutakee and Thumb Mountains is by far my favorite segment of the hike, and one of the most amazingly varied trails to be found in New Hampshire. After descending for the first 0.25 mile, the path swings left and flattens on a 0.75-mile journey to the base of Thumb Mountain. Within this distance, the Thumbs Up Trail leads hikers through emerald glades of ferns, delicate moss, colorful wildflowers, thick patches of blueberries, and stands of sugar maple regrown from long-ago logging days. Encounter ledgy flats, grassy clearings, rocky woodlands, duff-covered trail, and watery bogs in an endlessly changing scene. This kaleidoscope ends only when the Thumbs Up and Thumbs Down Trails meet on Thumb Mountain's eastern slope.

The 0.25-mile hike west from the Thumbs Up/Thumbs Down junction to the summit of Thumb Mountain is strictly an option. The short, steep segment that is visible from the intersection may dissuade some from making the effort. Near the top, a stone conversation pit offers a place to sit, but trees restrict the view largely to Mount Monadnock.

Bearing east on the return trip, the upper portion of the Thumbs Down Trail is noticeably steeper than the earlier Harriskat ascent. Before completing the circle, the Thumbs Down Trail enters a park-like setting of open woods on its approach to peaceful Jacks Pond. The height of land across the water is Skatutakee Mountain, the first summit you climbed on this engaging loop hike.

16 Mount Monadnock, Pumpelly Trail

General description:	A six- or seven-hour round trip on the longest, most diverse trail to the summit of Mount Monadnock.
General location:	About 12 miles east of Keene, and 35 miles west of Nashua.
Length:	9.0 miles round trip.
Difficulty:	Difficult.
Elevation gain:	1,700 feet.
Special attractions:	A quiet walk in the woods, a bumpy scramble above timberline, and the ultimate Monadnock view. Please note, however, that pets are not allowed in Monadnock State Park.
Maps:	USGS Monadnock Mountain 7.5 x 15, and Marlborough 7.5 x 15; also handout map of *Main Trails of Mt. Monadnock,* State of New Hampshire, Division of Parks and Recreation.
For more information:	Monadnock State Park, P.O. Box 181, Jaffrey, NH 03452, (603) 532-8862.

Key points:

2.2   Viewpoint at end of ridge.
4.5   Summit, Mount Monadnock.

Finding the trailhead: Begin at the conspicuous Dublin flagpole in the middle of the town of Dublin and literally in the middle of New Hampshire Route 101. Proceed west from the flagpole 0.4 mile and turn left onto Lake

Mount Monadnock, Pumpelly Trail • White Cross Trail

NORTH

0   0.5   1

MILE

To
Keene

Dublin Lake

101

To
Dublin

Lake Road

Hike 16—Pumpelly Trail

PARK BOUNDARY

PRIVATE

To
NH 101

Gilson
Pond

Mount Monadnock
Summit

Monte
Rosa

White Dot Trail

Upper Jaffrey Road

Thorndike
Pond

Visitor
center

P

Toll

To
Jaffrey

Road. Drive past an earlier turn marked with a sign for Monadnock State Park. That option is explored in Hike 17.

Follow Lake Road as it begins to circle Dublin Lake. In another 0.4 mile look for the trailhead on the left as an obvious path into the woods, marked with a sign for the Pumpelly Trail. Parking is limited to the side nearest the mountain. It may be best to pass the trailhead by about 70 yards and park off the pavement near a point where the road and lakefront meet.

The hike: The Pumpelly Trail from Dublin Lake to the top of the region's namesake peak is really two hikes in one. The first half is a pleasant walk through woodlands brimming with reminders of the area's agricultural history. The second is a scrambling roller-coaster ascent over a ridge that extends northeast from Mount Monadnock's summit. It's the ridge section, gaining and losing altitude in 10- and 20-foot increments, that earns this hike its difficult rating and adds substantially to the elevation gains predicted by topographic maps. Still, the dual personality of this hike commends it as the only single trail that samples the full geographic range of the beautiful Monadnock Region.

Near the lake, the trail makes some unusually sharp turns as it skims past private land in an area of attractive summer homes. Respect the No Trespassing signs and stay strictly to the trail. The route is not marked in this section except by an odd collection of signs and arrows at critical junctures. Before long the trail leaves modern civilization behind as it climbs easily along an old woods road that parallels a stone wall.

In time, the trail bears left off the farm road onto a path that continues its rolling journey through open woods. The chameleon forest reveals clues to its history—now new growth, now mature trees, now pasture pine, now pure stands of birch. It's hard to imagine the days when farmers logged this land with horses, and sheep grazed behind stone walls that march straight as an arrow through a backcountry of growing woods.

At about the midpoint, the character of the journey drastically changes. The trail steeply ascends the end of the ridge for about a quarter of a mile, then flattens for a short stretch before climbing several boulders to a ledge with views to the north and northeast. Cairns mark the path through the spruce and outcroppings along the ridge. Here hikers are forced to scramble over rocks and avoid falling off boulders. Exploration of this trail's higher reaches is not recommended in wet or foggy weather.

This ridge is composed of two distinct levels. The end of the upper ridge, with its bulbous promontory, hides its length from view until nearly its top. In other words, the summit of Mount Monadnock is farther away than it looks. After you make this discovery, take the time to relax on the open rock at the end of the upper ridge, and enjoy the fine views off to the north and east. From this point on, you can at least see the terrain ahead, and hiking becomes easier in these areas of low evergreens with the promise of the bald mountain peak offering incentive to toil on.

On the final, steep climb up the bare summit cone, reflect on the immense glacial power that left obvious gouges in the rock at your feet and smoothed the surrounding valleys into their present, gentle contours. The view from the top encompasses Pack Monadnock, Crotched Mountain, the Uncanoonucs, Kearsarge, Cardigan, and many more mountains that stretch to the far horizons and focuses on the intriguing texture of the Monadnock Region that is substantially closer at hand. Numerous lakes, ponds, rivers, and scattered villages tucked into the rolling hills of old farming country give this corner of New Hampshire a unique nubby look, as idealized by Currier and Ives. Part of the vista also includes a glimpse of Dublin Lake, a friendly reminder that you still have quite a hike before returning to your car.

17 Mount Monadnock, White Cross Trail

See Map on Page 64

General description: A traditional hike to the summit of Mount Monadnock from the mountain's most popular trailhead. A three- to four-hour round trip for hikers of all ages.

General location: About 15 miles east of Keene, and 35 miles west of Nashua.

Length: 4.4 miles round trip.

Difficulty: Moderate.

Elevation gain: 1,800 feet.

Special attractions: Historic views of beautiful landscapes on one of the world's most popular mountains. Please note, however, that pets are not allowed in Monadnock State Park.

Maps: USGS Monadnock Mountain 7.5 x 15; also handout map of *Main Trails of Mt. Monadnock,* State of New Hampshire, Division of Parks and Recreation.

For more information: Monadnock State Park, P.O. Box 181, Jaffrey, NH 03452, (603) 532-8862.

Key points:

- 0.5 Lower junction, White Cross and White Dot Trails.
- 1.9 Upper junction, White Cross and White Dot Trails.
- 2.2 Summit, Mount Monadnock.

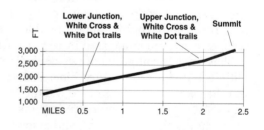

Finding the trailhead: Begin again at the Dublin flagpole (see Hike 16), but travel only 0.25 mile west on New Hampshire Route 101 before turning left onto Upper Jaffrey Road, which twists and turns in classic New England manner. Pass the park's Gilson Pond section, and turn right into the

Afternoon views on Mount Monadnock.

inconspicuously marked main entrance of Monadnock State Park, 4.8 miles from Route 101. The tollbooth and parking area are less than a mile up the access road. The trailhead is farther uphill, adjacent to a cabin at the far side of a circular driveway, just beyond the entrance to a campground.

The hike: A solitary peak with centuries of tradition, Mount Monadnock is one of the world's most frequently climbed summits, New Hampshire's version of Mount Fuji. Even on a weekday, I've never hiked this mountain without seeing at least a dozen other people. During the busy fall-foliage season, you may even be part of the crowd diverted to the overflow trailhead a few miles up the road.

With so much company, some may wonder why anyone should bother to hike these trails at all. Aside from a majestic peak and tremendous views, a collective memory of naturalist history emanates from this trailhead, which was well known by the likes of Emerson and Thoreau. Footsteps on this mountain lead into geographical realms that conserve part of our cultural heritage. A scattering of cabins under ancient trees creates an aura akin to visiting a grandparent's old summer place, a sense of retained legacy that no one could ever duplicate. This hike is a rare chance to both climb a mountain and connect with American tradition.

Across from the visitor center, a large sign for the White Dot, White Cross, and other trails designates the trailhead. Initially, all routes proceed up a wide, shaded path through beautifully mature woodlands sprinkled with a gleam of white birch. After about half a mile there is a major trail junction where the White Cross Trail diverges to the left. The White Cross and White Dot Trails run parallel to one another and reconnect short of the summit. The White Dot Trail is more direct, but it's also steeper, with sections over smooth rocks that may prove tricky in the rain. I recommend a climb of the more varied White Cross Trail, reserving White Dot as an alternate means of descent if the weather is dry.

The White Cross Trail gains much of its elevation by alternating two sets of diagonal side-hill stretches with two direct climbs of boulder-strewn trail. The scramble up the second slide area ends at a rock ledge with natural seating overlooking fine views to the south. Beyond this overlook, the trail wends through sparse woods before breaking onto open ledges with views to the southeast and a glimpse of Monte Rosa, a notable prominence on Mount Monadnock's southwestern shoulder.

The main peak remains hidden from view until the trail circles to the right as it aims to rejoin its companion path 0.3 mile from the summit. From this junction, the route is marked by white dots as it traverses a section of low spruce and scales Mount Monadnock's steep, glacier-scoured dome.

There are many ways to enjoy this summit. Stand proudly on the very peak and survey vast landscapes in all directions, or find a small niche out of the wind to enjoy a comfortable lunch with magnificent views. Children especially love Mount Monadnock and its various paths that ramble around the peak. Surrounded by 360-degree views, there are plenty of rocks to clamber about and trails that lead to stone formations with names like The Tooth, Doric Temple, and Emerson's Seat. Make sure children stay within sight while they have fun investigating the mountain. By the time the hike is over, the kids won't even notice that a tradition has passed to a new generation.

18 Pack Monadnock, Wapack Trail

General description:	A three- to four-hour ridgeline walk from summit to summit and back again. An auto road to the starting point furnishes barrier-free access to long-distance views.
General location:	On New Hampshire Route 101 about midway between Nashua and Keene.
Length:	4.0 miles round trip.
Difficulty:	Moderate.
Elevation gain:	About 1,200 feet, down and up both peaks.
Special attractions:	A superb view of Mount Monadnock on a trail that begins at its highest point. Picnic grounds and scenic outlooks for casual visitors and hikers alike.
Maps:	USGS Peterborough South, Greenville, and Greenfield quads.
For more information:	Manager, Miller State Park, 26 Pine Street, Peterborough, NH 03458, (603) 924-3672.

Pack Monadnock, Wapack Trail

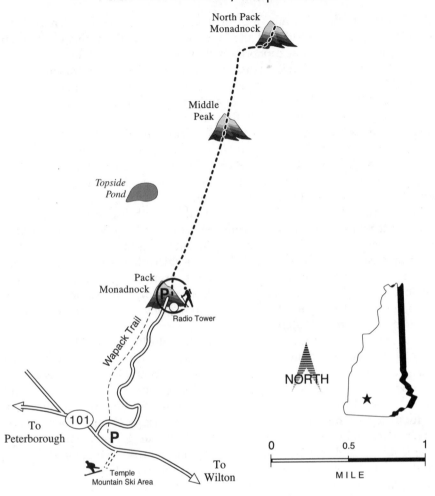

Key points:

    0.6   Low point in intervening col.

    1.1   Cairn on middle peak.

    2.0   Summit, North Pack Monadnock.

Finding the trailhead: From the traffic lights on New Hampshire Route 101 in Peterborough, travel east 3.9 miles to the access road for Miller State Park. The turn is across the highway, 0.1 mile west and almost within sight of the entrance to the Temple Mountain Ski Area. Because it's very steep, has hairpin turns, and has no guardrails, the road to the top of Pack Monadnock is not for the squeamish, and camper vehicles are not allowed. A parking area and trail directory are located at the base of the mountain for those who care to walk up the mountain. The hike described here leaves from the summit, immediately to the left of a distinctive stone hut.

The hike: The Wapack Trail is a 21-mile path that originates in northern Massachusetts, follows the ridge of the Wapack Range, and terminates only 1.5 miles beyond the summit of North Pack Monadnock Mountain. The access road to Miller State Park allows hikers to intercept the Wapack Trail and enjoy the highlights of an upside-down hike along the northern section of the route.

Like a ski area with its base lodge at the top, it seems odd to begin a hike by traipsing down a mountain. In fact, this walk on the Wapack Trail begins and ends at its highest point on the 2,310-foot summit of Pack Monadnock Mountain (also referred to as South Pack Monadnock). Before this hike is through, you'll descend to the bottom of an intervening col and climb the summit of North Pack Monadnock to stand at the midpoint of your journey only 32 feet lower than where you began.

Miller State Park provides even non-hikers with a mountaintop picnic area, vast panoramas of the glorious Monadnock Region, and a stunning view of renowned Mount Monadnock. In spite of its fame, a comprehensive look at this larger mountain is sometimes difficult to achieve, except by ascending a peak such as Pack Monadnock. From this vantage, the unique geological significance of southwestern New Hampshire's dominant peak becomes instantly apparent, a paradigm for a glacier-resistant core standing tall above a contoured plain.

Better views are promised by North Pack's alluring summit that seems to lie just beyond the stone hut near the end of the parking circle. Yellow triangles mark the trail as it leaves to the left of the hut and descends almost immediately to a picnic area on a rocky ledge with more views west and north. Beyond the ledge, the trail steadily descends what will be the most arduous part of the return journey. Following the ridge, the path then crosses a wet area on a bridge of decaying logs and climbs an elongated knoll through maple, birch, and spruce, before crossing and re-crossing a stone wall. The trail ascends through a concentration of red pine to the top of a larger knoll, sometimes referred to as Middle Peak, which is marked by a cairn but provides limited views. Bear left at the junction with the Cliff Trail and descend to a bog enclosed by another stone wall built by forgotten farmers many years ago. The final leg of the hike to the summit of North Pack Monadnock ends with long, looping zigzags up a wooded, southern slope.

Two large cairns occupy the flat top of North Pack Monadnock, which is covered with a heavy growth of evergreens. Explore the circumference of this summit to secure views that may stretch to the far White Mountains if the air is clear. The unencumbered view of Mount Monadnock is less dependent upon the weather, so relax and enjoy the scenery before retracing your steps and returning to the trailhead on South Pack.

For those in a lazy mood or with limited time, the short Red Dot trail circles South Pack Monadnock's perimeter. This fifteen-minute walk drops just below the driveway level near the park ranger's booth, circles to the picnic area near the Wapack Trail crossing, and returns to the parking area on the side of the summit opposite from where it began.

19 Pisgah State Park, Kilburn Loop

General description:	A quiet afternoon stroll through the woodlands of New Hampshire's largest state park.
General location:	Near Keene, in the extreme southwest corner of New Hampshire.
Length:	5.4 miles.
Difficulty:	Easy.
Elevation gain:	Less than 200 feet.
Special attractions:	Mountain laurel, blueberries, rustling woodlands, and the secluded shore of an unspoiled pond.
Maps:	USGS Winchester 7.5 x 15; trail maps are available from the address below, or from the mailbox at the trailhead.
For more information:	Pisgah State Park, P.O. Box 242, Winchester, NH 03470, (603) 239-8153.

Key points:

- 0.4 Inlet, Kilburn Pond.
- 1.0 Junction, Kilburn Road and Pisgah Mountain Trail.
- 1.3 Junction, Pisgah Mountain Trail and Kilburn Loop.
- 3.0 Crossing, Kilburn Brook.

Finding the trailhead: From Keene, drive about 11 miles west on New Hampshire Route 9, then turn south onto Route 63. Pass through the hilltop village of Chesterfield and ignore signs to a different Pisgah trailhead. About 4.4 miles from Route 9, around a sweeping left turn in the highway, turn left into a small gravel parking area marked with a sign for Pisgah State Park, Kilburn Road Trailhead.

The hike: Too often we think of wilderness as a remote area with spectacular natural scenery or herds of exotic and dangerous animals. We overlook the more workmanlike natural areas where human intrusion is minimized and the earth and water provide a home to mundane, unthreatening creatures—land that holds the rest of the world together. Such a place is Pisgah State Park. Over 13,000 unprepossessing acres of wooded ravines, marshes, and ponds compose Pisgah, New Hampshire's largest state park. A quiet wilderness.

Like the park, this hike neither dazzles with mountain vistas nor tests hikers' stamina. Instead, it's a mellow woodlands walk with a taste of everything that Pisgah has to offer. Of all the many trails in the park, it's also one of the few that's restricted to pedestrian use year-round.

After climbing to the top of the first ridge on a gravel path, the Kilburn Road quickly reverts to a mossy woods road, twisting and turning up and

Pisgah State Park, Kilburn Loop

To
Chesterfield

Davis
Hill

Baker
Pond

Lily
Pond

North
Round Pond

Baker Trail

P

Kilburn
Pond

Pisgah Mountain Trail

Pisgah
Mountain

Pisgah
Mountain Trail

Kilburn Brook

Kilburn Loop

Pisgah
Reservoir

63

Bishop
Mountain

NORTH

0   0.5   1

MILE

To
Hinsdale

around ridges and ravines through a cool New Hampshire forest. Mountain laurel seems to be everywhere, and in this park blueberries are more abundant than bugs. In about four-tenths of a mile, the trail bears left as it passes the return leg of the Kilburn Loop, and becomes a grassy path near a small bog at the inlet to Kilburn Pond, where a short detour leads to a view of the water.

About a mile from the trailhead, Kilburn Road intersects the Pisgah Mountain Trail, which departs to the right over a wooden footbridge visible from the trail junction. In the hilly section of the hike, the Pisgah Mountain Trail traces the contours of two small rises before meeting the beginning of the Kilburn Loop near the top of the third and largest rise. Marked with blue rectangles for cross-country skiers, the first half of the Kilburn Loop runs directly south, keeping to the top of the descending ridge that parallels Kilburn

Kilburn Pond, Pisgah State Park.

Pond's outlet brook. After more than a mile of woodland walk, the trail skirts an extended marsh and small pond where another short side trail leads to a view from shore.

At its most southerly point, the Kilburn Loop turns sharply right over a bridge where a small felled tree blocks the way straight ahead. The northern return trip on the opposite side of the watershed reclaims the elevation previously lost and again stays atop the ridge until returning to the south end of Kilburn Pond. The trail hugs this unspoiled shoreline for 0.75 mile with ample opportunities for wildlife viewing or waterfront relaxation under towering pines before completing the loop at Kilburn Road.

If you absolutely feel your hike must include a mountain view, continue on the Pisgah Mountain Trail about half a mile beyond the junction with Kilburn Loop. Then, either hike another 0.5 mile on the Baker Trail (loaded with blueberries) or continue about the same distance on the Pisgah Mountain Trail. Both have views of Mount Monadnock. These two paths are actually linked by the Reservoir Trail and form another loop, but that's a hike for another day.

20 Rhododendron State Park

General description:	A short, flower-filled walk through a national natural landmark. Portions may be enjoyed by persons with some types of physical disabilities.
General location:	10 miles southeast of Keene, near the village of Fitzwilliam.
Length:	0.6 mile, but meandering paths can double the distance.
Difficulty:	Easy.
Elevation gain:	Nominal.
Special attractions:	15 acres of native rhododendrons and an informative wildflower trail.
Maps:	A brochure with map and botanical information is available from the address below. Also USGS Monadnock Mountain 7.5 x 15.
For more information:	Rhododendron State Park, P.O. 181, Jaffrey, NH 03452-0181, (603) 532-8862.

Key points:

0.1   Junction Laurel Trail.
0.2   Optional trail to Little Monadnock.
0.4   Start of wildflower trail.

Botanical beauty at Rhododendron State Park.

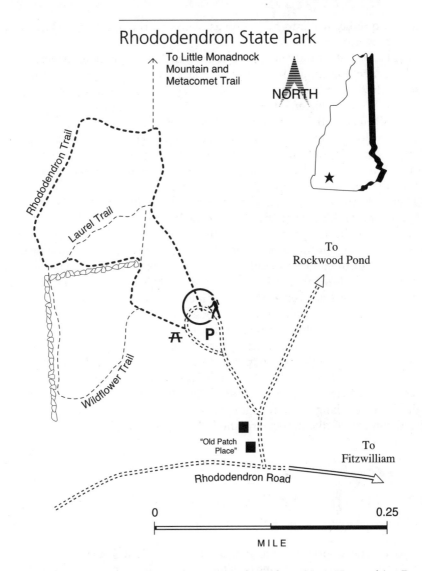

Rhododendron State Park

To Little Monadnock
Mountain and
Metacomet Trail

NORTH

Rhododendron Trail

Laurel Trail

Wildflower Trail

To
Rockwood Pond

"Old Patch
Place"

To
Fitzwilliam

Rhododendron Road

0

0.25

MILE

Finding the trailhead: From Keene travel south on New Hampshire Route 12 to the town of Fitzwilliam. At the blinker light at the intersection with Route 119, turn right (west) and drive 0.2 mile to a stop sign across from the historic Fitzwilliam Inn in the middle of the village. Turn left, staying on Route 119 for another 0.7 mile and bear right at the state park sign onto Rhododendron Road. The pavement ends after 2 miles; turn right onto Rockwood Pond Road, pass the old farmhouse, and bear left at a fork to the parking loop at the trailhead.

The hike: Designated a national natural landmark by the National Park Service, and New Hampshire's only botanic site, Rhododendron State Park draws visitors into its looping paths of delicate beauty. The 0.6-mile Rhododendron Trail commences through stone posts at the far end of the parking area and quickly leads to huge groves of native rhododendron shaded by oaks and evergreens.

Don't expect the gaudy profusion of blooms that occur on domestic rhododendron. Arching jungle-like overhead on 15-foot-high shrubs that nearly obscure the trail, these native plants display a refined beauty for the connoisseur. Broadly dispersed clusters of snowy blossoms range from white, to white fringed with blush, to the brilliance of shocking pink buds ready to burst into bloom. Benches are available to encourage contemplation and the passage of time required to appreciate these large flowers, here reaching skyward and backlit by the sun, there curving gently in the shade, soft against the rough texture of an old stone wall.

Thanks to the local garden club, a separate wildflower trail extends the height of the park's season into the spring, before rhododendron blossoms steal the show in mid-July. After ambling along the looping Rhododendron and Laurel Trails in the cool shade of the damp forest floor, most visitors will also want to include the informative 0.3-mile wildflower walk in their itinerary. This pleasant addition is a marvelous resource for anyone wishing to improve one's knowledge of native plants. Checkerberry, Indian cucumber, Clintonia, mountain laurel, and wood aster are a few of the many varieties clearly identified in their natural surroundings.

Avid hikers who feel the need to burn up extra energy can add their own 2-mile round trip on a moderate trail to Little Monadnock Mountain. The path departs from the northeast corner of the Rhododendron Loop and near its conclusion visits open ledges at its junction with the old Metacomet Trail. From this height, there is a nice view of Mount Monadnock and the ragged summit of distinctive Crotched Mountain.

21 Sheldrick Forest

General description:	A self-guided nature walk through a mature New Hampshire forest.
General location:	South-central New Hampshire, about 18 miles west of Nashua.
Length:	1.25 miles.
Difficulty:	Easy with moderate options.
Elevation gain:	Less than 200 feet.
Special attractions:	The Valley of the Giants and several natural history lessons in the woodlands of southern New Hampshire.
Maps:	Trail maps are available at the trailhead; also USGS Greenville quad.
For more information:	The Nature Conservancy of New Hampshire, 2 1/2 Beacon Street, Suite 6, Concord, NH 03301, (603) 224-5853.

Sheldrick Forest

Key points:

0.45 Valley of the Giants.
0.65 Laurel Ridge.
0.95 Stone culvert.
1.25 Return to trailhead.

Finding the trailhead: From the junction of New Hampshire Routes 101 and 31 South about 2 miles west of Wilton, continue west on Route 101 for 1.9 miles and then turn left onto Temple Road (just beyond Gary's Harvest Restaurant). Bear left at a fork after 0.3 mile and turn left again onto Town Farm Road just 0.1 mile later. Park in a well-marked field on the left 0.6 mile up Town Farm Road.

The hike: Inveterate hikers tend to dismiss Sheldrick Forest as "just" a walk in the woods. They're making a big mistake. Anyone who is used to hiking through the immature forests that blanket the White Mountains will marvel at this tract of towering trees in the state's southern tier. Saved from the whine of chain saws and preserved by The Nature Conservancy of New Hampshire, this extraordinarily diverse parcel of mature New Hampshire woodlands now serves as a living classroom where young and old can discover the special wonders of an undisturbed forest.

Unless you're an expert, "Everything Changes," the self-guided interpretive brochure prepared by The Nature Conservancy of New Hampshire, is indispensable to a full understanding of what Sheldrick Forest reveals. Topics that range from vernal pools to the effects of glaciation are explained in numbered chapters that correspond to numbered signs posted in the forest. Pick up a map of forest trails and a copy of the brochure from the information kiosk at the trailhead. Then relax in the sun, preview the guide, and gather some helpful hints on what the forest has in store.

More than 3 miles of trails explore Sheldrick Forest. For a good introduction, though, I suggest an elongated loop that combines sections of Helen's Path, the Charles Davisson Trail, the Laurel Ridge Trail, and the Swift Way to visit most of the highlights that reside in the forest's core.

Armed with map and brochure, walk north toward the edge of the field that serves as the parking lot. Follow signs for Helen's Path as it parallels the tree line, enters the woods on a worn track, and bends through a gap in a wall. Set amidst butternut, oak, ash, and cherry, signpost number 1 soon offers a thorough primer on tree identification before Helen's Path slowly descends to signpost number 2 where the trusty brochure helps you judge the age of various species that are growing all around you.

After crossing an old rangeway that separates two stone walls, Helen's Path continues to ease downhill, skirts the bank of Morgan Brook, and enters the Valley of the Giants. Walking between 165-year-old hemlock trees on the floor of this sheltered valley, hikers won't get a full sense of the size of these evergreen giants until they walk right over, touch a trunk, and look up to the sky. When you gaze at these immense conifers that soar into the blue, remember they were already taller than any hiker when President Abraham Lincoln gave the Gettysburg Address.

A little beyond signpost number 6, bear right for a short stint on the Charles Davisson Trail that crosses the brook on a split-log bridge and meets the junction with the Laurel Ridge Trail about 70 yards above the opposite bank. A right turn onto the Laurel Ridge Trail forgoes more than 0.5 mile of the Charles Davisson loop with its groves of majestic trees, but it gives hikers a chance to savor a walk on the crest of a narrow ridge that is sheathed with mountain laurel growing in bountiful clusters beneath maple, hemlock, and oak. Be forewarned, though, the Laurel Ridge Trail climbs surprisingly steeply to the top of a tall knoll, with correspondingly impressive views down its sharply angled slopes to the thread of Morgan Brook.

The Laurel Ridge Trail ends at its junction with the Swift Way at the base of the tall knoll. A right turn onto the Swift Way returns to the Valley of the Giants. I turned left instead for a roundabout return that crosses a stone wall, jogs left and right at the second intersection with the Charles Davisson Trail, and aims along a ridge beneath a canopy of old-growth trees. Interpretive lessons on beech and pine lead back to Morgan Brook, which hikers cross on a stone culvert that was made for teams of horses. Nearing its conclusion, the Swift Way gently winds through the forest before it discovers a second field that borders Town Farm Road. Angle right across the field, walk through an aisle in a patch of forest, and you'll find yourself back in the field where you parked your car just a few yards from the trailhead.

Dartmouth/
Lake Sunapee Region

It's curious that an Ivy League college and a popular lake lend their names to this west-central region. But the college in Hanover educated students before New Hampshire was born, and the lake and its mountain are a geographic center for year-round outdoor fun.

I like to think of this region where I live as New Hampshire in microcosm. The lakes are smaller and the peaks less awesome than in the rest of the state, but the combination results in a durable mix that bears up to frequent use. This is nature to visit when the spirit moves, and that fosters a quiet sense of comfort established with the passage of years.

Undiscovered pockets of natural beauty abound in this compact region. In Fox State Forest and Pillsbury State Park flourishing wildlife will cross your path, but you'll see few other people. If you know where to look, secluded walks can even be found close to more popular fare. Try the Andrew Brook Trail to Lake Solitude near Mount Sunapee's busy slopes, a waterfront stroll in a wildlife refuge on Lake Sunapee's thriving shore, or a walk through a bog on the edge of New London. After you explore these hidden treasures, a sociable swim or familiar views from the tops of Kearsarge and Ragged Mountain always await the active hiker.

22 Fox State Forest, Ridge Trail

General description:	A half-day excursion through a rich variety of wildlife habitats that echo with the history of human occupation. Accessible year-round.
General location:	In the town of Hillsborough, nearly midway between Concord and Keene.
Length:	About 4 miles.
Difficulty:	Moderate, but with shorter alternatives that are easy.
Elevation gain:	About 600 feet, including the ascent of Jones Hill.
Special attractions:	The quaking kettle hole of Mud Pond Bog, bear and deer habitat on Jones Hill, and memories of farmsteads along Concord End Road.
Maps:	A trail guide is available from a mailbox outside the headquarters building near the trailhead. Also USGS Hillsboro Upper Village quad.
For more information:	South Region Headquarters, Fox State Forest, P.O. Box 1175, Hillsborough, NH 03244, (603) 464-3453.

Fox State Forest, Ridge Trail

Key points:

0.2	Brook crossing.
0.9	Mud Pond.
2.7	Top of Jones Hill.
3.2	Valley Road Junction.
3.7	Brook crossing.

Finding the trailhead: From the direction of either Concord or Keene, follow New Hampshire Route 9 to Hillsborough. At the traffic lights in the middle of town, turn northwest onto School Street (opposite Route 149, which runs rapidly downhill to the southeast). School Street passes the post office and becomes Center Road at the outskirts of the village. The headquarters of Fox State Forest and trailhead parking are on the right immediately beyond two immaculate hilltop farms about 2 miles outside of town.

80

The hike: More than 25 miles of Fox State Forest trails lead to peat bogs, wandering brooks, oak-covered hilltops, cellar holes, and virgin forests that lie within 2 miles of a major state highway and are readily accessible throughout the year. The Ridge Trail hike along the perimeter of the forest's eastern quadrant is a contemplative excursion through a variety of geography and habitat, an adult adventure infused with a sense of expectant wandering. A great walk for observant naturalists, but not so appealing to children. A quick round trip to Mud Pond may be a better alternative if the younger set is along.

Trail signs near the edge of a paved parking area mark the start of a wide track swooping downhill by a row of pitch pine that line a clearing. The hike follows one of several paths that use the Valley Road to descend to the brook on the valley floor. Watch for the departures of the Tree I.D. and Mushroom Trails before the Ridge Trail, unmistakably blazed in white with red center, executes a short left-right jog across a wooden footbridge and turns downstream in the direction of Mud Pond.

As this well-marked trail bounces along between the stream and a stone wall, hikers are treated to a revolving mix of pine, spruce, hardwoods, and marsh thickets typical of New Hampshire lowlands. The route bears southeast toward a distant gap where converging ridges tail off into wetlands, but the path swings uphill to the left before reaching this elusive goal. In a few yards the white-blazed Mud Pond Trail diverges to the right.

Mud Pond Bog is prettier than its name and is one of the highlights of the hike. The boardwalk that penetrates the bog is less than half a mile from the junction with the Ridge Trail via a path that ascends a low hill, crosses a small forest road, and descends easily to the shore. This small glacial kettle hole, partially capped with a quaking cover of sphagnum moss, harbors a conglomeration of unique trees, shrubs, orchids, and even insect-eating plants. For a real education in bog ecology, try to obtain the guide to Mud Pond *(Fox Forest Saunters #2)* from Fox State Forest headquarters before you go.

To resume the journey on the Ridge Trail, it's not necessary to backtrack all the way to the Ridge/Mud Pond junction. As you return from the pond, just turn right (north) on the forest road near the top of the hill. Within a few hundred yards the Ridge Trail reenters from the left and joins the road for a short stroll. Soon, distinctive blazes mark a right turn onto a wooded path through a younger section of forest.

In the course of the next 0.35 mile, the trail flows along undulating ridges, over stone walls, past glacial erratics, and through changing patterns of forest vegetation. At the Bog 4 Corners entrance to Fox State Forest, the trail brushes a modern roadway on the right as it diagonally crosses Gould Pond Road. A left turn down the length of this old thoroughfare leads to the Concord End Road a little northeast of Gerry Cemetery, a logical shortcut for hikers who wish to avoid the long climb of Jones Hill.

North of Gould Pond Road, the ridges become sharper and the turns more erratic. This rough terrain is a precursor of the Ridge Trail's 0.5-mile ascent through woodlands that are scattered with large beech and oak. Deer and bears frequent this rugged area that most hikers never visit. If you tire on the long uphill haul, pause to look for signs of wildlife, or consider how it would have felt to build the stone walls that partition the side of this mountain.

On the terraced heights of Jones Hill, the view is enclosed by nearly pure stands of beech. Peace and solitude are found in this hilltop glade, where tree trunks stand like columns supporting a dome of green. Beyond the summit, the trail rapidly descends to civilization on the Concord End Road. Turn left, downhill, on this narrow byway, pass a curve at the intersection with the western end of Gould Pond Road, and look for cellar holes in the woods on the right, reminders of farmstead days.

Farther down the easing slope, take another minute to admire more remnants of long-lost human skills, as an old hand-laid stone culvert carries the road across a brook. The route continues to flatten near the Gerry Cemetery where stone walls hold back the encroaching woods. At the far cemetery wall, a left turn onto the Valley Road leads 0.6 mile along the familiar brook, which returns to the first Ridge Trail junction at the base of the hill below the trailhead.

23 John Hay National Wildlife Refuge

General description: A short family walk on a forest-ecology trail that visits a historic estate and a quiet Lake Sunapee shore.

General location: About 28 miles northwest of Concord in the town of Newbury.

Length: 1.8 miles.

Difficulty: Easy, but with instances of rough footing and small embankments.

Elevation gain: Less than 200 feet.

Special attractions: The manicured grounds of a summer estate, an informative forest-ecology trail, and waterfowl habitat on the shore of an unspoiled lake.

Maps: A trail guide and map are available at the visitor center or trailhead kiosk; also USGS Newport 7.5 x 15.

For more information: Refuge Manager, The John Hay NWR, Route 103A, P.O. Box 276, Newbury, NH 03255, (603) 763-4789.

Key points:
0.25 The Fells.
0.7 Shore of Lake Sunapee.
1.1 Beech Brook.
1.7 Return to trailhead.

Finding the trailhead: From exit 9 of Interstate 89, take New Hampshire

John Hay National Wildlife Refuge

Route 103 west about 13 miles to the town of Newbury, at the south end of Lake Sunapee. In the village, across from the large Safety Services building on the left, turn right onto Route 103A. The driveway for the John Hay National Wildlife Refuge, The Fells, is 2.1 miles north on the left. Look for masonry stone posts and vine-covered walls at the entrance. Once beyond the stone posts, a gatehouse and visitor center are on the left, and the parking area is immediately on the right.

The hike: Consider the plight of the rich and famous in the nineteenth century, before the comforts of air conditioning or the convenience of jet flights to Mediterranean shores. Surely, public figures and gentlemen of means were not expected to endure the sweltering summers of Washington or New York. What was a body to do? One answer survives here at The Fells, the summer home of John M. Hay, author, statesman, and confidant of President Abraham Lincoln.

A surprising aspect of this magnificent estate, sited on a hill above the cooling waters of Lake Sunapee, is that the formal gardens and 100-foot portico do not command sweeping lake and mountain views. In a likely concession to modern sensibilities, the forests have been allowed to reclaim all but a southerly outlook across manicured lawns to Mount Sunapee and a part of the lake at its feet. The balance is maintained as a national wildlife refuge and historic site that contain acres of stately grounds and a forest-ecology trail that touches the pristine shore of one of New Hampshire's most popular lakes.

The hike really begins from the parking area, although the official trailhead is close to the main house about a quarter of a mile down the driveway. The gradual descent along this gravel road was meant to be an impressive introduction to an idealized slice of nature. It is grandly successful. Stately oaks, maples, and a few immense white pines stand in splendid isolation on a cleared swath that borders the drive. Near the house, rhododendrons spread beneath huge beech trees and specimen plantings.

Heading downhill, pass just to the right of the main house to gain a taste of the geometry of the formal lawn and gardens that stretch behind the brick portico at the rear of the building. Look for the entrance to the house off the portico where tours of the home are available seasonally on weekends and holidays.

To find the trail proper, continue to the far (south) side lawn, enjoy the view over the top of the herb garden, and pass through the wall under the medallion to the right of the fountain. Quickly turn right at the lilac bushes and look for a trail sign and the beginning of yellow trail markers. Don't bear left, but follow a straight line that would be a continuation of the extended axis of the house. A second trail sign soon points the way into the woods on the right, as the trail angles down the hill back toward the portico side of the building.

Numbered posts correspond with the "Guide to the John Hay II Forest Ecology Trail," an informative introduction to the common and not-so-common plant species that have regenerated here. The route is a little obscure in spots, but in only a few hundred yards it leads to a largely undeveloped quadrant of Lake Sunapee's stony shore.

Nature's profusion on this extended coastal walk is in sharp contrast to the symmetry imposed at the top of the hill. A fresh, prevailing breeze sweeps down from the low hills across the lake and kicks small breakers against the shore. The path leads past an off-lying island to a gravel beach with a sweeping Sunapee view. Waterfowl nesting sites are located in this vicinity; be cautious of where you step.

Beyond the beach, the trail loops up an embankment and quickly crosses a mossy brook. The stream's tiny ravine leads the trail uphill, as the top of its ridge grows higher with increasing distance from the lake. Near the crest of the hill, the trail re-crosses the brook and climbs 50 yards to meet a grassy woods road that runs at the top of the ridge. A left turn onto this old road ends the loop with a birch-lined stroll back to the rhododendrons that line the driveway about 100 yards above The Fells.

24 · Mount Kearsarge, Rollins Trail

General description: A short hike to a popular peak with fine views of west-central New Hampshire. Suitable for the entire family.

General location: About 25 miles northwest of Concord in the town of Warner.

Length: 1.0 mile round trip.

Difficulty: Moderate, but very close to easy.

Elevation gain: 300 feet.

Special attractions: Picnic grounds and long-distance vistas near high-altitude trailhead parking, plus easy access to a fire tower with 360-degree views.

Maps: USGS Andover and Warner quads.

For more information: Manager, Rollins State Park, Box 219, Warner, NH 03278, (603) 456-3808.

Key points:

0.1   Picnic area.
0.25 Rest-stop boulders.
0.5   Fire tower on summit.

Finding the trailhead: From the south, take Interstate 89 to exit 8 and turn left at the end of the ramp. Go straight at the yield sign onto New Hampshire Route 103 and continue 1 mile to the center of town. Just beyond the brick town hall, turn right onto Kearsarge Mountain Road, following signs for Rollins State Park. The state park tollbooth is 5 miles from the center of town, but once in the park, the paved access road winds another 3.5 miles up the mountain along Mission Ridge. Drive past several picnic sites and outlook turnouts to reach the upper parking area adjacent to the trailhead.

From the north, depart Interstate 89 at exit 9. A left turn at the ramp onto Route 103 leads to the center of town. The turn onto Kearsarge Mountain Road is on the left, just beyond a bank.

The hike: The southerly approach to the summit of Mount Kearsarge through Rollins State Park is a perfect outing for an entire extended family. Thanks to an auto road that scales most of the mountain, even the very young or very old can enjoy a picnic with a view, hike the moderately easy trail to the summit, or learn the workings of an active fire tower.

John Hill welcomes visitors to a working fire tower.

Mount Kearsarge, Rollins Trail • Winslow Trail

11

To
Andover

To
New
London

Kearsarge Mountain Road

WINSLOW

STATE PARK

Toll booth P

Kearsarge Valley Road

Bradley Brook

Summit, Mount Kearsarge X

P

Little
Mountain

To
Interstate 89

Black
Mountain

NORTH

MISSION RIDGE

Meadow Brook

French Brook

ROLLINS
STATE
PARK

0   0.5   1

MILE

Gore Road

Toll
booth

Kearsarge Mountain Road to Warner

On the upper side of the parking lot, a sign reading "Picnic Area" marks the beginning of the 0.5-mile trail to the summit. About 50 yards up the hill, a grassy expanse filled with picnic tables, fire grates, and birch trees overlooks wide-angle views to Mount Monadnock 50 miles to the south. Many may be satisfied to relax here, break out the food, and call it a day. Others will prefer to increase their appetites by bearing right and continuing on the trail to the peak.

The first half of the Rollins Trail is rocky, but the grade is moderate as it wends its way up slopes of spruce and pine. Children seem to enjoy scrambling up this path, and even a toddler holding a parent's hand can navigate most of the way. Recent ditching efforts have mitigated this trail's former gully look.

Just shy of the halfway mark, large boulders on the right provide a rest stop with expansive views. Look for the Blackwater River, the Contoocook Valley, and Mission Ridge that extends south just beyond the corner of the parking lot.

The trail resumes across wooden planks that bridge a wet area and ascends gradually on a smoother path of thin soil and exposed ledge. As the trail swings left to avoid a large outcropping, blueberries are found interspersed among boulders and small evergreens, until all vegetation gives way to gray granite slabs. Painted white arrows and crosses and an occasional cairn mark the best route over steeply slanted bedrock, before the top of the fire tower guides the final course up the bare summit dome.

Mount Kearsarge is an observation point for much of west-central New Hampshire, featuring tremendous views in all directions. Pleasant Lake, Lake Sunapee, Mount Sunapee, and Ragged Mountain command the immediate foreground, while the ski mountains of neighboring Vermont and the peaks of New Hampshire's White Mountains rim horizons to the west and north.

On blustery days, the spectacle seems even better if observed from the enclosed comfort of the fire tower deck. When it's staffed, hikers are welcome to visit this working tower during the summer and active fall seasons. Use caution on the narrow metal stairs, and knock on the counter-weighted door for entry. The lookout staff seems unfailingly willing to explain their duties and identify landmarks, especially for curious youngsters. There should be enough time to take a site on the range finder before heading back down the trail to picnics that await.

25 Mount Kearsarge, Winslow Trail

See Map on Page 87

General description: A half-day family hike on a gradual trail that ascends the full height of Kearsarge Mountain.

General location: About midway between Concord and Claremont in the town of Wilmot.

Length: 2.0 miles round trip.

Difficulty: Moderate.

Elevation gain: 1,100 feet.

Special attractions: A longer and less crowded route to a popular summit with fire tower views in all directions.

Maps: USGS Andover, Bradford, and New London quads.

For more information: Winslow State Park, P.O. Box 192, North Sutton, NH 03260, (603) 526-6168.

Key points:

0.7 Viewpoint to the west.

1.0 Summit of Mount Kearsarge.

Finding the trailhead: At exit 10 of Interstate 89, northbound travelers turn right at the end of the exit ramp, and southbound travelers turn left. About 80 yards northeast of the highway, travelers from both directions then turn right at a T intersection onto North Road. Proceed 0.4 mile to a sweeping left turn onto Kearsarge Valley Road, which intersects with Kearsarge Mountain Road after another 3 miles. The right turn onto Kearsarge Mountain Road is marked by a "Winslow State Park" sign adjacent to a field with full views of Kearsarge Mountain. The tollbooth and parking area are about 2 miles up the road. Note that this is NOT the same Kearsarge Mountain Road that provides access to Hike 24.

The hike: On these slopes in 1868, Civil War hero Admiral John A. Winslow attended the grand opening of a resort hotel named in his honor. In the modern age of interstate highways and rapid access to the spectacular White Mountains, it's hard to believe that resorts once flourished on peaks like modest Mount Kearsarge. In fact, many of our ancestors contented themselves with the simple pleasures of nature conveniently found in these nearby locales. Only a trace of the Winslow Hotel remains, but the beauty of the trail from Winslow State Park to the summit of Mount Kearsarge endures on this straightforward, no-nonsense hike that befits the memory of a naval officer.

The foundation stones of the old Winslow House hotel encircle a spreading birch tree and picnic table in the parking area at the end of the access road. From the lawn, look for the fire tower on the summit and views of the Dartmouth/Lake Sunapee Region lying to the west. Two trails now leave the upper end of the parking area from a signboard in a clearing. The new Barlow Trail is more gradual but wet. I prefer the Winslow Trail, which follows a well-trod dirt path through a stand of evergreens.

The climb of Mount Kearsarge from the Wilmot side is a great family hike, but requires more effort than most people expect. The rocky and root-bound trail almost immediately begins a moderate climb of the highest peak in Merrimack County. Proper footwear and adequate clothing are needed to protect from strong winds and changeable weather.

About two-thirds of the way to the summit, the trail eases a bit, allowing hikers to catch their breath and steal a quick glance through spruce and fir trees to the views that appear at their backs. Short of the summit, the rocky climb soon reaches a large boulder that guards extensive local vistas of King Ridge, New London, and Pleasant Lake with the Green Mountains of Vermont forming an impressive backdrop.

Vegetation becomes stunted as the soil thins and the trail ascends the solid incline of the summit ledges. All around are signs of the area's geology. Parallel lines gouged into the rock beneath your feet are striations carved by mile-thick ice about 10,000 years ago, while exposed 60-million-year-old bedrock supports your final steps up the summit cone.

The greatest joy of this hike is in circling the lookout tower and bounding about the rounded summit dome, exploring all points of the compass. Try to spot Mount Monadnock well to the south, Franconia Notch to the north, Camel's Hump to the west in Vermont, or Boston's glass-and-steel towers in the haze that spreads southeast. A declivity in the rock provides a picnic spot complete with a picnic table protected from prevailing winds. Check out the fire tower's observation deck, and remember to follow the red blazes on your return. White blazes are for Hike 24.

26 Philbrick-Cricenti Bog

General description:	A nature walk on a mat of living vegetation that floats on a kettle-hole pond.
General location:	In New London, just 1.5 miles from the center of town.
Length:	0.75 mile.
Difficulty:	Easy.
Elevation gain:	Virtually none.
Special attractions:	Pitcher plants, orchids, and arctic species that grow in a quaking bog.
Maps:	A map with descriptive brochure is usually available at the trailhead.
For more information:	New London Conservation Commission, Town Hall, New London, NH 03257, (603) 526-4821.

Key points:
0.2 Peek Hole Loop.
0.3 Quaking Loop.
0.75 Return to trailhead.

Philbrick-Cricenti Bog

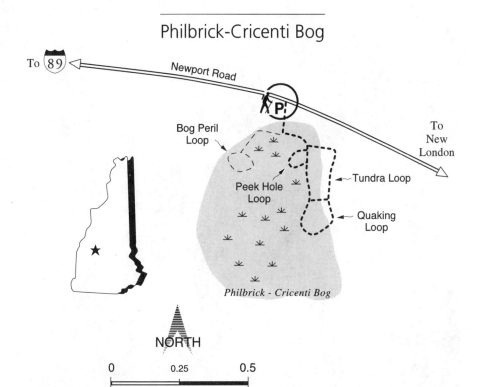

Philbrick - Cricenti Bog

NORTH

0   0.25   0.5
MILE

Finding the trailhead: Beginning near Colby-Sawyer College in the center of New London, drive north on New Hampshire Route 114 (also known here as Main Street). Bear left onto Newport Road at a blinking traffic light where Route 114 continues straight ahead. Look for the New London Post Office on the left just 0.7 mile

past the blinking light. Park in a wide gravel area on the left (south) side of Newport Road 0.2 mile beyond the post office.

From the opposite direction, the parking area is on the right side of Newport Road 1.6 miles south of exit 12 off Interstate 89.

The hike: If you'd like to walk on water, you'll find your perfect chance at Philbrick-Cricenti Bog. Formed by arctic plant species that grew across the top of a glacial pond, a living mat of moss and sedge, dwarf spruce and tamarack now floats on 20 feet of murky water. Walking a squishy trail, you can venture out to the middle of this ancient pool, measure the depth of the water, and feel the unmistakable bounce of the mat of a quaking bog. *One serious note, though.* This walk is only possible because of a boardwalk trail maintained by the town of New London. Hikers who leave the path risk sharing the fate of wandering livestock at the bottom of the pond. What looks like solid ground may be a trap for the unwary. *Be sure to stay on the trail and leave your pets at home.*

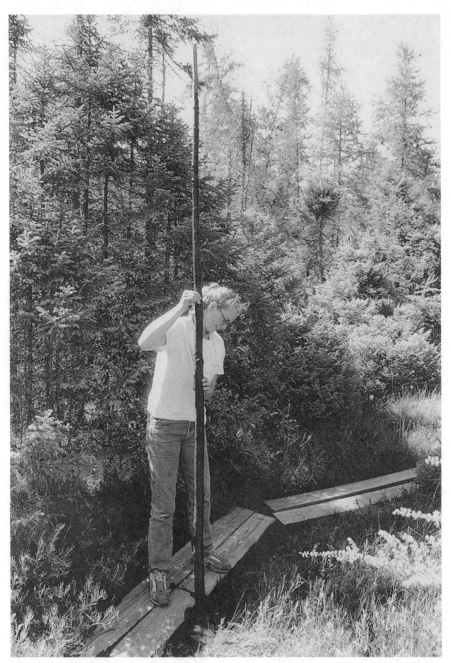
Checking the depth of Philbrick-Cricenti Bog.

Wildflower enthusiasts will take special pleasure in Philbrick-Cricenti Bog. Set amid ferns and saw grass 10 feet down a dirt path that leaves the side of the road, a welcoming sign makes note of particular flowers that may be blooming from time to time. On my last visit in late July, clusters of brilliant white-fringed orchids added a delicate splash of contrast to the bog's ever-greens. Pitcher plants, leatherleaf, and bog rosemary are always on hand to add to the arctic mix, but observant hikers will also spot flowers such as yellow-horned bladderwort and even calla lilies blooming in their season.

Beyond the welcoming sign, a damp access path leads through waist-high ferns and grasses growing beneath red maple trees in a shallow part of the bog that rims the ancient shore. Black spruce trees dominate as the path advances towards the edge of the floating mat and arrives at the first trail junction 0.1 mile from the road. The collection of looping paths here is short enough that even casual walkers can explore all trails at their leisure, but the Peek Hole, Tundra Garden, and Quaking Loops quickly guide visitors to the highlights of the bog.

Turn left at the trail junction and follow a boardwalk path that roams across a mat of sphagnum moss floating above several feet of submerged peat, a layer of once-living vegetation now preserved by the highly acidic water of the bog. Tiny tamarack trees sprouting elegant evergreen tufts seem to be on loan from a Japanese garden as you pass through a tundra land-scape of brilliant wildflowers on a platform of rusty moss.

Be sure to take the next right onto the short Peek Hole Loop. Here you'll find abundant orchids and proof that you're walking on water. Reach down and pull up the pole that sticks out of the mat by the side of the boardwalk path. A little messy perhaps, but solid confirmation that you're standing above 20 feet of watery ooze.

The Quaking Loop carries walkers nearly to the center of the bog, where pitcher plants are plentiful and a platform of wooden planks lets you bounce on the quaking mat. Wear waterproof footgear as you walk this peaceful trail and gaze across the thin skin of tundra vegetation that hides the open water. Inspect the array of arctic plants that intertwine at your feet and look for the flag of a white-tailed deer that bounds away from danger between the trees that line the bog.

Both the Quaking Loop and the Tundra Garden Loop return to the first trail junction through the woods above the shore. Rocks and roots in this woodland section might pose a problem if you planned on an easy hike. It's simple enough to backtrack and return the way you came, but you'll miss the frogs and calla lilies that call these damp woods home.

27 Pillsbury State Park, Monadnock-Sunapee Greenway

General description:	A five-hour circuit through a lake-filled park to the Monadnock-Sunapee Greenway. A remote campsite allows overnight use.
General location:	30 miles west of Concord and 15 miles southeast of Claremont.
Length:	About 8.5 miles.
Difficulty:	Moderate.
Elevation gain:	900 feet.
Special attractions:	Glimmering lakes and ponds, forests filled with wildlife, views from Lucia's Lookout, and a rare chance to backpack in southern New Hampshire.
Maps:	Trail maps are available from the park office; Monadnock-Sunapee Greenway Trail Guide, published by the Society for the Protection of New Hampshire Forests; also USGS Newport and Lovewell Mountain 7.5 x 15.
For more information:	Pillsbury State Park, Washington, NH 03280, (603) 863-2860.

Key points:

0.7 Junction, Bear Pond and Pamac Trails.
1.7 Junction, Bear Pond Trail and Greenway.
4.4 Lucia's Lookout.
7.8 Return to junction, Bear Pond and Pamac Trails.

Finding the trailhead: Take New Hampshire Route 10 south from Newport and continue through the village of Goshen. Bear left onto Route 31, and drive southeast 4.7 miles to the entrance to Pillsbury State Park. After checking in at the ranger's office, proceed about a mile through the park to a turnaround at the end of Mill Pond. A short walk up the spur road that branches from the turnaround leads to the trailhead at a gate that prevents vehicular access.

The hike: The Monadnock-Sunapee Greenway links Mount Monadnock and Mount Sunapee on a rolling, north/south, ridgeline route that covers almost 50 miles of south-central New Hampshire. I came to Pillsbury State Park

Pillsbury State Park, Monadnock-Sunapee Greenway

knowing that its trails connect to the greenway, providing a rare opportunity to backpack in southern New Hampshire. What I found was a gorgeous, virtually undiscovered park, teeming with wildlife and very few people. Moose, beavers, turtles, and loons make their home around the beautiful lakes and small ponds that lie below the shallow greenway ridge. Campers, canoeists, and day hikers couldn't ask for a more marvelous backcountry setting.

The hike begins by following a jeep road along a ridge above the northwest shore of Mill Pond. The path is initially signed as the Five Summers Trail, corresponding with the name in the Monadnock-Sunapee Greenway Trail Guide, but recent park maps also call it the Pamac Trail. By either name, the route crosses a wooden bridge over a flowage connecting North

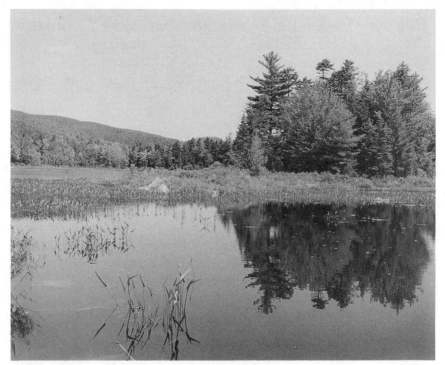

Mill Pond, below the Monadnock-Sunapee Greenway ridge.

and Mill Ponds and quickly comes to a fork where the Bear Pond Trail diverges to the right.

Keep right on the Bear Pond Trail and pass through brambles and low brush of premier moose habitat for what should be a 1-mile, easterly hike up the low, wooded ridge to the greenway junction. Apparently, I was not the first hiker on this route to mistake a game path for a detour around a beaver flowage and end up bushwhacking to my destination. Before you set out, check on current trail conditions with the ranger on duty, and by all means carry a compass.

The Monadnock-Sunapee Greenway is a well-defined path that provides easy walking as it rolls gradually along a wooded ridge, but long pants will be appreciated in some areas where heavy undergrowth and prickly berry bushes crowd the trail. At a low point on the ridge, about 1.5 miles north of the Bear Pond Trail junction, a blue-blazed side path leads to a campsite surrounded by beech, maple, and small evergreens on the top of a tiny knoll. Backpacking to this spot as part of an easy overnight trip on the Pillsbury Park circuit is only one way to enjoy this rare, southern New Hampshire backcountry site. With judicious car shuttling, hikers can also make this stop part of an extended cross-country trek that connects to Mount Sunapee State Park over the most northerly segment of the Monadnock-Sunapee Greenway (see Hike 29).

Beyond the campsite spur, the route negotiates more than a mile of hilly terrain before it rendezvous with the northern end of the Five Summers

(Pamac) Trail. For beautiful, southerly views down the entire length of the greenway, delay your return on the Pamac Trail, continue 0.2 mile north on the greenway, and climb steeply over and around rock outcroppings to reach Lucia's Lookout. An exploration of this minor summit will yield views of Mount Monadnock to the south, Kearsarge and Ragged Mountains to the north, and tranquil May Pond to the southwest near the trailhead.

Through hikers may continue north on the greenway about 3.25 miles to the summit of Mount Sunapee. Others need to backtrack to the Five Summers Trail and bear right (southwest) at its junction, for the 3.9-mile hike back to the trailhead. The trail angles gradually off the ridge, includes a long stretch over a badly eroded logging road, but ends happily by traversing the entire length of serene North Pond.

To reverse the loop, care is needed after ascending about halfway up the Five Summers Trail where only a handmade sign marks a right turn at a junction of old logging roads. It's the only similar option along this route, so you really shouldn't go wrong. If you crest over a small rise and the road turns back on itself sharply to the left, you'll know you just missed your turn.

28 Ragged Mountain

General description:	A spirited climb to a small peak on a newly established greenway.
General location:	About 23 miles northwest of Concord, near the town of Andover.
Length:	6.0 miles.
Difficulty:	Moderate.
Elevation gain:	1,200 feet.
Special attractions:	Buswell Ridge, wildlife, and views of central New Hampshire from the peaks of Ragged Mountain.
Maps:	USGS New London and Andover quads.
For more information:	Sunapee-Ragged-Kearsarge Greenway Coalition, P.O. Box 1684, New London, NH 03257-1684.

Key points:
- 1.2 Junction, Ridge Trail.
- 2.4 Ragged Mountain ski peak.
- 3.2 West Peak.
- 4.4 Crossing of skier's bridge.
- 6.0 Proctor Academy Trailhead.

Finding the trailhead: New Canada Road: From the junction of New Hampshire Route 11 and U.S. Highway 4 West in Andover, drive north on US 4

Ragged Mountain

West 1.8 miles and turn right onto New Canada Road. The trailhead is on the right after 0.9 mile. Look for a sign for the Ragged Mountain Trail and park in the spaces provided on either side of the road.

Proctor Academy: From the junction of Route 11 and US 4 West in Andover, drive east on Route 11 for 1.5 miles and turn left onto Field House Lane in the center of the village. Park near the tennis courts on the left. The trailhead is just beyond the tennis courts on top of an embankment.

The hike: The trail over Ragged Mountain has now become part of a new addition to New Hampshire's hiking scene. Thanks to the dedicated efforts of the Sunapee-Ragged-Kearsarge Greenway Coalition a 70-mile network of hiking paths, logging trails, and old town roads circles Sunapee Lake and links the principal summits of the Dartmouth/Lake Sunapee Region. Aside from locating routes and blazing trails, the coalition has been hard at work preparing a trail guide and sponsoring a series of guided hikes on their annual Walkabout. Each of their half-day or day-long hikes is described in its own brochure and explores a different segment of the large greenway network. While these guided walks serve as the perfect introduction to the greenway every fall, hikers can always pick their favorite section of trail and discover this great new resource on their own in any season.

The New Canada Road to Proctor Academy segment may be the most energetic link in the greenway chain. Exploring an unspoiled pocket of central New Hampshire, this portion of the greenway wanders through sidehill forests that teem with wildlife and tops a peak that sees little traffic, at least during the summer. By spotting a car, this vigorous segment is perfect for end-to-end hikes in either direction, but rapid access to remote woodlands and fun-to-hike Buswell Ridge makes New Canada Road the better trailhead for starting a round trip.

A comfortable backcountry feeling greets you at the trailhead. Stepping off from the gravel edge of New Canada Road, the greenway follows an overgrown swath that curls into the woods and passes through a former logging yard after only 50 yards. Guided by white blazes with a long trapezoidal shape, the route tracks a logging road through a forest of hemlock and pine, darts through a gap in a stone wall, and enters another clearing. To the left, at the far end of this second logging yard, blazes mark a skidder path that crosses a small brook and continues to rise through the quiet woods at an easygoing pace.

Beech trees and small oaks are plentiful on the approach to Buswell Ridge as the trail becomes more challenging and offers a grand chance to test your tracking skills. Did a hiker or a lone moose last walk this forest path that angles left off the skidder road, wanders through a patch of level woods, and gently rolls to the Ridge Trail at a sign that says that you've already walked 1.4 miles from the trailhead?

Turn left (northeast) on the Ridge Trail (blazed with small metal squares) as it dips into a gully and immediately conquers a rock outcrop with views of the summit ahead. For more than a mile, the erratic Ridge Trail tutors hikers on the meaning of "Ragged" Mountain as it rambles along the crest of the ridge, bouncing up and down and alternating the cool of the woods with sunny blueberry patches. Watch for a 30-yard detour to views of Mount Kearsarge, before the trail drops into a rocked-walled col and the Ash Trail leaves to the right. Bear left along the Ridge Trail that parts a field of ferns, climbs through a cut in the wall of the col, tops a small outcrop, and ascends sharply through a switchback to the top of the Ragged Mountain Ski Area.

Like many of New Hampshire's smaller summits, the top of Ragged Mountain has recently been marred by the addition of a cell phone tower. Most hikers will probably race past the shiny, new fenced enclosure, following either a path through the woods or a 50-yard access road that leads to a chairlift station in the middle of a grassy slope. With open space all around, you've reached the logical turnaround point for a round-trip hike. You'll even find a picnic table at the edge of a ski slope for relaxed viewing of Newfound Lake, Cardigan Mountain, and Mount Moosilauke beyond.

If you're hiking end-to-end, walk west past the north side of the ski patrol hut, cross a power-line cut, and step onto a steep path that immediately enters the woods and plunges down the mountain. Once off the upper cone of the Ragged Mountain ski hill, the path eases through evergreen woods until its abrupt arrival at the base of West Peak. From this low point on the ridge, the trail climbs about two-tenths of a mile in a series of sudden bursts, pauses for a wetland interlude, and then charges up the steep slope one last time. The Ridge Trail actually misses the very top of West Peak, but a spur path on the right leads to a perfect perch. Check the view of Cold Pond and Mount Kearsarge to the south, look west toward Lake Sunapee, or chart your earlier course on bumpy Buswell Ridge that rises to meet the grassy swaths of Ragged Mountain's ski peak.

About 70 yards beyond the outcrop perch, the route becomes confusing. Hike east on the West Ridge or greenway route where a yellow-blazed trail marked "MT TR" turns downhill to the right. Pass a spur to another lookout, and descend to a shallow col where the Balanced Rock Trail also turns down-hill to the right. The greenway route follows the Balanced Rock Trail (not the less-used, smaller path that continues to East Peak).

After a rough drop of 0.2 mile down the Balanced Rock Trail, a brief detour on the left leads to a large glacial erratic stuck on a narrow ledge. You may not be wholly impressed by the sight of balanced rock, but the best view from the eastern side of the mountain lurks at the end of the detour about 50 yards beyond.

Pressing on after the detour, do not return 0.2 mile uphill to the ridge, but follow white painted blazes and aluminum trapezoids as the greenway route steadily falls downhill to the left. This no-nonsense descent cruises skidder paths and washed-out logging roads until a blue sign steers the route onto a narrow ski trail that veers off to the left. Enjoy your secluded forest stroll as you cross a skier's bridge and twist through woods on a well-marked trail that includes an odd uphill turn around a section of timberland that has recently been logged. Turn right when you meet a woods road and right again 0.15 mile later when the woods road ends at a fork. The last 0.1 mile of your forest walk concludes at the edge of the woods where a white blaze and a "Carr Trail" sign at the top of a small embankment look across the tennis courts to the Proctor Academy lot where your second car is parked.

29 Mount Sunapee, Andrew Brook Trail

General description:	A half-day family hike to a hidden lake suspended on the slopes of Mount Sunapee.
General location:	30 miles northwest of Concord in the town of Newbury near the south end of Lake Sunapee.
Length:	About 6.5 miles round trip.
Difficulty:	Moderate.
Elevation gain:	1,400 feet.
Special attractions:	Distant mountain views overlooking Lake Solitude, a contemplative pine-shaded shore, and refreshments at the summit.
Maps:	Maps of Sunapee State Park Hiking Trails; also USGS Newport 7.5 x 15.
For more information:	New Hampshire State Parks, West Region Office, P.O. Box 123, Greenfield, NH 03047, (603) 547-3373.

Key points:

0.1   Crossing Andrew Brook.
1.7   Lake Solitude.
2.1   White Ledges overlook.
3.2   Mount Sunapee summit.

Finding the trailhead: New Hampshire Routes 103 and 103A intersect in front of the Newbury Safety Services building near the south end of Lake Sunapee. From this landmark, proceed southeasterly on Route 103 for 0.8 mile and turn right onto Mountain Road about halfway down a long hill. The trailhead is 1.2 miles up Mountain Road just before crossing a small bridge with wooden guard rails. Although there is presently no trail sign and the yellow blazes are quite faint, look for an obvious opening into the woods and oversized gravel shoulders for parking.

From the opposite direction, the left turn onto Mountain Road is 5.3 miles west of the junction of Routes 103 and 114 in the town of Bradford.

The hike: I've always thought of the Andrew Brook Trail as being located on Mount Sunapee's back side. No disrespect intended, but the trail ascends this gentle mountain on its quiet southeastern slopes out of sight of Sunapee Lake and the always busy ski area that lies on the north side of the hill. Mount Sunapee's summit is graced by a snack bar with all the accouterments, and, even in summer, hosts sedentary types who arrive by chairlift to enjoy the limited view. Fortunately, inveterate hikers can avoid all this commotion by circling around back and walking directly to the mountain's genuine attractions about a mile below the peak. Few chairlift passengers ever discover the contemplative shore of tranquil Lake Solitude and the wondrous views from the top of White Ledges that are really the highlights of this hike.

Mount Sunapee, Andrew Brook Trail

Beginning at Mountain Road, the trail climbs cautiously in the first 100 yards, levels to cross Andrew Brook after 0.1 mile, and bears right, delaying the inevitable turn up the slope that awaits on the left. The route narrows to a maple-shaded path as it re-crosses the brook and steadily climbs along the ravine. When the trail next turns left across the brook, it has gained about two-thirds the height of the ridge that holds Lake Solitude.

At the fourth and last crossing, the brook is a mere summertime trickle high on the mountain's slope. The trail commences a long, cross-hill traverse, gently ascends the shoulder of the ridge, and opens onto a clearing near the north end of the lake. Footpaths weave among the evergreens, visiting a multitude of secluded outlooks along the eastern shore. These are fine places to converse, examine lily pads, or view the bare cliffs of White Ledges reflecting in the clear water.

To resume the journey, make your way to a trail junction beneath huge trees that crowd the water at the northern tip of the lake. To the left, white blazes lead south on the Monadnock-Sunapee Greenway along the western shore. To the right, the greenway and the orange-blazed Solitude Trail lead north to White Ledges and the summit of Mount Sunapee. Don't put much weight in the trail-sign distances posted here. They are badly overstated.

Ascending north away from the lake, the trail quickly turns back on itself and surmounts open boulders at the top of White Ledges. A short detour along the ledge instantly reveals how this curious rock got its name, and unveils fabulous views overlooking Lake Solitude. *Be cautious! This small but very real cliff tolerates no false steps.* Below, the pond levitates on its ridge amidst hills that evaporate in summer haze.

If you really can't resist an icy drink or hot snack, follow the trail as it descends into a col and swings northwest on a fairly level, heavily forested path. Before long it pops out onto a ski slope with partial views of Mount Kearsarge and Lake Sunapee. Follow the ski run uphill and under a chairlift to reach the top of the mountain. The views are restricted, but the smell of grilling hamburgers may be enticement enough.

For long-distance hikers, Mount Sunapee is the northern terminus of the Monadnock-Sunapee Greenway, and Lucia's Lookout (see Hike 27) is only 2.5 miles south of the trail junction at the north end of Lake Solitude. The outlooks along the trail are rapidly being overgrown by evergreens, but mountain views still remain. Backpackers need to know that camping and open fires are prohibited on Mount Sunapee. Head south instead to the campsite described in Hike 27.

Lake Solitude, high on Mount Sunapee's slope.

Lakes Region

Ask anyone about the Lakes Region and what immediately come to mind are beaches, boating, ice-cream cones, condominiums, and waterslides. With 273 lakes less than two hours north of Boston, this east-central portion of the state is ready-made for high-volume recreation. Squam, Winnipesaukee, Winnisquam, The Weirs, and Newfound Lake clearly sound like lots of fun, but is there anything here for us hikers?

Resoundingly, the answer is Yes! The Lakes Region takes full advantage of its water-flecked terrain by boasting a remarkable mix of trails that entertain hardy hikers and vacationing families alike. At White Lake, the Loon Center, and Paradise Point, young or old can amble beside quiet wooded shores, while a natural education waits for all at the Science Center at Squam Lakes. Before going for a swim, the beach crowd might like an overview of the area. Mount Major, Belknap Mountain, and West Rattlesnake all serve this noble purpose, with short climbs to low-lying summits above glistening New Hampshire lakes.

Mountain hikers have no need to feel left out. Capping the region to the north and west, Mounts Passaconaway, Cardigan, and Chocorua fringe the lakes with alpine silhouettes and generate their own authentic sense of backcountry hiking adventure.

30 Mount Cardigan, West Ridge Trail

General description:	A three- to four-hour loop on the easiest trail to the summit of Mount Cardigan. A good intermediate hike for children.
General location:	About 20 miles east of Hanover and Lebanon.
Length:	3.5 miles round trip.
Difficulty:	Moderate.
Elevation gain:	1,300 feet.
Special attractions:	A junior-sized peak with a big mountain feel. Unique views of Vermont, the Lakes Region, and the Connecticut River Valley.
Maps:	USGS Mount Cardigan quad.
For more information:	Regional Manager, Cardigan State Park, Box 273, West Ossipee, NH 03890, (603) 323-2087; or New Hampshire State Parks, West Region Office, P.O. Box 123, Greenfield, NH 03047, (603) 547-3373.

Mount Cardigan, West Ridge Trail • Manning Trail

Key points:

  0.5   Lower junction, South Ridge Trail.
  1.0   Footbridge over brook.
  1.5   Summit, Mount Cardigan.
  1.9   Top of South Peak.
  3.0   Return to lower junction, West Ridge and South Ridge Trails.

Finding the trailhead: Follow New Hampshire Route 118 as it branches north from U.S. Highway 4 at the triangular traffic island and town common in the village of Canaan. As you pass the fire station, the tower on the bald peak of Mount Cardigan is plainly visible on the right. One-half mile from US 4, turn right onto the access road designated by a Cardigan State Park sign, and bear right at an intersection with a dead-end road after crossing the Orange town line. The pavement ends 2.7 miles from Route 118, and 0.7 mile later the access road forks left to the parking area and picnic grounds. The trailhead is on the left behind a shelter and picnic tables. In the off season, the last 0.7 mile of the access road may be closed; park in the space provided at the last fork in the road. This closure adds 1.4 miles to the hike and about 160 feet of elevation gain.

The hike: Mount Cardigan's West Ridge Trail may be the most deceptive hike in New Hampshire. Although the path is often broad and ascends at a reasonable pace, the upper reaches traverse almost a quarter of a mile of the mountain's bare summit cone. Because this innocent trail quickly transports hikers to an exposed peak with all the attendant risks of a larger mountain, Mount Cardigan has taken on the aspect of a proving ground for each generation of new, young hikers. It's a great place to bring the kids, but make sure to pack adequate clothing, and keep a sharp eye on the weather.

The West Ridge Trail climbs easily through a white-birch forest for the first 0.5 mile to arrive at the lower junction with the South Ridge Trail, the return route if the weather is good. For now, continue left on the West Ridge Trail that leaves the flank of the mountain and climbs easily through mixed hardwoods that shelter plentiful partridge.

The path broadens and is often muddy on portions of its middle segment, which doubles as a snowmobile route. A small brook can be heard well before it appears to the left of the trail. After crossing the brook and climbing more directly up the slope, the path reaches a footbridge over a second brook 0.5 mile from the summit.

Once beyond the footbridge, woodlands give way to shoulder-high spruce clinging to granite slabs. Eventually, even the evergreens yield to Labrador tea and mosses sticking like mortar to fissures in the rock. On the upper section, white blazes, arrows, and stone cairns replace the painted orange rectangles that usually mark the trail. If you cover the last few feet to the summit by walking directly toward the fire tower, you won't even realize that you've been on the Clark Trail until you check the directory signs clustered below the southwest base of the tower.

On clear days, the spectacular view from Mount Cardigan includes unique vistas not seen on mountains farther north. Miles of the fertile Connecticut

Cardigan Mountain as seen from Firescrew summit.

River Valley stretch north to south, while to the west, ski slopes rise randomly over what looks like most of Vermont. Winnipesaukee, Squam, and Newfound Lakes sparkle in hollows between the Ossipee and Belknap Mountains that block the view to the east.

The West Ridge Trail is well marked with cairns near the summit, not nearly as steep as the alternate route, and it is the safest means of descent if the weather turns bad. But if weather and moderate steepness don't deter you, completion of the loop on the South Ridge Trail will add spice to your hike with a great change of perspective on Mount Cardigan's bald peak.

Return to the trail-sign cluster below the fire tower, and descend the summit dome to the south in the direction of the Clark Trail arrows. Before losing sight of the signs, look for painted marks suggesting the trail and the roof of the warden's cabin at the bottom of the slabs. The route to the South Ridge Trail passes directly in front of the cabin, and 0.1 mile later turns left at a trail marker toward South Peak and Rimrock. As you approach the large cairn on South Peak, the view back to the tower on Cardigan's summit conveys a surprisingly rugged image to summarize your hike.

The rimrock segment follows white painted rectangles and small cairns along the mountain's shoulder and offers interesting views of approaches from the south. Another trail junction atop Rimrock 0.8 mile from the summit leads you along the South Ridge Trail that completes the loop back to the lower junction with the West Ridge Trail, 0.5 mile from the trailhead.

31 Mount Cardigan, Manning Trail

See Map on Page 105

General description: A half-day walk from campground or lodge to the summits of Firescrew and Mount Cardigan.

General location: About 20 miles northwest of Franklin, and 8 miles due west of Newfound Lake.

Length: 6.0 miles round trip.

Difficulty: Moderate.

Elevation gain: 1,700 feet.

Special attractions: Classic views of Cardigan's peak, panoramas of the western Lakes Region, and south-facing slopes with extra early spring flowers.

Maps: USGS Mount Cardigan quad.

For more information: Regional Manager, Cardigan State Park, Box 273, West Ossipee, NH 03890, (603) 323-2087; and Manager, AMC Cardigan Lodge, RFD 1, Box 712, Bristol, NH 03222, (603) 744-8011.

Key points:

0.4 Holt Trail junction.
1.7 Scenic ledges.
2.4 Firescrew summit.
3.0 Summit, Mount Cardigan.

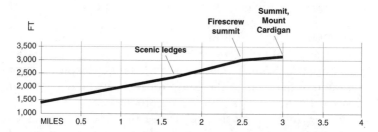

Finding the trailhead: Depart Interstate 93 at exit 23, and proceed west on New Hampshire Route 104 for 5 miles to the junction with Route 3A in the town of Bristol. Turn right (north) on Route 3A for about 2 miles to a set of blinker lights at the intersection with West Shore Road. There is a church on the corner, and the south end of Newfound Lake glistens through the trees. Turn left on West Shore Road passing the developed edge of Newfound Lake. In 1.8 miles, leave West Shore Road by continuing straight at mail-route signs pointing to Alexandria.

After Mount Cardigan becomes visible across a large farm field, do not turn left to the town of Alexandria, but bear right at the junction with the Fowler River Road. This junction, and all following junctions, should be marked with directional signs to the AMC Lodge that is also your destination.

Stay on the paved Fowler River Road after 3.2 miles where it bears left at an intersection with a gravel road. Continue 1.1 miles and turn right onto a gravel portion of the road, and bear right again in 0.1 mile for the final 1.3 miles to the lodge. The trailhead is beyond the lodge near the apple trees by a pond.

The hike: Except at the windy summit, the eastern approach to Mount Cardigan bears little resemblance to the West Ridge Trail (Hike 30). An additional 400 feet of elevation gain over steeper terrain makes vistas at the end of the Manning and Mowglis Trails seem especially well earned. But early spring wildflowers and views from the open ledges below Mount Firescrew's summit will be just compensation for all the added effort.

This hike meets the Manning Trail near its midpoint, adjacent to the Cardigan Lodge. This remote hiker's retreat is operated by the Appalachian Mountain Club and provides family-style meals and bunkroom accommodations similar to the AMC's White Mountain huts. Walk-in campsites are also available in several locations along the early stretches of the trail. This is not wilderness camping, of course, but a far cry from the usual developed campground, and an attractive option for day hikes and weekend excursions.

A signpost near the swimming pond notes that the Manning Trail initially shares the path with other routes to Cardigan's summit. In this stretch, hikers pass several campsites along a gentle woods road, but don't be tempted by the trail junction that appears in less than half a mile. Although the Holt Trail is the most direct route to the summit, it's extremely steep and potentially dangerous in certain conditions. Bear right on the more enjoyable Manning Trail for the 1.3-mile walk to the ledge and the 2 miles to the Firescrew summit.

Soon after the Holt Trail junction, the Manning Trail leaves the broad lane and angles to the right as a more typical mountain path. Interrupted only by a plateau in the birch woods, this segment eases up the side hill of a sunny, south-facing slope, an ideal environment for the early blooming of trout lily, trillium, violets, and other woodland flowers.

Beyond the side hill, the trail zigzags more steeply to the first of three ledges with picturesque views of the Ragged Mountain, Mount Kearsarge, and Mount Cardigan summits. As you climb each ledge in turn, the views open to encompass the full panoply of vistas from northeast to southeast with Newfound Lake and Cardigan Lodge prominent in the foreground.

The final ledges are largest and steepest, and lead into the woods for the steep climb to the windswept Firescrew summit. Devoid of substantial growth for reasons implied by its name, this level summit instills an enjoyable top-of-the-world feeling—except, of course, for Cardigan Mountain looming 0.6 mile to the west. The Manning Trail ends just beyond the Firescrew summit. Turn left onto the Mowglis Trail, blazed with painted white rectangles, as it dips briefly into a wooded col and then abruptly climbs the steep Cardigan summit cone. Before returning, have a snack by the fire tower and enjoy sweeping views of much of New Hampshire and Vermont from the barren granite slabs that are Mount Cardigan's peak.

32 Mount Chocorua, Liberty Trail

General description:	A less-traveled, southern approach to one of the state's most popular summits. A five- or six-hour day trip, with an optional overnight stay at a cabin near the peak.
General location:	About 10 miles southwest of Conway, between the Lakes Region and the White Mountains.
Length:	About 7.4 miles round trip.
Difficulty:	Moderate to the cabin shelter. Difficult in the last 0.5 mile to the peak.
Elevation gain:	2,600 feet.
Special attractions:	High-altitude shelter, impressive views of the White Mountains, and a firsthand look at the unique Chocorua peak.
Maps:	USGS Mount Chocorua quad.
For more information:	Saco Ranger District, 33 Kancamagus Highway, Conway, NH 03818, (603) 447-2166.

Key points:

2.7   Junction, Liberty and Hammond Trails.
3.3   Liberty cabin.
3.5   Junction, Liberty and Brook Trails.
3.8   Summit, Mount Chocorua.
7.0   Junction, Brook Trail and Paugus Mill Road.

Finding the trailhead: From New Hampshire Route 16 turn west onto Fowler's Mill Road, 5.7 miles north of the junction of Routes 16 and 25, or 9.5 miles south of the junction of Route 16 and the Kancamagus Highway (Route 112). Fowler's Mill Road is recognizable from the main highway as the unmistakable dirt road that crosses a photogenic wooden bridge with spectacular views of Mount Chocorua across Chocorua Lake. After stopping to take a few pictures, follow the twists and turns of this dirt road as it bears left at a fork after 1 mile and continues straight at an intersection in another 0.8 mile. About 3.4 miles from Route 16, just before a bridge, turn right onto a forest road that should be marked with a sign for the "Mt. Trail." The parking area and trailhead are 0.7 mile down the forest road.

Mount Chocorua, Liberty Trail

NORTH

Summit, Mount Chocorua

■ Jim Liberty Cabin

Hammond Trail

Liberty Trail

Brook Trail

Claybank Brook

Durrell Brook

0   0.5   1

MILE

Paugus Brook

P

Paugus Mill Road

NATIONAL FOREST BOUNDARY

James Pond

Fowler's Mill Road

To NH 113A

To NH 16

Chocorua's view of Mount Washington.

The hike: Patriotic enthusiasm had nothing to do with the naming of this trail. That honor was bestowed on a peak in Franconia Notch. Instead, the name preserves the memory of Jim Liberty, who hacked and blasted this bridle path to the upper reaches of Mount Chocorua out of strictly pecuniary interests. Unfortunately, the three-story Peak House resort he helped to build was literally blown off the mountain in 1915. On top, note the massive chains that pass over the roof of the cabin that now occupies the site.

The trail begins along a broad, smooth path up a modest grade surrounded by scattered hardwoods that survived recent logging. This is a wonderful trail for horses, an Achilles-stretching experience for hikers. After flattening to cross two brooks, the path becomes a little rockier, the woods lose the just-logged look, and the gradient remains moderate with steep sections, if you can call them that, aided by convenient stone steps. Eventually the pitch increases, spruce and fir trees predominate, and the trail climbs via quick switchbacks to enter the summit's Forest Protection Area. Soon, the Hammond Trail enters from the right (east), while the course swings left across the face of a steep incline and then twists back again up a stony ledge with southern views of the Ossipee Mountains rising to the east of Squam Lake.

Approaching Mount Chocorua's flat upper shoulder, a short descent leads to open rock ledges that offer an astounding perspective. Pastel hues and green-stained striations appear on a summit that looks from here to be a transplant from southern California. Soon after exposing this startling view, the trail arrives at the Jim Liberty Cabin, picturesquely standing in the shadow of the angular peak.

The robust alpine location succeeds in making this shelter magnificent, not the accommodations. The rudimentary cabin holds only a shelf for dining and nine plywood bunks. Overnighters will need a backpacker's stove; fires are not permitted. The cabin is operated on a first come, first served basis. Contact the USDA Forest Service Saco office for reservations and more information.

Apparently, the bridle path never extended beyond the cabin. In its final stages, the trail circles left across the face of steep rock slabs where horses would be loathe to travel. *Be very wary here of short, severe pitches that are doubly dangerous in wet conditions.* The Liberty Trail ends at the junction with the Brook Trail about halfway between the cabin and the peak. Follow the painted orange blazes of the Brook Trail that lead over steep slabs and rock scrambles 0.3 mile to Chocorua's summit.

The panorama from the top of Mount Chocorua is staggering. To the west, Mounts Whiteface, Passaconaway, Tecumseh, and the Tripyramid stand impressively close at hand. To the north, Mount Washington grandly rises above the Presidential Peaks, while Crawford Notch carves its niche in the middle distance.

To create a loop hike on your return, simply follow the Brook Trail downhill instead of the Liberty route. This alternate trail ends about 0.4 mile farther up the forest road, northwest of the closed gate at the Liberty Trailhead. The Brook Trail is steeper, rockier, and bypasses the great views near the Jim Liberty Cabin, so I prefer the original route.

33 The Loon Center at the Markus Wildlife Sanctuary

General description:	A one- to two-hour nature walk near the shore of Lake Winnipesaukee.
General location:	About 18 miles northeast of Laconia, in the town of Moultonborough.
Length:	About 2 miles round trip.
Difficulty:	Early portions are easy, but the trail to the loon-nest overlook is often rocky and rough.
Elevation gain:	Nominal.
Special attractions:	Lakeside woods and wetlands, a loon educational center, and a view of nesting loons.
Maps:	Trail maps are available at the Loon Center, the Loon's Feather Gift Shop, and from a mailbox near the trailhead.
For more information:	The Loon Preservation Committee, Audubon Society of New Hampshire, Lees Mills Road, P.O. Box 604, Moultonborough, NH 03254, (603) 476-LOON.

Key points:

0.2   Bench and viewing platform.
0.7   Fork in trail to start loop.
0.85 Loon-nest lookout.

Finding the trailhead: From exit 23 of Interstate 93, drive east on New Hampshire Route 104 for 8.3 miles, turn left at the light onto US Highway 3, and drive north 0.9 mile. Turn right onto Route 25 in the center of Meredith Village, pass through the town of Center Harbor, and turn right onto Blake Road (just beyond the Moultonborough Central School) 9.1 miles from Meredith Village. Blake Road ends at a T intersection after 0.9 mile. Turn right at the T onto Lees Mill Road. The entrance to the Loon Center at the Markus Wildlife Sanctuary is on the left after 0.2 mile.

The hike: A cherished symbol of wilderness, the loon is usually appreciated by paddlers on backcountry lakes, not by New Hampshire hikers. A rare chance to spy on nesting loons from a comfortable bench on shore is the main reason hikers visit the Markus Wildlife Sanctuary on the shore of Lake Winnipesaukee. But the sanctuary offers more. Operated by the Audubon Society of New Hampshire, this 200-acre preserve is also the home of the Loon Center and Loon Preservation Committee—a perfect place for hikers of all ages to learn all there is to know about these threatened waterbirds.

Visits to the Loon Center last longer than expected. Aside from a gift shop with a loon motif, the Loon Center has video displays, computer terminals, research books, an electric loon quiz, and several exhibits that pinpoint where loons are currently nesting in New Hampshire. In one stop, you can learn all about the life cycle of the loon, the dramatic rebound of

The Loon Center at the Markus Wildlife Sanctuary

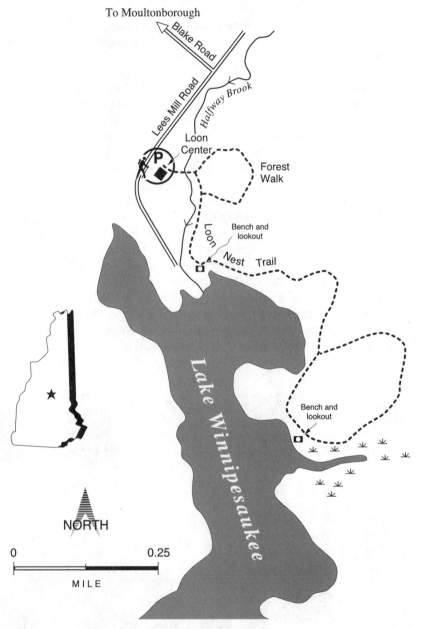

New Hampshire's loon population, the passage of legislation to remove deadly lead from fishing sinkers, and the effort to monitor local lakes for mercury and other contaminants to protect the loon's future.

Once your research is complete, simply follow the wooden arrows that guide you away from the screened porch at the end of the Loon Center and step onto a path that drops down a small embankment to a bridge that crosses a stream. Borrow a trail guide from the mailbox that stands near the end of the bridge, and watch for red and yellow arrows after you cross the wooden span.

Red arrows point left to the Forest Walk, an easygoing path that skirts the edge of the stream and loops a few hundred yards through a damp woodland environment. Especially in the spring, wildflowers and ferns line this simple stroll, and nesting boxes for wood ducks hang from the trunks of trees.

Yellow arrows point right to your main objective, the woodchip-covered Loon Nest Trail that tracks Halfway Brook to an arm of Lake Winnipesaukee. Split logs and small wooden walkways span sloughs and waterways as the trail eases through the forest near the muddy banks of the stream. In less than two-tenths of a mile, the path arrives at a cozy bench perched on a portable dock stranded on a dry shore. Depending where the loons nest, views from the trail's benches may vary from year to year. During my visit, this first platform was perfectly positioned to observe songbirds in a lily-pad marsh while I casually picked blueberries that brushed the top of my shoulder.

Beyond the first outlook, the Loon Nest Trail is a little less friendly as roots and stones intrude on the path, and the trail climbs 20 feet under hemlock and oak trees that cover a waterfront knoll. For the direct route to the Loon Nest Lookout, keep right when the trail branches to form a loop. Less than two-tenths of a mile from the junction, another bench sits high above the wetlands providing a view of a nesting box that looks like a clump of vegetation floating on the lake's surface about 60 yards out. Binoculars will help you keep track of the ever-vigilant loon, which sits on her minimal nest and even tolerates boat traffic that keeps a respectful distance.

Halfway Brook on the Loon Nest Trail near the shore of Lake Winnipesaukee.

Most visitors don't complete the loop that continues beyond the lookout even though it adds only 0.33 mile to the total hike. Don't make the same mistake. Even if you don't finish the whole loop, a short continuation will bring you to intimate views of grassy marshes and teeming wetlands that others seldom see. Walk slowly in this quiet realm where shy turtles sun themselves on rocks by lily pads and fluttering songbirds animate a very special corner of the loon's environment.

34 Hebron Marsh and Paradise Point

General description:	A visit to a barrier-free nature center, and two short family walks along the shore of Newfound Lake.
General location:	About 20 miles north of Franklin and 10 miles southwest of Plymouth.
Length:	Less than 1 mile.
Difficulty:	Easy.
Elevation gain:	Negligible.
Special attractions:	A nature center, a waterfront walk on a mountain-ringed lake, and a bench or picnic table overlooking Hebron Marsh.
Maps:	A visitor guide with trail map is available from the nature center, or from the address below; also USGS Newfound Lake quad.
For more information:	Audubon Society of New Hampshire, 3 Silk Farm Road, Concord, NH 03301-8200, (603) 224-9909.

Key points:

0.2   Gooey wetlands.
0.4   Paradise Point.
0.8   Dock near nature center.

Finding the trailhead: From exit 23 of Interstate 93, travel west on New Hampshire Route 104 about 5 miles to the intersection with Route 3A in the town of Bristol. Turn right (north) on Route 3A and enjoy 9.1 miles of beautiful views on the eastern shore of Newfound Lake before turning left onto North Shore Road. Trails at Paradise Point are accessed by turning left into the steep driveway 1 mile west on North Shore Road, and walking the last 100 yards from the parking lot to the nature center.

The path at Hebron Marsh is reached by driving an additional 1.2 miles along North Shore Road to the bright red Ash Cottage at the Hebron Marsh Wildlife Sanctuary.

The hike: Need a family activity for a summer morning not yet warm enough to swim, or are you trying to occupy the kids on one of those gray afternoons when the sun has completely failed to appear? The Paradise Point Nature Center may be just the diversion you're looking for. Lakefront, woodlands, wetlands,

Hebron Marsh and Paradise Point

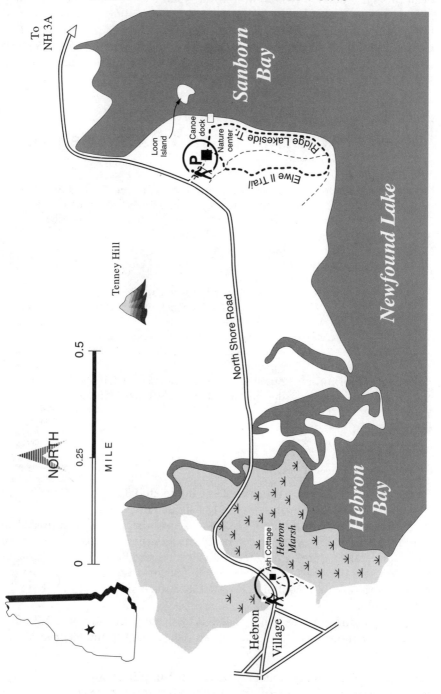

To NH 3A

Sanborn Bay

Loon Island

Canoe dock

Nature center

Ridge Lakeside Tr.

Elwe II Trail

Newfound Lake

Tenney Hill

North Shore Road

Hebron Bay

Ash Cottage

Hebron Marsh

Hebron Village

NORTH

0   0.25   0.5

MILE

and nature center will pique the curiosity of the younger crowd, and give the entire family a chance to watch nature in clean air by a pristine lake.

The starting point is the small, barrier-free nature center, a resource offering summertime educational programs, wildlife exhibits, and general information. Displays are designed to make learning fun for budding naturalists. Check out the tracking exhibit and the Loon Menu featuring Perch Patties, Breaded Leach Sticks, and other avian delicacies.

The Loop, Ridge/Lakeside, and Elwell Trails fan out from the front porch of the nature center. All of these paths could be explored in a couple of hours, but an oblong hike combining the Elwell Trail and the waterfront portion of the Ridge/Lakeside Trail offers the greatest variety in a single package. Under the hemlocks at the top of the knoll, look for the red markers of the Elwell Trail, but don't follow these blazes by turning left at the first junction. Instead, continue a few more yards and bear left onto the second prong of the Elwell loop.

Most children experience a stage when gooey wetlands, bogs, frogs, and salamanders are irresistible. These kids will be in their element, as the Elwell Trail parallels a moss- and fern-blanketed swamp for most of its length before crossing a small brook near the end of Paradise Point. Several paths wander amongst the trees on the point, leading to water-lapped boulders with views encompassing the low-lying mountains that surround Newfound Lake.

Following the shore north, yellow markers identify the return route on the Ridge/Lakeside Trail. Beginning high above the water on a wooded embankment, the route inclines to the same level as waves that wash the forest's stony edge. Listen for loons and mergansers that inhabit the waters to the right. Look for a vast array of mosses and lichens that cling to boulders near the shore, and be alert for mink that live in waterfront rocks by the canoe dock, just down the hill from the nature center.

An outlook more attuned to adult interests can be found just down the highway at Hebron Marsh. From the Ash Cottage and Audubon Nature Store, a short loop hike skirts the edge of a field where a bench and picnic tables overlook the marsh. Acres of grassy wetlands emerging from the shallows of Newfound Lake forge a marvelous wide-angle view. Regrettably, an observation deck has now been removed, so you'll need to bring binoculars to spot any details in this picture. Focus closely on a rock-steady heron, standing still as a statue to spear its dinner, or the low-level reconnaissance flights of a marsh hawk, searching for its next meal with swooping dives and impossible stalls.

35 Mount Major

General description: An afternoon diversion to a popular summit with panoramic views of New Hampshire's largest lake. A very popular family destination.

General location: South of Lake Winnipesaukee between Laconia and Alton Bay.

Length: 3 miles round trip.

Difficulty: Moderate.

Elevation gain: 1,100 feet.

Special attractions: Wide-angle views of Lake Winnipesaukee spread before a backdrop of White Mountain peaks.

Maps: USGS West Alton quad.

For more information: Director, Division of Forests and Lands, P.O. Box 1856, Concord, NH 03302-1856; (603) 271-2215.

Key points:

1.25 Viewpoint slabs.

1.5 Summit, Mount Major.

Finding the trailhead: Head north on U.S. Highway 3 toward Laconia and turn right onto the limited access US 3 and

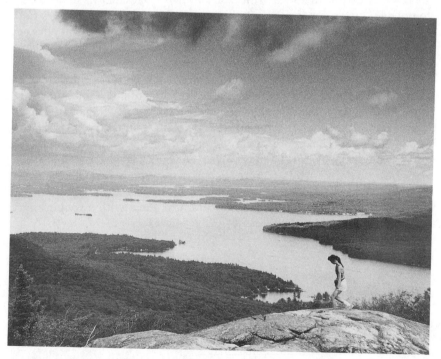

Squalls over Lake Winnipesaukee; time to leave Mount Major.

Mount Major

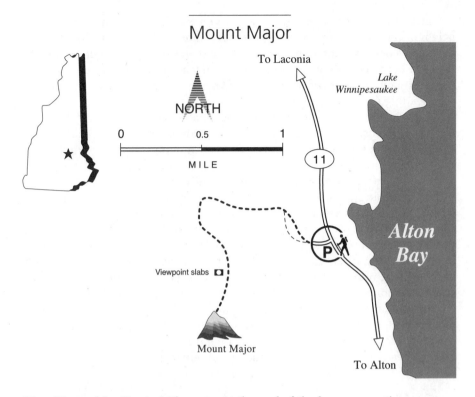

New Hampshire Route 11 bypass. At the end of the bypass, continue east on Route 11 past Ellacoya State Beach and the waterfront resorts in Gilford. After about 10.6 miles, look for a right turn into the trailhead parking area marked by a conspicuous state highway sign. From the opposite direction, the entrance to the trailhead is about 4 miles west of Alton Bay.

The hike: Locate a short hike to a beautiful view on one of the main tourist arteries in the Lakes Region and you're sure to generate plenty of interest. Within easy driving distance of Meredith, Weirs Beach, and Laconia, this well-trod path to the summit of Mount Major is a convenient family outing with sufficient challenge to give those who climb it the feeling they've completed a "real" hike. From the summit, a unique summertime vista also encompasses two Mount Washingtons, the White Mountain peak on the northern horizon, and the historic steamship that plies the waters of Lake Winnipesaukee.

Follow a gravelly jeep path from the trailhead for only 0.1 mile to a fork where the hiking trail diverges to the right. The jeep track to the left is a smoother path, the hiking trail a bit more scenic, but both routes gain moderate altitude and ultimately converge farther up the slope.

The rejoined trails enter a long, level section that smoothly leads away from the lake through quiet woodlands to the base of Mount Major. Here, the trail turns sharply left, ascending gently up the hill, and soon encounters sloping granite slabs, most of which can be avoided by staying well to the right.

These lower slabs open into engaging views of Lake Winnipesaukee and neighboring mountains beyond its northern shore. Most visitors opt to pause on these slopes to picnic, rest, enjoy the view, or complete conversations fostered in the course of the easy hike. Many simply choose to end a relaxing afternoon without proceeding up the more challenging path that can be seen leading to the summit ahead.

To attain the peak, the main trail negotiates several moderately steep pitches of exposed rock that some may find unnerving. If you become uncomfortable, it's generally possible to keep moving upward on a web of easier detour routes that meander all about the higher slope. It's all good exercise for parents and a grand, scurrying adventure for the kids.

The sweeping panorama from the broad, open summit is spectacular, with an angle that exaggerates the concave curve of Lake Winnipesaukee's southerly shore. The effect is to place you on the point of a pivot. A thin, watery arm stretches 4 miles southeast to Alton Bay, while curving around in the opposing direction the lake's northwestern expanse is dotted with islands. In the middle view, directly north, a foreshortened perspective makes shore-side communities appear to be neighbors of White Mountain peaks. On certain days, you can stand comfortably on this sunny perch, watching menacing storm clouds escape the grip of northern summits and race their shadows across a lake-speckled plain. Be sure to leave time to get back to the trailhead should any black clouds head your way.

36 Mount Passaconaway, Dicey's Mill Trail

General description:	An all-day hike through historic foothills to a peak that straddles the Lakes Region and Waterville Valley. A shelter and campsites provide overnight options.
General location:	About 20 miles northeast of Plymouth near the settlement of Wonalancet.
Length:	About 9 miles round trip.
Difficulty:	Moderate.
Elevation gain:	2,800 feet.
Special attractions:	A touch of antiquity in scenic foothills, and relaxed hiking in the mellow woodlands of the Sandwich Range Wilderness.
Maps:	USGS Mount Chocorua and Mount Tripyramid quads.
For more information:	Saco Ranger Station, 33 Kancamagus Highway, Conway, NH 03818, (603) 447-2166.

Mount Passaconaway, Dicey's Mill Trail

Key points:

0.2   Farmhouse.
0.4   Wilderness boundary.
2.3   Brook crossing.
3.8   Camp Rich.
4.5   Summit, Mount
        Passaconaway.

Finding the trailhead: From Interstate 93, exit 24, take U.S. Highway 3 to Ashland and then Holderness. Turn left on New Hampshire Route 113 in Holderness and drive 11.5 miles paralleling the entire length of Squam Lake. Stay on Route 113 where it turns left in the village of Center Sandwich, and 3.7 miles later continue straight on Route 113A where Route 113 turns right in North Sandwich.

Follow Route 113A for 6.6 miles to a point where the road makes a sharp turn to the right. Ferncroft Road (unmarked) exits left at this curve. Look for signs for Wonalancet. The parking lot for several trails in the area is 0.5 mile down Ferncroft Road at the far end of a large field on the right.

The hike: The old homes tucked into the narrow valley at the start of the Dicey's Mill Trail are reminiscent of many early New Hampshire settlements, nestled into protective folds of remote foothills. It seems appropriate, then, that this hike explores summits with names that recall an era when neither Native American nor European dominance of this region had finally been established. Ahead stands Mount Passaconaway, honoring the sachem of the Pennacook Confederation of the 1600s, hidden behind smaller Mount Wonalancet, recalling the son and successor who maintained coexistence with English authority. Unseen to the north, Mount Kancamagus and the Kancamagus Highway commemorate a grandson whose subsequent history unfortunately proved to be considerably less auspicious.

To begin the hike, return on foot to Ferncroft Road and turn right in the direction of Mount Wonalancet. The dirt lane leads beyond a white house in the field on the right to an old, Capestyle home that sits close to the road supervising the intersection with the Blueberry Ledge Trail. Departing left on a bridge across Wonalancet Brook, this alternate hike climbs steeply to Mount Whiteface, the summit with exposed stone cliffs that rises directly ahead.

Dicey's Mill Trail continues straight, northeast of the brook, on a narrowing lane that passes between a barn and a brown house that hugs the stream. A brief walk through the woods ends at the entrance gate to another large field that holds an old farmstead resting in the shadow of Mount Wonalancet. Pedestrians need not be dissuaded by the Private sign on the gate, but visitors will no doubt realize how critical it is to remain strictly on the path and do their part to preserve the aura of antiquity and peace that surrounds them.

The lane passes directly in front of the farmhouse and is guided by trail signs and stone walls back into the woods at the far end of the field. Rising slowly, the route now traverses an old logging road and crosses the wilderness boundary into the national forest less than two-tenths of a mile from the last farmhouse.

The objective of the next 1.5 miles is to circle to the back of Mount Wonalancet while avoiding its steep western slope. The trail briefly adopts a course high above and parallel to the brook, turns right for a short, steep ascent, and then flattens as it curls up the valley on a wonderfully peaceful woodland walk. The path descends, bearing right at a trail junction, and continues a shallow descent to an easy stream crossing at about the halfway point of the hike. The gurgling water and inviting woods make the large clearing at this crossing a favorite rest stop and a well-used campsite.

Leaving the stream near a hulking glacial erratic, the second half of the hike begins a long, gradual ascent of the ridge that extends south from Mount Passaconaway. Angling upward for more than a mile, the trail exchanges a clear view of Mount Wonalancet to the rear for a glimpse of Mount Passaconaway's summit a little to the right of dead ahead. Near the top of the ridge, the Rollins Trail diverges left to Mount Whiteface, and the route to Mount Passaconaway meanders through wet ledges on a ridgetop plateau.

The trail crosses a small brook on split logs about 10 yards before a fork where the Dicey's Mill Trail bears left toward the peak. Almost immediately beyond this junction, watch for the metal gleam of the roof of Camp Rich about 100 yards farther up the slope. This log shelter for eight is in rough condition, suggesting that its removal may not be far off. For the present, its setting near tall, open pines makes a pleasingly remote overnight destination within easy striking distance of the top of the mountain.

The last 0.7 mile of trail from Camp Rich to the summit gains about 500 feet in elevation. Except for a fairly steep, rough, and rocky climb over the last 0.2 mile, the zigzag course is much easier than it looks. The best viewpoint is found about 50 yards before the junction with the Walden Trail and overlooks the outside curve of Mount Tripyramid's eastern wall. The Dicey's Mill Trail ends at the Walden Trail junction. Restricted views on the absolute summit are found to the right, another 50 yards up the Walden Trail.

Frankly, the summit is not the highlight of this hike, and you may be tempted to skip it altogether. On the other hand, I recall a sunny September day, lying on warm summit boulders, watching hawks and bald eagles spiral south on the updrafts. You never know what you might be missing up there.

37 Squam Lakes Natural Science Center

General description:	A short, animal-packed nature walk for children and parents.
General location:	In the village of Holderness at the northwest end of Squam Lake.
Length:	1 mile.
Difficulty:	Easy.
Elevation gain:	Nominal.
Special attractions:	Black bears, deer, red foxes, bobcats, otters, bald eagles, and a children's activity center with giant spider web and track making.
Maps:	Trail maps and brochures are available from the science center. Also USGS Holderness quad.
For more information:	Squam Lakes Natural Science Center, Route 113, P.O. Box 173, Holderness, NH 03245, (603) 968-7194.

Key points:

0.1 Lower pond and exhibit loop.
0.7 Upper Pond.
0.75 Marsh Pond.
1.0 Return to science center.

Finding the trailhead: From exit 24 of Interstate 93 follow U.S. Highway 3 to Ashland and then Holderness. In Holderness, turn left onto New Hampshire Route 113. The entrance to the science center is 0.2 mile on the left.

The hike: Did you know that black bears do not really hibernate? Can you recognize the scent of a red fox? Have you ever figured out the difference between ravens and crows? If you have no clue how to answer these questions, you may need to consult with some knowledgeable youngsters. Each year, over 40,000 school children enjoy learning about this state's natural environment at the Squam Lakes Natural Science Center. Ideally located in the heart of the Lakes Region, this popular resource also features informative family trails that easily accommodate small legs and strollers.

The center is open daily, May through October, from 9:30 A.M. to 4:30 P.M., and an admission fee is charged. The Exhibit Trail leads past ponds, brooks, fields, and shaded woods on a manicured path where black bears, bobcats, and other native New Hampshire species are on display. Clearly, this is no traditional hike, but a guaranteed child-pleaser nonetheless. Everyone has a chance to have some fun while learning about ravens or getting a pungent whiff of that cute little red fox.

I particularly enjoyed the raptor exhibit of hawks and eagles typical to New Hampshire and the otter house with above- and below-water viewing of the playful antics of these sociable mammals. For anyone sensitive to the

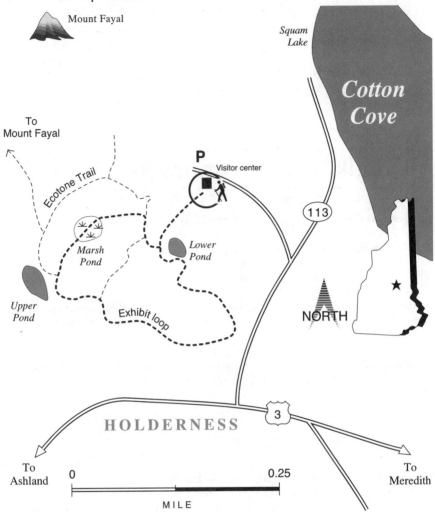

Squam Lakes Natural Science Center

Mount Fayal

Squam
Lake

*Cotton
Cove*

To
Mount Fayal

Ecotone Trail

P
Visitor center

Marsh
Pond

Lower
Pond

Upper
Pond

Exhibit loop

113

NORTH

★

3

HOLDERNESS

To
Ashland

To
Meredith

0

0.25

MILE

exhibition of animals, be assured that the residents are mostly orphaned or injured creatures who would be unable to survive in the wild. It's also reassuring that the purpose of this non-profit center is to educate about nature in a respectful way. Almost every animal is paired with a creative, hands-on exhibit explaining specific aspects of its natural history.

An ecotone is a border between adjacent ecological communities. Departing from the circular Exhibit Trail just beyond the raptor house, the Ecotone Trail loop explores the forest/field transition zone on a more natural path that includes the grassy banks of a tadpole-filled pond. Signs explain the importance of these areas to wildlife and identify many of the typical plant species that thrive here. The Ecotone Trail is an interesting detour, but a tough choice, as you look down across a sloping field to intriguing wetlands that this trail avoids. If you have children with you, they may rightfully demand to retrace your steps to complete the full circle of the Exhibit Trail and explore the floating walkway over sunny Marsh Pond.

A steeper, alternate path departs the Ecotone Trail and climbs to the summit of nearby Mount Fayal. This trail will provide moderate exercise and offers a glimpse of beautiful Squam Lake. For stunning lakeside views, however, drive 5 miles to the West Rattlesnake overlook (Hike 39), which can easily be completed in the same afternoon.

38   Belknap Mountain, Red Trail

General description:	A simple family hike to a low summit with extensive Lakes Region views.
General location:	Due east of Laconia near the town of Gilford.
Length:	1.6 miles round trip.
Difficulty:	Moderate.
Elevation gain:	700 feet.
Special attractions:	An easily accessible outlook to Lake Winnisquam and the city of Laconia, plus a summit fire tower with a full circle of lake and mountain views.
Maps:	USGS West Alton and Laconia quads.
For more information:	Director, Division of Forests and Lands, P.O. Box 1856, Concord, NH 03302-1856, (603) 271-2215.

Key points:

0.1   Garage on carriage road.
0.2   Red Trail departs carriage road.
0.8   Fire tower at summit.

FT | Fire tower
2,500
2,000
1,500
1,000
MILES   0.5   1

Finding the trailhead: From exit 20 on Interstate 93, drive north 6.3 miles on U.S. Highway 3 toward Laconia to the US 3 and New Hampshire Route 11 bypass. Follow the bypass 3 miles, turning right onto Route 11A toward Gilford Village. Stay on Route 11A for 2.3 miles, past the middle school on the right, and turn right at the blinker lights onto Belknap Mountain Road. Drive through Gilford and carefully follow the twists and turns of this road, especially at a junction 1.3 miles from Route 11A where the road turns 90 degrees right at an intersection with a dead-end street. Turn left at a sign for Belknap Mountain 2.4 miles from Route 11A.

Trailhead parking is reached in another 1.5 miles along this half-paved carriage road that pursues a steep and narrowly winding course up much of the mountain. The gate to the carriage road is locked overnight. Be mindful of the closing hours posted near the entrance.

The hike: Belknap Mountain rises 600 feet above the bald pate of Mount Major (Hike 35), yet thanks to the carriage road, the walk to its summit is

Belknap Mountain, Red Trail

To Gilford Village

Belknap Mountain Road

Gunstock Mountain

Ski lift

NORTH

Saddle Trail

Red Trail

Green Trail

Belknap Mountain

P

0   0.25   0.5

MILE

much less demanding than the ascent of its smaller neighbor. More than a map of New Hampshire is required to identify landmarks from the fire tower on Belknap's wooded peak. I find it surprising then, that this mountain's more natural environment receives fewer visitors than the lower summit to the southeast. The easy walk and fantastic views add up to a delightful family hike, and a logical destination when spring or fall weather makes northern peaks inaccessible.

For an enjoyable preview of the hike, look for a path that leaves the upper side of the parking area between two large stones.

The trail ascends about 100 yards through small oaks and maples to a beautiful overlook of Laconia and Lake Winnisquam lying to the west. From this vantage point, your final destination is partially obscured by trees at your back. The hill that is clearly visible beyond the parking area is Mount Piper, not Belknap Mountain.

Several colorfully named trails depart for the summit of Belknap Mountain from a brown garage on a continuation of the carriage road, which is closed to motor vehicles. From the overlook, try to spot the garage through the trees, about 75 yards down a path that runs east through the woods perpendicular to the road.

Of the red, blue, and green summit trails, choose the red. The blue trail is much longer and circuitous, while the green trail ascends on a direct route that is gravely, steep, and shares much of the course with utility lines. The red trail's woodsy, gradual path is a pleasing compromise.

The green trail departs the carriage road first, followed by the red trail in another 30 yards. There are plenty of signs, arrows, and blazes for guidance, as well as a gnarled maple tree acting as a trail guide in its declining years. The red trail slabs easily to the left along a birch- and beech-covered hillside, interrupted by two swings to the right that challenge the slope. Reaching patches of exposed ledge beyond the halfway point, the route turns still farther right, slabbing upward to arrive at a small, intermediate outlook.

After a brief view, the path edges left, ascending into a realm of spruce and fir typical of moderate elevations.

A few more yards of easy hiking suddenly end the trail among scattered evergreens that obstruct the view and crowd the base of the tower.

A sign advises that you climb the tower at your own risk. The wooden steps and metal railings seem like a reasonable gamble in exchange for magnificent 360-degree views. From Mount Washington to Mount Kearsarge, virtually all of central New Hampshire is gloriously visible. A clear day will reveal peaks in Vermont, as well as the wide-open spaces of Maine. Nearer at hand, Mount Major obscures the southeasterly arm of Lake Winnipesaukee, while Gunstock and Piper Mountains invite exploration along the Belknap Ridge.

For those who desire a longer hike, the Saddle Trail leads north from the fire tower less than a mile to the Gunstock summit and passes the upper end of the blue trail in the intervening col. As with the red and green routes, the blue trail returns to the old carriage road just above the trailhead's brown garage.

39 West Rattlesnake

General description:	A very short family outing to a spectacular overlook of Squam Lake.
General location:	About 6 miles northeast of Holderness on the northwesterly shore of Squam Lake.
Length:	1.8 miles round trip.
Difficulty:	Easy.
Elevation gain:	450 feet.
Special attractions:	Large, open ledges for sunning or picnicking and a panoramic view of New Hampshire's most beautiful lake.
Maps:	USGS Squam Mountains quad.
For more information:	Manager, Woodlands Office, 102 Pettee Hall, University of New Hampshire, Durham, NH 03824, (603) 862-3951.

Key points:
0.9   Boulder ledges overlooking Squam Lake.

West Rattlesnake

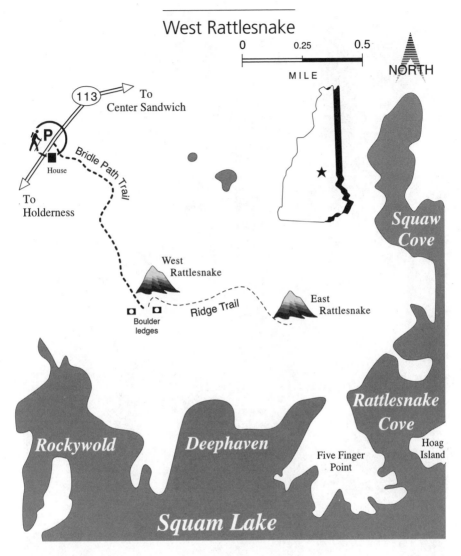

Finding the trailhead: From exit 24 on Interstate 93 take U.S. Highway 3 to Ashland and then Holderness. Turn left onto New Hampshire Route 113 in Holderness, passing the Squam Lakes Natural Science Center (Hike 37). The trailhead is 5.5 miles from US 3, and 0.5 mile beyond the intersection with Pinehurst Road

(Rockywold, Deephaven). A trail sign is located on the right (southeast) side of Route 113 about 30 feet into the woods just beyond an area cleared for a newer home. Parking is about 70 yards beyond the trailhead on the opposite side of the highway. Look for an open white gate in a gap in a stone wall. The parking area also serves a trail to another mountain on the northwest side of the road.

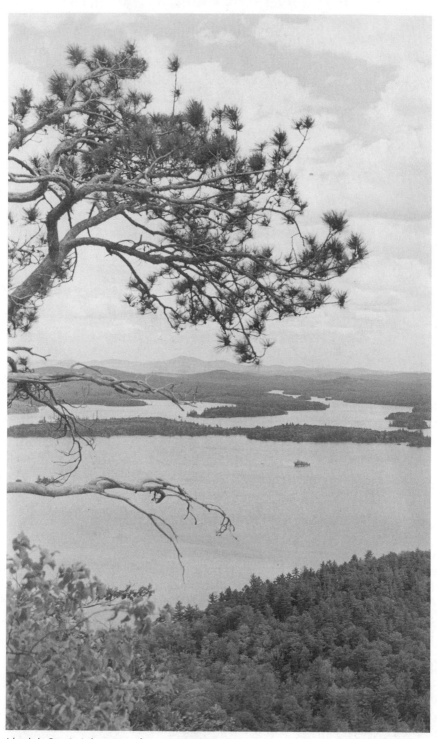

Islands in Squam Lake as seen from West Rattlesnake.

The hike: The journey from Route 113 to the top of West Rattlesnake Mountain is pleasant enough and immensely popular. Hikers from three to seventy-three tramp along the well-worn Bridle Path Trail on its gradual ascent through sun-filled birch woodlands. This easy walk over rocks and gnarled tree roots affords moderate exercise, but its real function is to heighten anticipation of the view that lurks just beyond the small oak trees near the summit.

Topping out on this low mountain, the trail blossoms onto large boulder ledges with stunning panoramas of Squam Lake and the many small peaks of the Lakes Region spreading to the south. This is no mere long-distance, lakeside overlook. The broad sweep of the lake exceeds the peripheral scope of the human eye. You simply cannot take it all in at once. An exploration of the curving ledges reveals the changing facets of the island-dotted water spreading out below.

There is a certain intimacy to this perch that is high enough to reduce the lake to storybook proportions, yet low enough to absorb the details of its life. Sounds come wafting up: the buzz of a motorboat arching through the cove or the thump of a hammer repairing a porch roof. In the distance stand mountains and the reflections of other lakes, while ravens drift on invisible currents above the trees.

It is no wonder that these ledges are regarded as one of the state's premier picnic spots. They're easy to reach for all members of the family, have a view that can entertain you for hours, and catch a breeze that normally can be counted on to keep summer insects at bay. Kids love it here. Just be certain to keep an eye on younger children who will need supervision at several places along the precipitous face of the ledge.

40 Three Ponds Trail

General description:	A four- to five-hour loop hike through a backcountry watershed with easy-to-find campsites on remote White Mountain ponds.
General location:	Near Stinson Lake about 10 miles northwest of Plymouth.
Length:	5.3 miles round trip.
Difficulty:	Moderate (because of distance).
Elevation gain:	440 feet.
Special attractions:	Ponds, wetlands, and wildlife on a little-used backcountry trail.
Maps:	USGS Mount Kineo quad.
For more information:	Pemigewasset Ranger District, RR#3, Box 15, Route 175, Plymouth, NH 03264, (603) 536-1315.

Three Ponds Trail

Key points:
- 0.1   Junction, Three Ponds Trail and Mount Kineo Trail.
- 1.0   Snowmobile bridge over Sucker Brook.
- 2.3   Three Ponds shelter at middle pond.
- 3.6   Junction, Donkey Hill Cutoff and Mount Kineo Trail at Brown Brook.
- 5.2   Return to junction, Three Ponds Trail and Mount Kineo Trail.

Junction, Three Ponds Trail & Mount Kineo Trail

Junction, Donkey Hill Cutoff & Mount Kineo Trail

Junction, Three Ponds Trail & Mount Kineo Trail

Snowmobile bridge

Three Ponds shelter

FT

2,000
1,500
1,000
0

MILES 1 2 3 4 5 6

Finding the trailhead: From the traffic circle at the junction of New Hampshire Routes 3A and 25 in West Plymouth, travel 3.4 miles west on Route 25 and then turn right onto Main Street in Rumney. (Look for signs for the Mary Baker Eddy historic home and Quincy Bog.) Pass the Rumney town common and continue straight at the intersection with Quincy Road. Bear left at the junction with Mill Street where Main Street becomes Stinson Lake Road. Continue nearly 4 miles to the Stinson Lake Store. A Forest Service parking lot is located on the left side of Stinson Lake Road 1.8 miles beyond the store.

The hike: If you're looking for a mellow backpack trip with a sense of exploration, this loop through a rolling watershed that feeds the Baker River may be just what you had in mind. Streams, bogs, wetlands, and ponds are the theme of this backcountry trek that successfully avoids nearby peaks and the onslaught of other hikers.

Split-log walkways greet you just a few paces from the trailhead, as the Three Ponds Trail crosses a small brook, passes under birch trees, and begins its 2.3-mile jaunt to a trio of backcountry pools. After only 0.1 mile, a signpost at a side-hill junction points right along the Mount Kineo Trail (your likely route of return) as the path to Three Ponds continues straight ahead and gains much of the day's elevation in the next 0.25 mile.

After cruising along the rolling path that spans the first 0.5 mile, most visitors actually turn left toward the knobby summit of Carr Mountain, a 2.9-mile detour that might be fun on another day. For now, though, ease downhill on the Three Ponds Trail to another split-log crossing near the outlet of a marsh at the base of Black Hill. The easygoing trail soon completes another descent, steps over a seasonal brook, and crosses a stream on a hiker's bridge before spanning impressive Sucker Brook on a large wooden (snowmobile) bridge about a mile from the trailhead.

At the far end of the snowmobile bridge, the trail turns right on an old woods road that follows the brook upstream. Look for spots to sit on a log and savor a view of the water as this wide woodland thoroughfare ascends a moderate slope. After 0.1 mile of climbing, the path veers right off the woods road, touches the bank of the stream, and leads to a well-maintained beaver dam that holds the waters of a flooded swamp shadowed by a nearby hill.

After briefly rejoining the woods road, the Three Ponds Trail again reverts to a smaller path and makes three crossings of Sucker Brook in the next 0.33 mile. Beyond the third crossing, a newly cut section of trail angles to the right away from the stream and climbs a low ridge before dropping down to the southeast corner of the middle of the three ponds. An undisturbed sense of backcountry surrounds these hill-rimmed waters that are lined by evergreen woods and punctuated by grassy marshes that attract wildlife.

Edging the eastern shore, the trail runs north for only a few paces before a spur path climbs a bank to a large Adirondack shelter that overlooks the pond and the blueberry and raspberry bushes that cluster close to the water. Near the north end of the middle pond, the main trail skirts a marsh and arrives at a trail junction where a right turn onto the Donkey Hill Cutoff continues the loop hike. Before starting this return, though, backpackers and curious hikers should tiptoe across the ruins of a beaver dam that carries the main trail left. This short detour on the Three Ponds Trail discovers peaceful campsites with views of middle and north ponds within only 0.2 mile.

The Donkey Hill Cutoff curls slightly south and crosses a small brook as it works around a wetland and finally turns northeast. Sometimes muddy and often rough, this 1.1-mile link passes hundreds of acres of bogs, ponds, and marshes—prime habitat for moose—and a pocket of low-country wilderness where wildlife watchers will want to linger. Climbing a ridge at the edge of a marsh, the cutoff finally swings southeast as it circles Black Hill and wanders to a junction on the southwest side of Brown Brook where it meets the Mount Kineo Trail.

Continue straight (southeast) on the Mount Kineo Trail following a faded sign that points to Ellsworth Road in 1.6 miles. Keep in mind, though, that after the old sign went up, the trail was rerouted and no longer ends at Ellsworth Road. The new route follows the bubbling course of Brown Brook for just about a mile before turning right on a new section of trail that completes the circle of Black Hill by climbing a low divide and ending back on the Three Ponds Trail 0.1 mile from the trailhead.

41 White Lake State Park

General description:	A short, wooded stroll around a swimming hole, with a nature trail loop to pitch pine and bog. Barrier-free campsites, beach, picnic area, and bathhouse.
General location:	About 12 miles south of Conway between West Ossipee and Tamworth.
Length:	About 1.75 miles including pitch pine loop.
Difficulty:	Easy.
Elevation gain:	Nominal.
Special attractions:	Sandy beach with mountain views, giant trees in a pitch pine forest, and varied habitats for birds.
Maps:	USGS Ossipee Lake quad.
For more information:	Manager, White Lake State Park, Box 41, West Ossipee, NH 03890, (603) 323-7350.

White Lake State Park

Key points:

0.2 Junction Pitch Pine Trail.
0.5 Northwest end of White Lake.
1.75 Return to snack bar and beach.

Finding the trailhead: The entrance to White Lake
State Park is on the west side of Route 16, 1.2 miles north of the junction of
New Hampshire Routes 16 and 25. Once on the entrance road, continue
straight past the tollbooth to the beach parking area. The trailhead is on the
far side of the bathhouse to the left.

The hike: Imagine one of those hot summer days when a brilliant sun
steams through the haze of a high, pale blue sky, and the air of early morning promises scorching heat by noon. A day when the most dedicated hiker
would just as soon hit a sandy beach and swim in a clear lake with mountain peaks a shadow on the northern horizon. A late afternoon, when you
might be persuaded to slip on a pair of sneakers with your wet bathing suit
and walk a mile or two along an easy trail to bird watch and build up your
appetite before the burgers go on the grill. On such a day consider White
Lake State Park.

A large campground and protected beach make White Lake State Park a
popular over-night stop for vacationers traveling to and from the north country and a pleasant spot for day-tripping sun worshipers as well. All facilities,
including designated campsites, beach, bathhouse, snack bar, and picnic

area, are barrier free. In sultry weather, the comfortable beach and clean, cool waters can easily convince most of us to forsake the wilderness for a day. Besides, escape from the crowd is as easy as walking a few hundred yards up the sandy trail.

If you assume that the beach is located at 6 o'clock on this essentially circular lake, then Mounts Whiteface and Passaconaway reflect on the rippled surface at about 12. The trail begins by heading clockwise beyond the bathhouse at the left end of the beach. Almost immediately, huge specimens of unusual pines dominate the landscape, ducks and gulls populate the lake, and songbirds skitter in the brushy undergrowth along the shore.

At about 9 o'clock, the Pitch Pine Trail turns away from the lake on a long, looping detour through blueberries, pine, and scrub oak. This wandering path is a highlight of the walk as it passes through groves of lacy, long-needled pitch pine and visits a small marsh with abundant bird life. The detour is marked with white blazes, but be alert for an indistinct right turn at a junction where the orange blazes of another path suddenly appear.

The Pitch Pine Trail returns to the circumference of White Lake at about 11 o'clock in a quiet corner of watery environment punctuated by the sounds of red squirrels and the occasional call of a loon. The mountain view, now behind you, is replaced by sight of the diminutive beach far across the lake. The remainder of the walk follows the well-worn path along the water's edge in shaded woodlands and sparse undergrowth on the eastern shore. As the mountains slide back into view, the trail nips a corner of the campground and returns to the position of 5 o'clock at the end of the inviting sand. With proper timing and a little luck, someone else may start the charcoal while a cool swim completes your day.

The White Mountains

Nearly 800,000 acres of White Mountain National Forest cut a grand swath across north-central New Hampshire and preserve New England's premier recreational environment. Although one-third the size, this eastern forest entertains more hikers, skiers, and tourists than Yellowstone National Park. Each year, at least 6 million visitors are drawn to this legendary region of mountains, streams, and forests that embraces more than 1,200 miles of hiking trails, 20 developed campgrounds, and 53 shelters, cabins, and tent sites scattered throughout its enveloping woods.

Four wilderness areas in five ranger districts spread from the border of Maine to the foothills northwest of Plymouth. There's simply too much here to describe, with features too varied to typify. We've divided the White Mountain National Forest into ten distinct regions, but readers should avoid drawing hasty conclusions about the character of any zone. The Presidential Peaks are justly famous for soaring alpine heights, but they also shelter outstanding hiking in the Great Gulf's hidden depths. The Pemigewasset Wilderness is widely known for gentle backpacking routes but also rises to hard-won views on the wind-scoured Bondcliff peak. Franconia Notch, Crawford Notch, and the Kancamagus Highway are familiar to many readers, but look in these pages for less-frequented routes in these often-visited areas, and check out excursions in the Carter, Pilot, and Sandwich Ranges that are sure to broaden anyone's White Mountain hiking perspective.

WATERVILLE VALLEY

Waterville Valley means skiing, but it hasn't always been that way. In prior centuries before condos and resort hotels flanked the waters of the rushing Mad River, this isolated valley in the southern White Mountains meant logging, homesteading, or simply traversing miles of formidable forest.

In settling the area, our ancestors did not literally pave our way, but traces of their efforts remain useful to those who wish to explore the region today. Once a common thoroughfare, the Sandwich Notch Road now weaves a narrow dirt track out of Waterville Valley and over a low divide that gives modern drivers a seasonal taste of the hardships of earlier days. This picturesque route through encompassing woods may very well jar your teeth, but it also leads to reclusive trails that penetrate the enticing wilderness of the secluded Sandwich Range.

Most people who come to Waterville see a valley enclosed by mountains, but another relic, the Livermore Road, once joined a maze of logging paths that penetrated the circling summits and connected to outlets further north. This elderly route and its sprouting branches bless current generations of hikers with comfortable trails that wend their way to Mount Osceola, Mount Tripyramid, and the gorgeous Greeley Ponds, all part of a sprawling watershed fanning out from the head of the valley.

Of course, hikers can enjoy more recent developments, too. For a pleasant change of pace, you may want to discover how a return from Mount Tecumseh makes the most of alterations in the valley.

42 Mount Tripyramid, Livermore Road

General description:	A seven- to eight-hour day hike to the triple peaks at the head of Waterville Valley. More leisurely as an overnight backpack that could include Hike 43 or 44.
General location:	20 miles northeast of Plymouth near the ski resort town of Waterville Valley.
Length:	12.1 miles.
Difficulty:	Moderate, but some will find the descent of the Southslide difficult.
Elevation gain:	2,600 feet.
Special attractions:	Woodland strolls, mountain vistas, a unique look down Waterville Valley, and an unforgettable Southslide descent.
Maps:	USGS Mount Tripyramid and Waterville Valley quads.
For more information:	Pemigewasset Ranger Station, RR#3, Box 15, Route 175, Plymouth, NH 03264, (603) 536-1315.

Key points:

0.2	Depot Camp.
2.6	Junction, Livermore Trail and Southslide Trail.
3.8	Junction, Livermore Trail and Scaur Ridge Trail.
5.8	Summit, North Peak.
6.5	Summit, Middle Peak.
7.0	Summit, South Peak.
9.5	Return to junction, Livermore Trail and Southslide Trail.

Finding the trailhead: Follow New Hampshire Route 49 East from the Campton, Waterville Valley exit of Interstate 93 (exit 28). Stay on Route 49 for 11 miles past all the condos, campgrounds, and ski areas, then turn right by a golf course onto Valley Road. Drive another 0.4 mile to an intersection

Mount Tripyramid, Livermore Road

Waterville Valley

Depot Camp

P

Mad River

Library

49

To Interstate 93

Livermore Road

Avalanche Brook

0 — 0.5 — 1

MILE

NORTH

SANDWICH RANGE WILDERNESS BOUNDARY

Slide Brook

Southside Trail

Livermore Trail

Scaur Ridge Trail

Northslide Trail

Pine Bend Brook Trail

Scaur Peak

South Peak

Middle Peak

North Peak

where the tiny Osceola Library stands on the opposite corner. Turn left, following signs for Woodstock and Lincoln, and in 0.7 mile, just before a bridge, turn right into a gravel driveway that's marked with a sign for the Livermore Road. Park in the large parking area with a trailhead sign at the other end.

The hike: Welcome to the Livermore Road! If the prospect of hiking a road sounds uninspiring, consider that this former logging route between Waterville Valley and destinations north of the Kancamagus Highway now exclusively serves as a scenic thoroughfare for hikers and wildlife to easily penetrate a rugged, mountainous region west of the Sandwich Range Wilderness. A base camp established at any one of several sites along its length also permits exploration of the Cascade Path (Hike 44) and Greeley Ponds (Hike 43) on trails that branch off this major access route to the Tripyramid summits at the head of Waterville Valley.

Curiously, Mount Tripyramid is less well known for its unique triple summit than for the immense rockslides that appear as bright scars on its spruce-covered North and South Peaks. Popular trails dissect both slides, but the ledges of the Northslide Trail are too steep and unreliable to be a recommended route. I prefer to add twenty minutes of hiking on my way to these connected summits by taking a less direct approach on the Scaur Ridge and Pine Bend Brook Trails, which circle behind North Peak on a ridge at one end of the valley. After sweeping the mile-long crescent at the top of the Tripyramid peaks, this adventurous journey ultimately loops back to the Livermore Road by descending the imposing slide that plunges down South Peak.

The first 2.5 miles of the hike are an easy ramble, so smooth that you can focus on trillium and violets lining the Livermore Road or scan beyond the treetops for a glimpse of nearby peaks. The gradual ascent traverses Depot Camp and quickly passes the Greeley Pond Trailhead, rapidly breezing up the valley.

After the Southslide Trail departs to the right, the road passes a meadow that was the site of a former logging camp, and the route becomes rough and overgrown in segments now signed as the Livermore Trail. In another mile, at the junction with the Northslide Trail, the path turns back on itself to the left and seems to head in the wrong direction. Within a short distance, opt for a more logical course by turning right onto the Scaur Ridge Trail at a sign that also points to the Pine Bend Brook Trail and the summit of Mount Tripyramid.

Ascending this moderate slope avoids the glistening slabs of granite now visible on North Peak. The climb on the Scaur Ridge Trail is steep enough as it gains the top of the ridge. At the crest, turn right onto the Pine Bend Brook Trail, which leads along a narrow, wooded spine with mountain views on either side.

Climbing steeply on a trail that still may have sizeable patches of ice and snow as late as the middle of May, you'll unexpectedly pop out of evergreens onto North Peak's tiny summit. Step up onto boulders and look over the tops of trees for distant views of other White Mountains peaks.

In the col between North and Middle Peaks, pass the Sabbaday Brook Trail that departs for the Kancamagus Highway before you begin the easy climb of Middle Peak for the best views of the hike. Scrambling onto this summit's boulders garners tremendous vistas of Mounts Chocorua and Passaconaway to the east, as well as Tecumseh and Osceola, which dominate the western view down the length of Waterville Valley.

Even without a summit view, South Tripyramid nevertheless manages to provide the most memorable moments of this hike. Some will be intimidated by the Southslide Trail; most will be simply awed. Gleaming in the afternoon sun is a boulder-strewn, loose-gravel slope that drops 800 feet down the mountain, looking not like the top of the world, but only like its edge. If you can avoid looking at this remarkable trail, you'll find superb views of the Sandwich Range and glimpses of the large New Hampshire lakes that lie even farther south. Care and caution are required in descending the South Peak slide. Go slow, check your footing, be cautious of loose gravel or unstable rocks, and be thankful you didn't try to climb up this trail.

Bring plenty of water on this hike. After reaching the bottom of the South Peak slide, there's nothing thirstier than returning to the Livermore Road immersed in the babbling sounds of Slide and Avalanche Brooks while walking with an empty canteen.

43 Greeley Ponds and Mount Osceola

General description:	An easy family hike to the scenic Greeley Ponds, with an optional climb to extensive views from the east peak of Mount Osceola.
General location:	20 miles northeast of Plymouth near the ski resort town of Waterville Valley.
Length:	About 6.5 miles round trip to the ponds. Add about 3.5 round-trip miles to include East Peak.
Difficulty:	Easy to Greeley Ponds; difficult to East Peak.
Elevation gain:	500 feet to Greeley Ponds; 2,500 feet to East Peak.
Special attractions:	Two beautiful ponds encircled by forested slopes in the cleft of Mad River Notch. A delightful overview of Upper Greeley Pond and the Kancamagus Highway from Mount Osceola's East Peak.
Maps:	USGS Mount Tripyramid, Waterville Valley, and Mount Osceola quads.
For more information:	Pemigewasset Ranger Station, RR#3, Box 15, Route 175, Plymouth, NH 03264, (603) 536-1315.

Greeley Ponds and Mount Osceola

To Kancamagus Highway

Mad River Notch

Upper Greeley Pond

Lower Greeley Pond

East
Peak

Mount
Osceola

NORTH

0   0.5   1

MILE

Mad River

Brook

Livermore Road

Depot Camp

To Tripoli Road

P

49

WATERVILLE
VALLEY

To Interstate 93

Key points:

0.2   Depot Camp.
0.5   Convergence with
      Mad River.
3.5   Upper Greeley
      Pond.
5.2   Summit, Osceola
      East Peak.

Finding the trailhead:
Same as Hike 42.

The hike: I suspect that the popularity of this hike has something to do with the average person's innate sense of proportion and scale. The Greeley Ponds are large enough to shelter quiet gravel banks and grassy lawns along their shores, but small enough to comprehend with a single view. The surrounding peaks that closely encroach upon the waters are tall enough to suggest enclosure but not so immense as to cause a troublesome sense of foreboding. Overall, we regard these magical ponds as cozy and comfortable wilderness spots that are now, regrettably, closed to camping because of their inordinate appeal.

A much shorter, northern access to Greeley Ponds is available from the Kancamagus Highway, but the approach along the Mad River from the Livermore Road places the ponds in better context and passes several tent sites for those who may wish to linger in the presence of a mountain stream. From the parking area, follow Livermore Road north 0.2 mile to the broad clearing of Depot Camp, a remnant of logging days. Turn left onto the Greeley Ponds Trail at the large directory sign just beyond the brook at the edge of the woods on the far side of the clearing.

Running northeast under firs and young maples, the Greeley Ponds Trail traverses an old jeep track and converges with the Mad River, which enters on the right after about half a mile. The trail continues for the next 0.6 mile as an easy upriver amble above the clear waters. After a bridge crossing that places the river on the left, the trail narrows, spans a tributary on a second bridge, and passes through another old logging camp, now just a small clearing filled with brambles and goldenrod. The trail becomes muddy in sections but eventually reverts to a gravel path that follows the Mad River, now babbling along as a gentle mountain stream. Several trails diverge in this section, and campers will find pleasant tent sites near various water crossings.

About a third of a mile before reaching the lower pond, signs announce entry into a reserved scenic area where camping is prohibited. A few hundred yards later, it's easy to miss a left turn where what appears to be the main course leads straight ahead to a limited water view. Look for an arrow sign and retaining logs stepping down to a stream crossing.

The path quickly reaches the lower pond and skirts its western shore. Beautiful views of subordinate summits of Mount Kancamagus rise across the water as the trail passes ready-made picnic grounds on a gravel beach at the wide north end of the pond.

145

The even more attractive upper Greeley Pond lies 0.2 mile north through woods webbed with pathways to former camping sites. As you approach the south end of the upper pond, cross the outlet brook on a side trail that features its own impressive view up the length of the mountain-rimmed waters to the height of the notch beyond. This side path ends at my favorite spot, a grassy clearing at water's edge with unobstructed views of the cliffs on Mount Osceola's north spur. What a perfect spot to relax in the sun, dabble hands and feet in the quiet waters, and gather resolve to explore the rock faces that stare back from across the pond.

Over the years, I've heard a variety of scary descriptions of the ascent from the Greeley Ponds to Mount Osceola's East Peak. It is difficult, and not for everybody, but it's not as if a Clint Eastwood character is about to cut your rope. The first thing to know is that the trail to the east peak does not leave directly west of the upper pond as current maps suggest. Walk about a tenth of a mile north of the pond (heading toward the Kancamagus Highway) for the left (west) turn onto the trail that now curves south below and parallel to the cliff face that you saw from the grassy clearing. The trail meets the old route at a sharp right turn about eight-tenths of a mile from the last trail junction.

I counted three difficult passages on the ascent of the East Peak: a tricky scramble over a few feet of rock 0.15 mile past the sharp right turn; a diagonal crossing of a steep, rough-textured stone face; and the last few feet of a

Upper Greeley Pond.

loose-gravel chute as you top out on Osceola's ridge. Since the view from the wooded peak is poor, my compromise is to stop at the base of the diagonal rock-face crossing, where you'll find the best views on the mountain and avoid two of the most difficult parts of the climb. Be cautious of your footing on the crumbling stones while you look out over a vast sea of mountaintops, the Kancamagus Highway, and the secluded beauty of upper Greeley Pond.

If you must attain the summit, be careful not to overshoot the mark. After scrambling up the loose-gravel chute to the top of the ridge, the route becomes quite moderate. If you encounter a substantial descent, you've begun a rugged, mile-long hike to a different Osceola peak.

44 Cascade Path

General description:	A looping, two-hour family hike to the falling waters of Cascade Brook.
General location:	20 miles northeast of Plymouth in the ski resort town of Waterville Valley.
Length:	2.7 miles.
Difficulty:	Moderate, but shading toward easy.
Elevation gain:	400 feet.
Special attractions:	Beautiful falls on Cascade Brook and close-up views of Waterville Valley from ski trails on Snow's Mountain.
Maps:	USGS Waterville Valley and Mount Tripyramid quads.
For more information:	Pemigewasset Ranger Station, RR#3, Box 15, Route 175, Plymouth, NH 03264, (603) 536-1315.

Key points:

0.3   Left turn onto Cascade Path.
1.5   Cascades.
2.3   Top of ski slope on Snow's Mountain.
2.7   Return to trailhead.

Finding the trailhead: Follow the directions for
Hike 42 until you arrive at the intersection in Waterville Valley with Osceola Library on the opposite corner. Rather than turning left, continue straight through this intersection for 50 yards and enter the large ski-area parking lot on the right. The trail leaves from the far end of the parking area.

The hike: Hikers who love waterfalls, have an active family, or need something to do on a drizzly day should enjoy the Cascade Path. Since these criteria include most everyone sooner or later, it's no wonder that this easy trail, smack in the middle of Waterville Valley, has become a popular family hike.

A directory sign marks the trailhead in a grassy area at the far end of the parking lot. Ascending the middle of a green swath, a gravel path quickly

Cascade Path

rises past residences that line the bottom of a wooded slope. The gravel soon disappears in favor of a simple path, actually a ski trail. In about two-tenths of a mile, the route passes a gap in the trees signed as a cross-country ski trail that proves to be a false lead. Walk double this distance, and yellow blazes, a "Cascade Path" sign, and a noticeable flattening of the hill signal departure on a small dirt trail disappearing into the woods on the left.

Dense, immature hardwoods prevail as the level walk traverses a side hill, passes a trail to Elephant Rock, and rolls along for some distance before slowly losing altitude. The route crosses several small brooks, spans wet areas on log walkways, and bears right onto a large cross-country ski track near the junction with the Norway Rapids Trail adjacent to Cascade Brook.

Keeping the narrow channel of the brook to the left, the Cascade Path gently ascends about two-tenths of a mile past pools and streamside views on its way to the base of the cascades. Small evergreens clinging to a ledge surround a pool below the granite falls, where foaming water spews from a scoured notch and fans out on the rocks below. The path climbs past several smaller cascades, visits glistening pools, and looks precariously down into the churning chute of one of the upper falls. Be cautious with young children in this vicinity. Less hazardous chances to approach the stream appear later, near the upper end of the cascades.

The Cascade Path ends at a gravel forest road on the south side of a wooden bridge just above the last cascade. Begin your return by turning right, away from the bridge. This well-trod highway leads gradually upward and slowly mutates into a pleasant walk along a grassy, graded path that leads to the top of the Snow's Mountain ski area. Looking straight down the hill to the base of the chairlift, you may recognize the red barn that stands at the opposite end of the parking lot from where you began. Before choosing a ski trail to complete your descent, be sure to enjoy the views of Mount Tecumseh far to the left, and Mount Osceola standing aloof from the bustling resort that carpets the valley floor.

Hikers and campers exploring Greeley Ponds, Mount Tripyramid, or the Livermore Road (Hikes 42 and 43) can easily access the Cascades. About 2 miles east of the Livermore trailhead, a major gravel forest road leaves Livermore Road bearing generally south across a large wooden bridge that spans Avalanche Brook. Look for signs on the bridge warning cross-country skiers that they are entering a fee use area. A 0.5-mile walk up this forest road leads to the wooden bridge near the intersection with the Cascade Path just above the cascades.

45 Sandwich Mountain, Algonquin Trail

General description:	A rugged, all-day hike off the beaten path to the summit of Sandwich Mountain.
General location:	Northeast of nearby Plymouth off the Sandwich Notch Road.
Length:	9.0 miles round trip.
Difficulty:	Difficult.
Elevation gain:	2,600 feet.
Special attractions:	Wildlife habitats near the trailhead and uncivilized Black Mountain views.
Maps:	USGS Squam Mountains, Waterville Valley, and Mount Tripyramid quads.
For more information:	Pemigewasset Ranger Station, RR#3, Box 15, Route 175, Plymouth, NH 03264, (603) 536-1315.

Key points:

0.9 Left turn off jeep road.

3.0 Ledges on Black Mountain.

4.5 Summit of Sandwich Mountain.

Finding the trailhead:

From Interstate 93, exit 28, take New Hampshire Route 49 east and turn right after 4.1 miles onto the Sandwich Notch Road. This historic link between the valley of the Mad

Sandwich Mountain, Algonquin Trail

River and the Lakes Region quickly reverts to a narrow dirt road that is seasonally suitable for family vehicles. The road climbs to a height of land, descends sharply, passes a farmhouse, and finally crosses a one-lane bridge. The trailhead is on the left about a tenth of a mile past the bridge and 3.5 miles from Route 49.

The hike: A mere 7 feet prevent Sandwich Mountain from being one of the most frequently climbed summits in New Hampshire. By measuring only 3,993 feet, however, it escapes the rapt attention of peak baggers pursuing their list of 4,000-foot mountains. One happy consequence of this lack of stature is that the Algonquin Trail provides a refuge for hardy hikers who wish to avoid crowds and explore the edge of the Sandwich Range Wilderness.

The trail begins with almost a mile of easy walking along an old jeep road through damp New Hampshire forests. A fine prospect for an early spring or autumn hike, the route rises gently past the oxbow of a stream and skirts several marshes where naturalists should stay alert for signs of wildlife. After 0.9 mile, a well-marked woodland path bears left off the jeep road and ascends gradually to a set of stone stairs that signal the end of this effortless leg.

The trail gains elevation rapidly over the span of a few hundred yards, moderates briefly through the woods, and climbs sharply again to flat blueberry ledges with views to summits ahead. There is a problem here of nomenclature. At various times the name Black Mountain has been applied to several of the peaks and prominences in this area. I believe the route first reaches a very sizable, unnamed knoll, then Black Mountain, and finally Sandwich Mountain (also known as Sandwich Dome). The knoll and Black Mountain can be seen from these early ledges, while Sandwich Mountain remains hidden until much later in the hike.

Reentering the woods, the trail crosses a small drainage and eventually begins a very steep ascent beside the protruding knoll. Circling to the right of the peak, it avoids jutting boulders and meets the Sandwich Range Wilderness boundary as it dips into a shallow col.

The most difficult section of the hike lies halfway between the knoll and Black Mountain. Several scrambles over ledge and boulder outcroppings are required to gain Black Mountain's crest. You can try to circumnavigate the worst of these formidable pitches, but the detours can be indistinct and not

Backcountry views of the Sandwich Range.

all that easy themselves. If you're not too preoccupied with this challenging ascent, check from time to time on your way up the hill for glimpses of Dickey Notch and Bald Mountain on the opposite side of Waterville Valley.

With the hardest part of the hike behind, the walk along the top of Black Mountain offers the best views of the day. Tucked behind the Squam Mountains, the major lakes of central New Hampshire glisten to the south, while scenic ponds near the trailhead enhance the woodlands across the Sandwich Notch Road. My favorite view lies at the other end of a plunging side trail straight down at the base of the mountain, where secluded Black Mountain Pond peacefully waits for overnight guests (see Hike 46).

This exposed summit of low spruce and bare rock holds other simple diversions. Clouds blown free from White Mountain peaks give fascinating proof of the prominence of this Sandwich Range crest, which forms the southern wall of lower Waterville Valley. I could watch for hours as misty vapors scud across the ridge, their first resistance in 20 miles on a journey from Crawford Notch.

Leaving Black Mountain for the final third of the hike, the route dives deeply to reach a flat col before climbing the gradual slopes of remote Sandwich Mountain. At times, crowding evergreens form a solid canopy over the ascending path that ends a few yards short of the summit at the Sandwich Mountain Trail. Turn right to reach a peak where tiptoeing onto rocks will give you the boost you need to see Mount Tecumseh and Mount Tripyramid over the tops of surrounding trees.

46 Guinea and Black Mountain Pond Trails

General description:	A comfortable day hike to secluded ponds, or a confidence-building backpack for less experienced hikers.
General location:	Northeast of Plymouth off the Sandwich Notch Road on the way to Waterville Valley.
Length:	8.0 miles round trip.
Difficulty:	Moderate.
Elevation gain:	700 feet.
Special attractions:	Wetlands, wildlife, and lakefront campsites in the shadow of imposing Black Mountain.
Maps:	USGS Center Sandwich, Squam Mountains, and Waterville Valley quads.
For more information:	Pemigewasset Ranger District, RR#3, Box 15, Route 175, Plymouth, NH 03264, (603) 536-1315.

Guinea and Black Mountain Pond Trails

Black Mountain

NORTH

To Black Mountain

Black Mountain Pond

Shelter

Black Mountain Pond Trail

Beebe River

Guinea Pond

To Guinea Pond

Beebe River

To NH 49

Kiah Pond

Sandwich Notch Road

Guinea Pond Trail

Power line

P

| 0 | 0.5 | 1 |

MILE

Key points:

1.6   Junction, Black Mountain Pond Trail.

2.0   Guinea Pond via detour.

3.5   Spur to Mary-Cary Falls.

4.0   Black Mountain Pond.

Finding the trailhead: From Interstate 93, exit 28, follow New Hampshire Route 49 east 4.1 miles and bear right onto the Sandwich Notch Road. This route soon reverts to a narrow dirt byway, crosses a first bridge near the Algonquin Trail (Hike 45), and spans a second bridge 25 yards before the trailhead, 4.9 miles from Route 49. Parking is available on the left along the first 100 yards of the jeep track that forms the beginning of the Guinea Pond Trail.

The hike: When I first spotted alluring Guinea and Black Mountain Ponds far below me while trekking the heights of Black Mountain (Hike 45), I knew immediately that I needed to explore these isolated pools at the edge of the Sandwich Range Wilderness. Separated from larger recreational lakes to the south by miles of protective woodlands, these glistening miniatures promised waterfront camping in the shadow of remote mountain beauty. I was not to be disappointed with these peaceful ponds, but the discovery of picture-perfect vistas along the easy access route ultimately earned this hike a place in this hiker's guide.

Vehicle access to the Guinea Pond Trail is foreclosed by a metal gate at the top of the hill about 100 yards above the trail sign on the Sandwich Notch Road. In another 100 yards, the trail angles beneath power lines on a stone path and quickly reenters the woods on a dirt track that follows the gentle incline of an old, graded railroad bed. In the next 1.5 miles, the trail rises easily through the woods, skirts a host of swamps, bogs, and beaver ponds that are part of the Beebe River drainage, and parallels the ridge linking Sandwich and Black Mountains. This fascinating journey results in a changing collage of wildlife-rich wetlands reflecting the contours of the Sandwich Range hills. An especially attractive outlook is found on a wooded embankment shortly after the trail begins a detour to avoid a flood area, with Sandwich and Black Mountains sliding into view beyond the beaver's handiwork.

After crossing more wetlands on a series of plank-and-log walkways, the detour ends back on the old railroad grade about 50 yards before the junctions with the Mead and Black Mountain Pond Trails. Straight ahead, along 0.4 mile of wobbly streamside trail, lies Guinea Pond, easily reached and worth a day visit but with a low-lying shore and tent site that may be too damp for many.

Turn left (north), instead, over a brook on the yellow-blazed Black Mountain Pond Trail, which leads in 2.4 miles to a more appealing camping alternative. Initially, the trail twists and turns through birch woods in a vain attempt to stick to high ground, but the path eventually resigns itself to following the Beebe River up a low hill and crossing the outlet of a marsh below an old, breached beaver dam. Rejoining the stream at the far end of the marsh, the trail climbs a low divide to the Black Mountain Pond watershed.

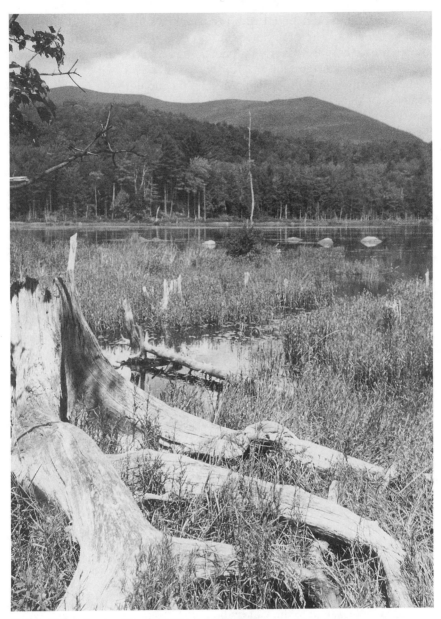

Shallow Guinea Pond on the edge of the Sandwich Range.

For a welcome break from uphill efforts, visit Mary-Cary Falls. This delicate waterspout over massive granite boulders is found to the left on a 0.1-mile side path, before the main trail concludes with a brief, moderate ascent to the top of the divide. A final, quick descent circling left over the river and a scramble up the opposite bank soon herald your arrival at Black Mountain Pond.

A log shelter is located at water's edge on the left (west) end of the lake. Vertical ledges prevent access to it along the shore, and the shelter is presently in very poor condition. Better to bring a tent, wander along the knoll that runs the length of the pond, and find a peaceful spot beneath the pines. Your campsite here will overlook quiet waters and the steep southern wall of imposing Black Mountain.

Theoretically, a path links Black Mountain Pond with the Algonquin Trail at the top of Black Mountain. On the pond end, the route is indistinct, and the effort akin to bushwhacking. Having slogged a few hundred yards in this direction, a look at the sheer slopes ahead easily persuaded me that it wasn't an option I wished to pursue.

47 Mount Tecumseh

General description:	A half-day hike to a peak that surmounts one of New England's major ski areas.
General location:	20 miles northeast of Plymouth at the ski resort of Waterville Valley.
Length:	About 4 miles, excluding the short loop to the absolute summit.
Difficulty:	Moderate.
Elevation gain:	2,100 feet.
Special attractions:	Wildflowers, sunshine, and spectacular views from meadows on mountain slopes.
Maps:	USGS Waterville Valley quad.
For more information:	Pemigewasset Ranger District, RR#3, Box 15, Route 175, Plymouth, NH 03264, (603) 536-1315.

Key points:

0.2   First stream crossing.
2.2   Summit of Mount Tecumseh.
3.0   Top of ski slope.

Finding the trailhead: From Interstate 93, exit 28, follow New Hampshire Route 49 east 10 miles and turn left onto Tripoli Road. Bear left again at a fork in the road following signs to the Waterville Valley Ski Area. At the base lodge, the trailhead is on the right, with trail signs posted near the far (wooded) end of parking lot number one.

The hike: Anyone who has watched *The Sound of Music* retains visions of the ecstatic Von Trapp family cavorting about luxuriant alpine meadows, regaling the peaks with their joyous songs. A little patience on this hike rewards hikers with a chance to duplicate these happy scenes on the open ski slopes of Waterville Valley. Each summer, vast acres of grass and wildflowers carpet the mountainside, offering a continuous panorama of Mount

Mount Tecumseh

Tripoli Road

Mount Tecumseh

Tecumseh Brook

Sosman Trail

Tecumseh Trail

Ski lift

Ski lift

Ski lift

Base lodge

P

X

WATERVILLE
VALLEY SKI AREA

Green
Mountain

NORTH

0   0.25   0.5

MILE

Tripoli Road
to NH 49

★

Tripyramid and the Osceola peaks across the resort-speckled valley. Allow your mind to edit out the chairlifts. Singing is purely optional.

The true summit of Mount Tecumseh stands aloof, a little to the north and higher than the ski slopes. The route to the peak begins to the right (north) of the base lodge and keeps out of sight of the open slopes on a wooded trail that immediately crosses two small brooks as it winds through mixed stands of beech and birch. The path parallels a larger stream that it keeps on the right and crosses after 0.2 mile. Soon, a new section of trail transforms what was a straight trudge up a logging road into a gently looping ascent of forested mountain terrain.

Having gained several hundred feet of elevation, the new route re-crosses the stream, executes several quick switchbacks, and climbs to meet a 20-yard spur trail that leads to a chairlift and early mountain views. After this diversion, the main trail reverts to a long, straight, steady ascent, parallel to ski runs hidden behind woods on the left. Eventually, the trail angles back to the right, away from the slopes and toward Mount Tecumseh's summit.

The Sosman Trail is encountered twice, both times entering on the left near the summit. The first junction leads directly to the top of the ski area, and serves as a good return path home. The second junction, about 100 yards uphill, is a short return leg on the loop to Tecumseh's peak.

The brief walk to the absolute summit is strictly optional. For a fair view of Mount Washington far behind the Osceola peaks, continue straight on the Tecumseh Trail, which spirals to the north side of the mountain. Be careful not to become disoriented when ready to leave this peak. Inadequate signs and unmarked paths can easily lead to confusion. Either return the way you came, or continue straight across the small, rocky top to depart on the Sosman Trail, which is hard to pick out without the help of a sign.

Once back at the first (lower) Sosman Trail junction, turn right (south) to begin the most rewarding portion of the hike. The trail ascends an intermediate knoll with a wonderful view back to Tecumseh's summit, and executes a surprisingly long traverse of the mountain's subordinate ridge. Along the way, engaging views are found in several clearings, including one with a bench for contemplative inspection of Mount Tripyramid. The Sosman Trail ends at the top of a ski slope. From here it's all sunshine and grassy meadows with constant views of the mountainous valley. Have fun! Between the chairlifts and ski-trail signs, you'll find your way back to the base lodge from here.

48 Welch and Dickey Mountains

General description:	A popular family loop hike over two picturesque peaks.
General location:	Northeast of Plymouth, about halfway between Interstate 93 and the town of Waterville Valley.
Length:	4.5 miles.
Difficulty:	Moderate.
Elevation gain:	1,600 feet.
Special attractions:	Open ledges with attractive views of the Sandwich Range, the Mad River, and the mountains of Waterville Valley.
Maps:	USGS Waterville Valley quad.
For more information:	Pemigewasset Ranger District, RR#3, Box 15, Route 175, Plymouth, NH 03264, (603) 536-1315.

Key points:

2.0   Summit, Welch Mountain.
2.5   Summit, Dickey Mountain.
4.5   Return to trailhead.

Finding the trailhead: From the Campton, Waterville Valley exit of Interstate 93 (exit 28) drive east on New Hampshire Route 49. Cross Route 175 and stay on Route 49 at the first junction with Upper Mad River Road (also Burbank Hill Road), which enters on the left 3.7 miles from the interstate highway. Turn left at the

Welch and Dickey Mountains

second junction with Upper Mad River Road after another 1.8 miles and cross the Mad River. Drive 0.7 mile and turn right onto Orris Road at a sign for the Welch-Dickey Trail. When Orris Road turns sharply left after 0.6 mile, continue straight on a dirt lane that ends at trailhead parking. (Note: by the time of publication, a new parking lot may be in the works on Orris Road about 300 yards before the present location).

The hike: If the Cascade Path (Hike 44) doesn't promise enough excitement, but a 4,000-foot summit is more than you're ready to try, Waterville Valley has a solution. Standing well under 3,000 feet, the summits of Welch and Dickey Mountains offer a moderate, half-day loop hike with all the satisfaction of a much more ambitious climb. Terrific views and the chance to scamper over bare ledges and faces of soaring granite make this hike a hit with kids. Just save it for a day when those sloping rocks are certain to stay dry.

The trail diverges to form a loop at a hiker's registration box just ten yards from the parking lot. The path on the right leads 2.0 miles to the summit of Welch Mountain. The path on the left climbs an equal distance to Dickey Mountain's higher top. A 0.5-mile connector trail links the twin peaks.

For no particular reason, I decided to turn right onto the Welch branch, following a path that quickly crosses a stream on a jumble of large stones. Hemlock and spruce mingle with hardwood forest, as the trail gently climbs through a watershed with the riffles and rills of a small brook visible on the left. After rising quickly for 100 yards, the yellow-blazed trail turns hard to the right between hulking glacial erratics about seven-tenths of a mile from the trailhead, wanders a few paces, and then zigs left again as it leaves the stream behind.

Patches of low-bush blueberries and the summer scent of pine surround the ascending trail as it curls over a slab of bedrock granite that only hints at the climb ahead. Painted blazes soon bend the path to the right across a flat mountain shoulder where the rolled edge of an open cliff makes a natural resting point. Enjoy the view of the Mad River Valley, distant Mount Tripyramid, and the nearby Sandwich Range, but don't be discouraged by Welch Mountain rising at your back. The climb to that looming summit isn't as difficult as it looks.

From the outlook ledge, the trail follows painted blazes into a grove of oak and beech and soon begins a sloping traverse with nearly continuous views. You'll forget how hard you're breathing on these steep faces of rock as a breeze springs up to cool you and vistas of Mount Moosilauke and the Pemigewasset Valley open to the west and south. Watch carefully for painted blazes as the trail twists and turns through rocky scrambles and squeezes between narrow cracks in giant granite boulders. Tracks worn into bedrock over eons by falling water rumple the path beneath your feet, as the trail begins the final push to the small, open summit. Finally perched on a split boulder at the top of Welch Mountain, you're greeted by wide-angle views that include Waterville Valley, the prominent ledges of Dickey Mountain, and the bumpy contours of central New Hampshire that fall away to the south.

The connector trail that links the peaks drops quickly from Welch's summit, weaves between rocks and boulders, and brushes through dense clusters of mountain azalea and Labrador tea. Passing a cairn with a stone post at the low point in the col, the trail wanders through evergreens and offers a new perspective on the summit you've just climbed.

After scrambling to Dickey's peak, the trail passes directly over the highest point on the mountain, but the best views and resting spots are found on a broad ledge 0.2 mile to the north (right). Without trampling the vegetation,

160

Arriving at a ledge-top rest below the summit of Welch Mountain.

try to follow a faint path that weaves across patches of rock to this large granite slab that adds impressive vistas of Franconia Ridge, Cannon Mountain, and the Kinsman peaks to your view of the Mad River Valley.

Zigzagging between blueberries and stunted evergreens, the return route down the western slopes of Dickey Mountain soon leads to a series of granite slabs with expanding southern views. Follow the cairns and painted blazes to the rim of these long ledges and turn for a summary look at the pair of peaks you just traversed. With a last glance over your shoulder, enter the nearby woods where a steep trail drops from the scenic heights and then descends steadily to join an old logging road that traces the valley floor. Turn left at the junction with the logging road for an easy 0.1-mile stroll that ends at the parking lot.

MOUNT MOOSILAUKE

The unique location of this westernmost, 4,000-foot summit largely accounts for the odd psychological distance that separates Mount Moosilauke from other White Mountain peaks. Usual means of access to trailheads in this region lead through towns like Wentworth, Warren, and Pike, smaller communities on the western fringe of the White Mountain National Forest that are linked more closely to an agricultural past than to alpine traditions found east of Franconia Notch. The result is a strong association between Mount Moosilauke and the upper portion of the Connecticut River Valley. This frame of reference leads to jolting surprises from the bald top of this hulking mountain, as you gaze directly down upon Lincoln and North Woodstock, at the entrance to the White Mountains' core. In the end, it's this extraordinary visual link, between a fertile farming valley and soaring mountain peaks, that makes the summit of Mount Moosilauke an exciting place to hike.

Lunch time on Mount Moosilauke.

49 Glencliff Trail

General description: A six- to seven-hour, western approach to the summit of Mount Moosilauke.

General location: About 20 miles northwest of Plymouth near Glencliff village.

Length: 8.0 miles round trip.

Difficulty: Moderate.

Elevation gain: 3,400 feet.

Special attractions: A pastoral trailhead, a ridge with mountain views, and broad summit lawns that encourage alpine wandering.

Maps: USGS Mount Moosilauke, Mount Kineo, and Warren quads.

For more information: Pemigewasset Ranger Station, RR#3, Box 15, Route 175, Plymouth, NH 03264, (603) 536-1315.

Key points:

0.3 Stream crossing near the edge of the woods.

3.2 Junction, Glencliff Trail and Moosilauke Carriage Road.

4.0 Summit, Mount Moosilauke.

Finding the trailhead: Depart Interstate 93 at exit 26 and take New Hampshire Route 25 west toward West Plymouth and Rumney. About 19 miles later, the solitary mass of Mount Moosilauke becomes visible from the town of Warren. The trailhead can be reached by following signs for the Glencliff Home for the Elderly and turning right onto High Street (Sanitorium Road) at the Glencliff Community Chapel, 25.1 miles from I-93. After another 1.3 miles, the trailhead appears on the right at a sign and wooden gate opposite a small field. Park in a gravel lot on the right about 100 yards beyond the trailhead.

The hike: Dairy cattle no longer linger near this once bucolic trailhead where an old, wooden pasture gate still waits by the side of the road. Instead of crossing the overgrown field that actually begins this route, most hikers duck past a different gate at the end of the parking lot and follow a farm road that merges with the Glencliff Trail in less than two-tenths of a mile. Also signed as a section of the Appalachian Trail, the merged routes skirt two upper pastures and duck under apple trees before swinging out of the field into the woods on the left.

Beyond the edge of the trees, the route immediately crosses a stream near a junction with the Hurricane Trail, 3.7 miles from Mount Moosilauke's summit. Weaving steadily upward, the path crosses several small brooks, and then swings farther left, aiming to connect with the top of a ridge that

Glencliff Trail

Mount
Clough

Mount
Blue

Mount
Moosilauke

Slide Brook

(Appalachian Trail)

Carriage Road

Gorge Brook

Still Brook

South
Peak

Glencliff Trail

Brook

NORTH

0   0.5   1

MILE

To NH 25

runs from the summit of Mount Moosilauke to the pinnacle of South Peak. A little more than 2 miles into the hike, having slabbed up part of the ridge, the trail finally turns right, eluding the sharpest pitches on South Peak in what still amounts to the steepest 0.5 mile of the hike. Surprisingly, still 0.8 mile from the summit, the Glencliff Trail ends at a carriage road that skims the top of the ridge.

Turning left toward the summit, it's daunting to consider that horse-drawn vehicles once rumbled up this road. Today, this former carriage track is merely an overgrown path bisecting a narrow ridge that is now, thanks to erosion, paved only with a chaos of stones. Mountain vistas slowly expand on this easy, upward tramp as you cruise into the alpine zone within sight of an arching trail that climbs to the treeless peak. The last stretch of the carriage road dips back into crowding spruce only to rise one last time to slant across rocky lawns blooming with alpine flowers.

Numerous paths approach Mount Moosilauke from all points of the compass and crisscross its open expanse. It's a popular destination, so don't expect to be alone with the wonderful views. Jumbled boulders and the ruins of a stone foundation hold hikers to this summit like a magnet. On a recent trip, even the thrill of being buzzed by a glider failed to shake hikers loose from this comfortable perch. For a bit of privacy before returning to the trailhead, try a short detour on the Benton Trail across sweeping acres of alpine lawns extending far to the north of the summit. A solitary lunch on the rim of these plains provides remarkable views of Franconia Notch and the neighboring Kinsman peaks.

50 Gorge Brook, Asquam Ridge Loop

General description:	A six-hour hike along a ridge of peaks to a summit that dominates the western White Mountains.
General location:	About 10 miles due west of Lincoln and North Woodstock.
Length:	9.3 miles.
Difficulty:	Moderate.
Elevation gain:	2,400 feet.
Special attractions:	A gradual ascent of a major peak at the headwaters of the Baker River, distant vistas from alpine lawns, and scenic views down Jobildunk Ravine from the slopes of Mount Blue.
Maps:	USGS Mount Moosilauke and Mount Kineo quads.
For more information:	Pemigewasset Ranger Station, RR#3, Box 15, Route 175, Plymouth, NH 03264, (603) 536-1315.

Key points:

1.5   Second crossing of Baker River.
1.9   Left turn at ski trail.
4.3   Junction, Asquam Ridge and Beaver Brook Trails.
5.6   Summit, Mount Moosilauke.
9.3   Return to trailhead.

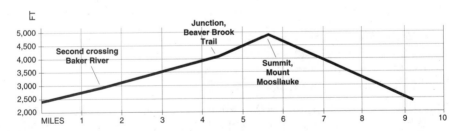

Finding the trailhead: From exit 32 of Interstate 93, travel west on New Hampshire Route 112 into North Woodstock. Cross U.S. Highway 3 and stay on Route 112 until turning left onto Route 118, 3.2 miles west of the village. Over the course of the next 7 miles, this twisting mountain highway gains almost 2,400 feet in elevation before descending slightly to meet a right turn

Gorge Brook, Asquam Ridge Loop

onto Ravine Road, a dirt access road marked with signs for the Moosilauke Ravine Lodge. Ravine Road deadends at the trailhead in another 1.5 miles.

From the west, the turn onto Ravine Road is 5.7 miles northeast of the junction of Routes 118 and 25.

The hike: At 4,802 feet, Mount Moosilauke dominates the western end of the White Mountains and separates the Baker and Lost River watersheds from the Connecticut River Valley. There are certainly easier routes to this mountain's expansive views, but none with the adventurous variety of this roundabout trail to the peak. The extended route along the Asquam Ridge, Beaver Brook, and Gorge Brook Trails traverses three other mountains, circles two watersheds, and provides southeasterly access to Mount Moosilauke through land owned by Dartmouth College. Hikers are welcome on this private land, but open fires and campers are not.

The Ridge Trail (or Asquam Ridge Trail) begins as a narrow extension of the access road. Pass a junction with the Gorge Brook Trail that exits to the left within only 100 yards. Continue straight on the narrow extension for a second 100 yards before taking the next left fork onto an old, overgrown logging road that ascends a gradual slope beside the rushing waters of the infant Baker River.

The early portions of this changeable hike rise steadily into the watershed, cross the river on a log bridge, and finally re-cross the flow to completely reverse direction. The trail angles southeast, away from the summit, on a side-hill climb of Blue Ridge, a crescent-shaped projection from Mount Moosilauke's eastern flank. After climbing more steeply at a sharp left turn at the junction with the Merrill Loop (ski trail), the route finally gains the end of the ridge where Mount Moosilauke and Mount Blue are visible through the trees.

Mount Waternomee, Mount Jim, and Mount Blue occupy the northern half of the Blue Ridge crescent, mere stepping stones on the way to Mount Moosilauke's major summit. The short climb to the top of Mount Waternomee and scattered steep pitches to the summit of Mount Jim constitute the most difficult portions of the hike. When the path finally descends Mount Jim, Mount Blue looms dead ahead.

The Ridge Trail ends in a large, flat col at the junction with the Beaver Brook Trail, 1.3 miles from Mount Moosilauke's summit. Turn left (northwest) on this boulder-strewn path, which quickly passes below steep cliffs that tumble down Mount Blue. The trail doesn't cross the true summit of this rugged mountain, but the jagged boulders overhead and the impressive views of the Baker River watershed at the bottom of Jobildunk Ravine offer a startling wilderness scene.

West of Mount Blue, the Beaver Brook Trail enters another flat col and circles easily between small evergreens on a gradual ascent of Mount Moosilauke. Lawns of alpine vegetation encircle craggy boulders covering the point of this windswept peak. The stones of an old foundation still provide shelter from breezes, and a full circle of mountain vistas rings the horizon. Look for North Woodstock village huddled at the base of Loon Mountain south of the row of pyramid peaks that line up on Franconia Ridge. A more practiced eye may also identify summits in Waterville Valley, several of the Presidential Peaks, or any number of mountaintops that spread west throughout Vermont.

Return to your vehicle on the Gorge Brook Trail, which you passed just before reaching the summit. This steep, more direct, and heavily used path departs almost due south of the peak, crosses a large alpine lawn, and enters a realm of scrub evergreens before dropping over a knoll. Tremendous effort has recently been expended to relocate the upper section of this route. Once off the heights, the last half of this journey descends the narrow Gorge Brook watershed, as both hikers and stream hurry south to meet the Baker River near the Asquam Ridge Trailhead.

FRANCONIA NOTCH

Aim an interstate highway at a narrow pass and few would believe that hiking, biking, fishing, camping, swimming, skiing, and sightseeing could peacefully coexist with the flow of constant traffic. Franconia Notch accomplishes this feat with a surplus of style and grace, as the highway shrinks to a two-lane road and discreetly weaves past delicate lakes on a course long familiar to throngs of White Mountain tourists.

The most heavily used of the mountain clefts that carry travelers north, Franconia Notch is best known as the home of The Old Man of the Mountain and the Cannon Mountain Tramway. Throughout the year, drivers crane their necks for a glance at the great stone face, while others pause in the course of their journey to stroll beside Profile Lake or ride up a mountainside. The Basin, The Flume, and Lafayette Campground also do their part to attract the passing crowd, with walks along the Pemigewasset River and views of soaring peaks that dominate the notch.

Don't make the mistake of thinking that Franconia Notch only appeals to tourists. Splendid family hikes lead to places like Lonesome Lake, Indian Head, or gorgeous Cloudland Falls, while Franconia Ridge and the Kinsman Peaks offer classic hiking adventures and the thrill of greater heights.

51 The Flume

General description:	A stroll on a boardwalk through a narrow gorge, with easy trails to pools and falls on the scenic Pemigewasset River. A wonderful one- or two-hour family walk.
General location:	Off the Franconia Notch Parkway at the southern end of Franconia Notch.
Length:	2.0 miles.
Difficulty:	Easy, but with hills to climb.
Elevation gain:	400 feet.
Special attractions:	The Flume, The Pool, Avalanche Falls, and the sparkling Pemigewasset River.
Maps:	Trail guides are available at the visitor center; also USGS Lincoln quad.
For more information:	N.H. Division of Parks and Recreation, Department of Resources and Economic Development, P.O. Box 1856, Concord, NH 03302-1856, (603) 271-3254. In season, The Flume, Route 3, Franconia, NH 03580, (603) 745-8391.

Key points:

0.7   Head of The Flume.
1.4   The Pool.
2.0   Visitor center.

168

The Flume

Sentinel pine covered bridge

Liberty Cascade

The Pool

To Parkway North

Pemigewasset River

Avalanche Falls

FLUME GORGE

Flume Brook

Old U.S. Highway 3

Parkway Service Road

Covered bridge

Cabin

NORTH

Visitor Center

P

P

0   0.25

MILE

To Exit 1

★

Finding the trailhead: Interstate 93 is redesignated as The Franconia Notch Parkway a little north of Exit 33. Leave the highway at Parkway exit 1 and follow the service road (old U.S. Highway 3) to trailhead parking at The Flume Visitor Center.

The hike: Years ago, someone knew a good thing when they saw it and beat us to The Flume with a visitor center, shuttle bus, graded path, and admission charge. I admit it! This hike is really a tourist attraction, and a few hard-core hikers may avoid The Flume on principle. Most of us, though, should not be deterred from enjoying the unique experience of this ideal family stroll.

Rising above the valley on the opposite side of the river, Mount Liberty and Mount Flume give a grand welcome to this Franconia Notch attraction. Pay the entry fee and start on the paved path that extends about 100 yards past the visitor center and becomes a wide gravel trail. Turn right after another 100 yards to head directly toward The Flume on a trail that zigzags downhill to a picture-perfect covered bridge across the Pemigewasset River. The trail passes a cabin that houses natural-history exhibits before rising gently on the southern banks of Flume Brook where glistening sheets of water race over slick granite in the vicinity of Table Rock.

After only 0.7 mile, you arrive at this hike's primary destination, an 800-foot-long gorge formed by the rapid erosion of lava dikes that penetrated cracks in the surrounding granite. This exceptional trail enters the gorge's narrow maw on boardwalks suspended near the base of 70-foot walls that

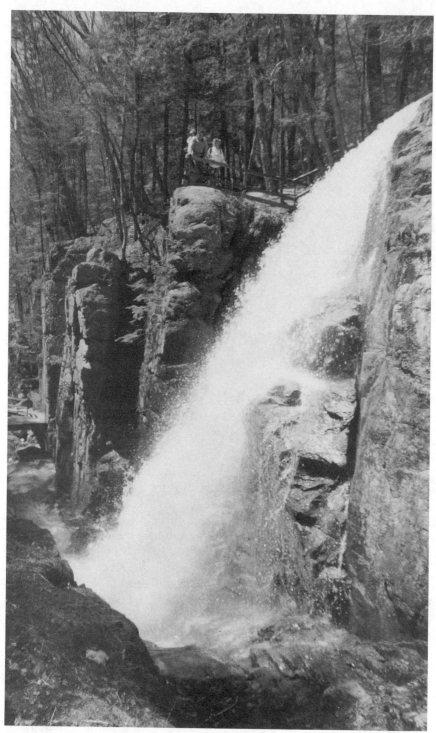

A grand entrance, Avalanche Falls at the head of The Flume.

channel the waters of Flume Brook. A cooling experience in midsummer, the boardwalk stroll above the sparkling stream allows firsthand views of unusual geology and moist mosses and ferns that cling to the side of the chasm. The boardwalk ends at fabulous Avalanche Falls where hikers can inspect the gushing cataract from above or below, and relax on natural stone seating that lines Flume Brook at a rest stop upstream of the falls.

It's possible to return to the trailhead on a path that parallels The Flume, but an added 0.6-mile walk completes a loop to engaging Liberty Cascade and The Pool on the Pemigewasset River. Take the Ridge Path northwest from Avalanche Falls on a long, downhill stroll to the floor of the wooded valley. The trail crosses Cascade Brook above its foamy falls and also circles The Pool, a gorgeous basin that lies far below a hiker-sized covered bridge across the river. To make the most of this walk, take time to explore several spur trails that lead to outstanding viewpoints overlooking the natural attractions. At the conclusion of this loop, many hikers will find that the steep climb out of the valley completely justifies ending their day by relaxing in sunny comfort, and enjoying a scoop of ice cream on the visitor center's deck.

52 Cannon Mountain, Kinsman Ridge Trail

General description:	An arduous, half-day hike to the top of Cannon Mountain.
General location:	About halfway between Littleton and Lincoln at the north end of Franconia Notch.
Length:	4.0 miles round trip.
Difficulty:	Difficult.
Elevation gain:	2,100 feet.
Special attractions:	Views of Franconia Notch from the Old Man's head, and an alternate route—a tramway ride.
Maps:	USGS Franconia quad or park maps from the address below.
For more information:	Franconia Notch State Park, Route 3, Franconia, NH 03580, (603) 823-8800.

Key points:

    1.5   Junction with spur to outlook near Old Man's head.

    2.0   Summit, Cannon Mountain.

Finding the trailhead: Drive north on Interstate 93 until it becomes the Franconia Notch Parkway. Take Parkway exit 2 following signs for the Cannon Mountain Tramway, and leave your car

Cannon Mountain, Kinsman Ridge Trail

To Twin Mountian

Echo Lake

NORTH

0   0.5   1

MILE

Exit 2

Profile Lake

Ski Tram

Ridge Trail

X Old Man of the Mountain

Cannon Mountain

Kinsman

The Cannon Balls

Hi-Cannon Trail

FRANCONIA NOTCH

Franconia Notch Parkway

To Kinsman Pond and Kinsman Junction

To Lafayette Campground

To Lincoln, N. Woodstock

in the ski area parking lot. The trailhead is immediately to the left of the base lodge, 150 yards down a dirt driveway to a picnic ground.

The hike: The Kinsman Ridge Trail runs almost 17 miles from the base of the Cannon Mountain Tramway, over Cannon Mountain and the Kinsman Peaks (Hike 55), to the Lost River Road in Kinsman Notch. Cannon Mountain has a solid following among aggressive skiers who ride the tramway 2,000 feet for a chance to bomb down expert slopes that end near Echo Lake. Hikers should get the message. The 2-mile segment of the Kinsman Ridge Trail that rises within sight of the tramway is a rough and difficult shortcut to beautiful mountain views.

Immediately to the left of the tramway cafeteria, signs point down a gravel driveway to a picnic area and trailhead. Near the end of the picnic-ground loop, a small field below an old ski trail looks up at a tramway tower and the eastern shoulder of Cannon Mountain, which you're about to climb. At the far end of this grassy field, a trail sign points into the woods to the left.

The route that weaves 1.5 miles up the imposing slope begins without hesitation and grows more demanding the higher it climbs. Some portions of this route are so vertical and wet they barely cling to the hill. Lower sections

172

imitate a gravel chute washed down from slopes above. The midriff presents slick facets of rock that glisten with constant runoff, and the upper reaches pose the more traditional challenge of a precipitous, rock-bound path.

Conditions improve markedly as the trail wanders through stunted evergreens on Cannon Mountain's eastern shoulder. The trail takes a hard right turn at a junction where a spur path leads straight ahead and curls onto bare, rolling cliffs. This may not literally be the top of the gentleman's head, but it's as close to the Old Man of the Mountain as most people will ever get. The views of Franconia Notch are superb, of course, looking down on Eagle Cliff and across the parkway to the entire length of spectacular Franconia Ridge.

Beyond the outlook spur, the Kinsman Ridge Trail descends to a low point on the ridge. As the trail climbs out of this saddle, the tramway terminal remains hidden on the far side of the summit, but an old fire tower is visible at the very top of Cannon's peak. The jumbled path switchbacks roughly up the rock- and scrub-covered cone, only to meet the Rim Trail and tourists dressed in casual clothes. The Rim Trail is a smoothly graded path that loops to and from the tramway by way of a lookout tower. To the right, the tramway is 200 feet distant. To the left, the Rim and Kinsman Ridge Trails join to skirt wonderful views of Franconia Notch. The Rim Trail returns to the tramway via the summit tower. The Kinsman Ridge Trail departs in the other direction on the way to Kinsman Notch.

I know this sounds like heresy, but if any of you are wondering, $6 is the present cost of a one-way tram ride. Just be prepared, as for any hike, and don't take the trip down lightly. The trail is difficult in both directions.

Echo Lake, Cannon Mountain, and the Franconia Notch Parkway viewed from Artists Bluff.

53 Mount Lafayette/Mount Lincoln, Bridle Path Loop

General description:	A classic circle to mountain peaks on the crest of Franconia Ridge. A long day hike that passes a hut to accommodate longer stays.
General location:	Between Littleton and North Woodstock off the Franconia Notch Parkway (Interstate 93) in the heart of Franconia Notch.
Length:	8 miles.
Difficulty:	Moderate, but requires stamina.
Elevation gain:	3,500 feet.
Special attractions:	Exhilarating panoramas from Mounts Lincoln and Lafayette, the knife-edge excitement of Franconia Ridge, and the calming waters of beautiful Cloudland Falls.
Maps:	USGS Franconia quad.
For more information:	Ammonoosuc Ranger Station, 660 Trudeau Road, Bethlehem, NH 03574, (603) 869-2626.

Key points:

0.2 Junction, Old Bridle Path and Falling Waters Trail.
2.5 Greenleaf Hut.
3.6 Summit, Mount Lafayette.
4.6 Summit, Mount Lincoln, near start of knife edge.
5.3 Summit, Little Haystack, beginning of return.
6.7 Cloudland Falls.
7.0 Stairs Falls.
7.8 Return to junction, Old Bridle Path and Falling Waters Trail.

Finding the trailhead: Follow Interstate 93 north until it becomes the Franconia Notch Parkway. Pass Parkway exit 1 as well as the unnumbered exit for The Basin, and turn off on the next unnumbered exit. Trailhead parking is about a quarter of a mile after the northbound highway narrows to one lane. The trailhead is on the far side of the parking lot.

Mount Lafayette/Mount Lincoln, Bridle Path Loop

The hike: Trailheads located within yards of an interstate highway seldom promise extraordinary mountain adventure. All the more special, then, is this classic loop hike that departs the Franconia Notch Parkway and intersects the most thrilling mile of Franconia Ridge, an elevated knife-edge walk that's a hallmark of New Hampshire hiking. Much of this route is exposed to the elements, but the isolated segment that ventures out onto Franconia's narrow crest carries you almost a mile from even minimal protection. For safety and enjoyment, be sure that your time on these marvelous heights corresponds with favorable weather.

Both prongs of this loop leave the parking area together, as the Old Bridle Path and the Falling Waters Trail follow a paved sidewalk for 50 yards before angling onto a gravel path 2.5 miles from the Greenleaf Hut and 3.6

miles from Mount Lafayette. In the cool shade of a hardwood canopy, about 70 yards after meeting Walker Brook, the Falling Waters Trail departs on a footbridge to the right, forcing a choice as to which route to follow. I prefer to ascend the Old Bridle Path, which offers wonderful mountain views during the climb, saving the picturesque falls and cooling pools as refreshments for the return.

The Old Bridle Path quickly peels away from Walker Brook, sedately eases north parallel to the slope of Franconia Notch, and begins a more purposeful climb of the ridge 0.3 mile beyond the stream. After another mile of good footing and moderate ascent, about two-thirds of the way to the hut, the trail turns sharply left at an overview of Walker Ravine. The pointed peak with deep scars, massive folds, and glistening ledges that stands across the valley is Mount Lincoln, 2,000 feet higher than this spot and a later stop on your itinerary.

Within 0.2 mile of the outlook, the path becomes steeper and the footing less reliable as the trail briefly rises above timberline to whet your appetite with spectacular views. Too soon, the path eases back into a wooded col, setting up for the steep 0.5-mile climb along the ridge that bursts into sunlight again only as it nears the hut. At various clearings, look for glimpses down the southern length of the notch, or across the valley to The Old Man's cliff and the plateau that holds Lonesome Lake beneath the Kinsman Peaks.

The Greenleaf Hut has a dramatic view, overlooking Eagle Lake below the bulge of Mount Lafayette. Because the tip of this mountain is out of sight behind the curve of its giant mound, the view belies the topo map, which shows that Mount Lafayette is nearly 200 feet taller than Mount Lincoln. From the hut, turn right (east) on the Greenleaf Trail, which dips down to Eagle Lake and ascends slightly more than a mile as it weaves a bouldery path up the treeless slope of Mount Lafayette.

The effort to attain the summit earns a sublime choice of alpine views. To the east: the Lincoln Brook Valley on the near side of Owl's Head Mountain with North Twin, South Twin, the Bonds, and Mount Guyot rising beyond the Pemigewasset Wilderness. To the west: the Franconia Notch Parkway emerges from both ends of Franconia Notch, where diminutive Echo Lake nestles below the rim of Eagle Cliff. To the north and south: the trail extends along the curve of Garfield Ridge and points toward the pyramidal peaks of Mounts Liberty and Flume.

A right (south) turn onto the Franconia Ridge Trail at the summit of Mount Lafayette commences a delightful 1.7-mile walk over legendary terrain. Accompanied by continuous views, the Franconia Ridge Trail plunges into a col with dizzying views into Walker Ravine, and then ascends the summit of Mount Lincoln, with ever more spectacular vistas to the south. Descending again from this pointy height, the path nips around a tower of boulders and tightropes the edge of the knife, where winds, weather, and incredible views sweep up from opposing valleys.

The return trip begins with a right (west) turn onto the Falling Waters Trail on the top of Little Haystack Mountain. Almost immediately, the route enters protective scrub and steeply descends for close to half a mile. It then zigzags and meanders to a right turn onto a gradual grade above Dry Brook. The path begins to live up to its name as the trail crosses the stream, virtually reverses direction, and descends on jumbled boulders to re-cross the stream at a substantially lower point. At the bottom of a narrow ravine, 1.4 miles from the top, the trail fords the water yet again, where the cascades of two small streams face one another at a 70-degree angle and join to form the single bridal veil of gorgeous Cloudland Falls.

The route passes swimming holes that attract the young and determined as it eases down a cut bank above the brook, crosses to the south side of the stream beneath charming Swiftwater Falls, and later glides by Stairs Falls, 0.8 mile from the trailhead. Within less than 200 yards, the route spans Dry Brook once and for all and leaves the stream at your back on a soothing walk that rejoins the Old Bridle Path at the crossing of Walker Brook.

For a trip that isn't nearly this long, consider the Falling Waters Trail between the notch and Cloudland Falls as a great family walk that beats the heat of scorching summer days.

54 Liberty Spring Trail, Mount Liberty/Mount Flume

General description:	A relentless but popular day hike over two 4,000-foot summits with classic Franconia Notch views. Tent sites also make this a convenient leg on longer cross-country routes.
General location:	About 22 miles north of Plymouth off the Franconia Notch Parkway at the southern end of Franconia Notch.
Length:	8.0 miles round trip.
Difficulty:	Moderate, but quite persistent.
Elevation gain:	3,000 feet.
Special attractions:	The granite ramparts of Mount Liberty's peak, wide-angle views of Franconia Notch, and convenient tent sites near the crest of Franconia Ridge.
Maps:	USGS Lincoln quad; also maps available from the Franconia Notch State Park information center at Lafayette Place Campground.
For more information:	Pemigewasset Ranger Station, RR3, Box 15, Route 175, Plymouth, NH 03264, (603) 536-1315; Franconia Notch State Park, Route 3, Franconia, NH 03580, (603) 823-8800.

Liberty Spring Trail, Mount Liberty/Mount Flume

To Twin Moutain

To Mount Lincoln

Franconia Ridge Trail

Liberty Spring Campsite

Mount Liberty

Mount Flume

Franconia Notch Parkway

Liberty Spring Trail

Whitehouse Trail

Flume Slide Trail

Flume Brook

P

Flume Visitor Center

Exit 1

To Lincoln

NORTH

0   0.5   1

MILE

★

Key points:

1.0   Liberty Spring Trailhead near bridge.

1.5   Junction, Flume Slide Trail.

3.7   Junction, Franconia Ridge Trail.

4.0   Summit, Mount Liberty.

FT

Summit, Mount Liberty

Junction, Flume Slide Trail

Junction, Franconia Ridge Trail

4,500
4,000
3,500
3,000
2,500
2,000
1,500
1,000

MILES   1   2   3   4   5

Finding the trailhead: Travel north on Interstate 93, past exit 33, until the highway becomes the Franconia Notch Parkway. Take Parkway exit 1 and drive north on U.S. Highway 3, 0.2 mile past the second driveway for The Flume. The trailhead turn-off is designated by a sign for Appalachian Trail Parking well before northbound US 3 reenters the Franconia Notch Parkway.

The hike: Pick up a map of hiking trails of Franconia Notch State Park and you're likely to conclude that Mount Liberty and Mount Flume lie on a convenient circular route similar to Hike 53. Sorry, but it doesn't work out that way! A double whammy of loose gravel and slick slabs on a steep mountainside makes Flume Slide one of those trails that most hikers should avoid. Happily, the other prong of this apparent loop makes up for what its

Franconia Ridge, Mount Lincoln from the top of Mount Liberty.

neighbor lacks. The Liberty Spring route tracks the Appalachian Trail to marvelous tent sites just below Franconia Ridge, then concludes with views from the fortress walls of Mount Liberty's awesome peak.

The blue-blazed Whitehouse Trail connects the parking area to the start of the Liberty Spring Trail. This wooded walk swings north parallel to US 3 and seems shorter than the 0.9-mile distance stated on a sign. It soon meets a paved bicycle path between the Pemigewasset River and the road. Bear left, watch for bikes, and walk 0.2 mile to the junction with the Liberty Spring Trail, which departs right (east) 200 feet beyond a large steel bridge.

This trail quickly turns to its work, steadily ascending Mount Liberty's western slopes on a popular, well-maintained route with stone steps and reasonable footing. In another 0.5 mile, the path reaches the junction with the Flume Slide Trail, now looking rather innocuous. Ignore the deception and stick with Liberty Spring. The trail levels off for 0.5 mile and crosses a sizable brook before resuming a moderate climb.

About half of the next 1.4 miles consists of an unrelenting trudge directly up the hill, including 60 yards of a boulder-strewn obstacle course. The effort eases slightly near the top, but the caretaker's tent at the campground is still a pleasant sight. Look for the spring on a spur trail on the right, complete with a rock bench in a clearing to enjoy refreshments and a view.

Beyond the campsite, the next 0.3 mile is another bit of a challenge, a bony, rock-bound path that meets a low point of Franconia Ridge at a junction 0.3 mile north of Mount Liberty's summit. Turn right (south) onto this Franconia Ridge Trail and scramble up the rocks to top out on an open knoll. Turn around, but be cautious. If the climb hasn't taken your breath away, the views of Mount Lincoln and Cannon Mountain will.

The massive granite ramparts that form Mount Liberty's awesome peak are only 150 yards past the knoll and are reached by an easy climb. The vistas that await are peculiar to the southern end of Franconia Ridge. Far across the notch, Mount Moosilauke's hulking form can be seen, while on the floor of the valley, Lincoln and North Woodstock stand before swaths of ski trails that swirl on Loon Mountain's peak. The mile-long path to Mount Flume can also be assessed from here, as it drops steeply into a col and gradually climbs the opposing side. The round trip to that largely wooded summit can be accomplished in under two hours, but the limited view adds nothing new, except for a chance to peer down the daunting slides that plunge nearly the entire length of the mountain's western slope.

55 Lonesome Lake and Kinsman Peaks

General description:	A varied day hike visiting two ponds, two summits, and lodgings along the way.
General location:	Off the Franconia Notch Parkway, on the west side of Franconia Notch.
Length:	11 miles for the complete round trip; 2.5 miles for the round trip to Lonesome Lake.
Difficulty:	Moderate, with steep ascents beyond Lonesome Lake.
Elevation gain:	1,000 feet to Lonesome Lake; more than 2,600 feet to Kinsman Mountain, South Peak.
Special attractions:	Lonesome Lake and Kinsman Pond where lake and mountains meet, plus views of Franconia Ridge from either Kinsman peak.
Maps:	USGS Lincoln and Franconia quads.
For more information:	Ammonoosuc Ranger Station, 660 Trudeau Road, Bethlehem, NH 03574, (603) 869-2626.

Key points:

1.2 Lonesome Lake.
3.4 Kinsman Junction near Kinsman Pond.
4.0 Summit, Kinsman North Peak.
5.8 Summit, Kinsman South Peak.

Finding the trailhead: Follow Interstate 93 north until it becomes the Franconia Notch Parkway. Trailhead parking for this hike is available on either side of the parkway. Northbound, pass Parkway exit 1 and the un-numbered exit for The Basin. After the road narrows to one lane in this direction, drive about a quarter of a mile farther and take the next unnum-bered exit for trailhead parking. This is also the parking area for Hike 53, but a pedestrian underpass allows hikers to safely cross the highway to reach the Lonesome Lake Trailhead.

Southbound, depart the highway at the well-marked exit for the Lafayette Place Campground. As you turn off the parkway, trailhead parking will be immediately on the left. If you wish to park on this side, but you're heading north, you must drive all the way through the notch to the Tramway exit (Number 2) and return southbound.

The hike: Part family outing to Lonesome Lake, part good old-fashioned mountain hike, the trail from Lafayette Campground to the Kinsman Peaks unveils two distinctive personalities. This dual disposition carries forward into overnight accommodations that satisfy varying styles, from comfort-able hut to basic tent sites beneath a mountain peak. Throw in diverse views

Lonesome Lake and Kinsman Peaks

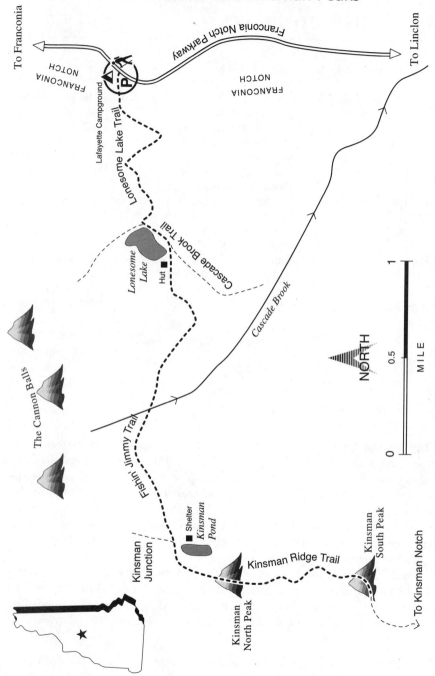

of 5,000-foot summits on beautiful Franconia Ridge, and you're likely to find something here that suits your hiking needs.

The Lonesome Lake Trail leaves the parking area on a footbridge that spans the nascent Pemigewasset River and enters Lafayette Campground. Yellow blazes guide the way past campsites, across the Pemi Trail, and into the woods to begin the climb of the 1,000-foot ridge that captures Lonesome Lake. Three long switchbacks and plank bridges at brook crossings are designed to make the AMC hut that lies near the end of the lake easily accessible to the vast majority of hikers.

Don't get confused at the trail junction shortly after cresting the ridge. Lonesome Lake Trail does not lead to the Lonesome Lake Hut. Turn left instead on the Cascade Brook Trail that runs the length of the lake—but first take a minute to rest at the outlook that's just across the junction. The rounded summits emerging beyond the far end of the water are Kinsman, North and South Peaks, your eventual destination.

The Cascade Brook Trail goes its own way at another junction near the outlet of Lonesome Lake. Bear right on the Fishin' Jimmy Trail, which continues to edge the water and comes to a "beach" and dock about 100 feet from the hut. The extraordinary view from this sunny spot largely accounts for the popularity of this hike. Who could resist whiling away blissful hours amidst views of an unspoiled lake, with shining facets on Franconia Ridge glistening beyond its shore?

The Fishin' Jimmy Trail passes the front steps of the Lonesome Lake Hut and commences a challenging 2.3-mile segment that ends near Kinsman Pond. The path starts off at a friendly pace, but soon tops a rough knoll within sight of the Kinsman Peaks. The ascent of these summits is really not as difficult as it may initially appear. The steepest sections total no more than half a mile, with a downhill run, several flat spots, and a few convenient wooden stairs to help.

Upon arrival at Kinsman Junction, a shelter and several tent sites are 0.1 mile to the left, down the trail to Kinsman Pond. Even day hikers owe it to themselves to walk down to the pond, casually stretched beneath the sheer ledges of Kinsman's wooded North Peak.

To reach the top of Kinsman Mountain, follow the Kinsman Ridge Trail from Kinsman Junction in the direction of Eliza Brook shelter. After 0.2 mile of comparatively easy climbing, the Mount Kinsman Trail departs amid stubby evergreens and expansive skies. Stay on the Kinsman Ridge Trail for the last 0.3 mile to Kinsman Mountain, North Peak, only one of many White Mountain summits now plainly within view.

A short side trail just before the peak leads to ledges with impressive views, a great spot to eat lunch and learn geography, too. Lonesome Lake lies straight ahead to the right of Cannon Mountain, identified by tiny ski lifts interrupting its curving brow. Between you and Cannon are the Cannon Balls, three rounded lumps in a row, while capping the scene above the lake is a string of 4,000- and 5,000-foot summits along jagged Franconia Ridge. From left to right: Lafayette, Lincoln, Little Haystack, Liberty, and

Flume with its hazardous slide, all pointing south to Loon Mountain's ski slopes on the Kancamagus Highway.

After attaining North Peak you'll probably debate whether another 1.8 miles of hiking to and from South Peak is really worth the bother. In good weather, it definitely is. Wandering from side to side on the nearly bare summit, encircled by mountain views, the expansive South Peak offers a slightly higher perspective on Franconia Ridge and makes an ideal turn-around point midway through the hike.

56 The Old Man and Profile Lake

General description: A brief, barrier-free visit to the Old Man of the Mountain.

General location: Off the Franconia Notch Parkway at the north end of Franconia Notch.

Length: A little more than half a mile round trip.

Difficulty: Easy.

Elevation gain: Nominal.

Special attractions: The Old Man, Profile Lake, Eagle Cliff, and beautiful Franconia Notch.

Maps: USGS Franconia quad; also maps available from the Franconia Notch State Park information center at Lafayette Place Campground.

For more information: Manager, Franconia Notch State Park, Route 3, Franconia, NH 03580, (603) 823-8800.

Key points:

0.25 View of the Old Man from the shore of Profile Lake.

Finding the trailhead: Interstate 93 transforms itself into the Franconia Notch Parkway north of exit 33. As the road narrows, the major exits are renumbered and some turnoffs for trailheads and scenic areas may not be numbered at all.

Signs advise northbound travelers of two exits for "Old Man Viewing." The first is unnumbered, has limited parking, but offers photographers the best angle to capture the Old Man. The second, at Parkway exit 2, enables you to turn left at the end of the exit ramp, cross under the highway, and follow signs to a large trailhead parking lot. Barrier-free parking is available at a lower level.

The hike: What stands 1,200 feet high and has a head 48 feet long? None other than New Hampshire's one-of-a-kind symbol, The Old Man of the Mountain, in remarkable Franconia Notch. Suspended near the top of Cannon Mountain's sheer eastern cliffs, the angular nose and jutting jaw of this handsome New Englander's great stone face can be recognized only from a northeastern aspect in line with Profile Lake.

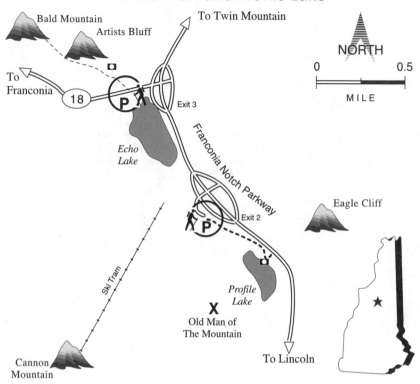

The Old Man and Profile Lake

Bald Mountain

Artists Bluff

To Twin Mountain

NORTH

0   0.5

MILE

To Franconia

18

P

Exit 3

Echo Lake

Franconia Notch Parkway

Exit 2

Eagle Cliff

P

Ski Tram

Profile Lake

X
Old Man of
The Mountain

Cannon Mountain

To Lincoln

The paved path that runs from the parking lot to the north end of Profile Lake is not the most adventurous trail in this guide, but it is without doubt the most easily recognized walk in the Granite State. With an interstate highway funneling traffic in and out of the notch, virtually every traveler on this major White Mountain route passes within yards of the convenient trailhead. It's easy, it's fun, and it's a surprisingly beautiful walk along the floor of Franconia Notch.

From the trailhead, a walkway drops down a small embankment and meets the access point for persons with disabilities at the bottom of the slope. A flat path parallels the inlet to Profile Lake, overshadowed by ski slopes, the walls of Cannon (Profile) Mountain, and jagged Eagle Cliff at the far side of the notch. Look up to the skyline for the silhouette of a granite artillery piece that gives Cannon Mountain its name. Just past an interpretive center housed in a small stone hut, hikers quickly arrive at a turnaround point on the northern shore of the lake. Here you can sit and enjoy the view of the massive mountain rising beyond the water and inspect the countenance of the famous face perpetually staring at Mount Lafayette.

If ambling down to Profile Lake doesn't satisfy your urge to hike, a short, moderate climb to a wonderful view is only 0.75 mile up the road. Return to Franconia Notch Parkway and drive north to exit 3. As you turn left at the

Profile Lake.

end of the exit ramp, look for a bare outcropping across the highway that marks the end of the notch. Park in the lot for nearby Echo Lake to access a trailhead immediately on the west side of the parkway and on the north side of Route 18. The 0.3-mile climb to the top of the ledges on Artists Bluff grants exquisite views of Echo Lake, the ski slopes of Cannon Mountain, and the 5,260-foot summit of Mount Lafayette towering above Eagle Cliff.

57 Mount Pemigewasset

General description:	A family hike to White Mountain views from the brow of Indian Head.
General location:	Off the Franconia Notch Parkway at the southern end of Franconia Notch.
Length:	3.1 miles.
Difficulty:	Moderate.
Elevation gain:	1,150 feet.
Special attractions:	A mountaintop ledge with overlook views of Kinsman Ridge, Franconia Notch, and the Pemigewasset Valley.
Maps:	USGS Lincoln quad.
For more information:	Franconia Notch State Park, Route 3, Franconia, NH 03580, (603) 823-8800.

Mount Pemigewasset

Key points:

0.2   Highway underpass.
1.45 Junction, Indian Head Trail.
1.55 Brow of Indian Head.

Finding the trailhead: Same as Hike 51. Park at the north end of the northernmost lot at The Flume Visitor Center. Look for signs for Indian Head or Mount Pemigewasset and a paved bicycle path.

The hike: I remember Franconia Notch before it had a parkway. Driving north on U.S. Highway 3, visitors would pass tourist cabins and stop for "Indian Head Viewing." For a small fee, you could climb a tower, peer through binoculars, and gaze at a mountain across the road that bore a vague resemblance to an Indian with a prominent nose. Now bypassed by a parkway, the cabins have lost their luster; however, the tower still survives, and the mountain of legend where Chief Pemigewasset maintained a silent lookout still offers sweeping views.

By far the most popular route to the top of Indian Head (also known as Mount Pemigewasset), the trail departs from the northern end of the northernmost parking lot at The Flume Visitor Center. Walk 150 yards north on a

187

paved bicycle path that runs the length of Franconia Notch, and take your first left turn onto a gravel path at a sign for Mount Pemigewasset 1.5 miles from the summit. The Mount Pemigewasset Trail immediately crosses US 3 with the aid of an underpass, spans a brook on a wooden bridge, and tracks south in an island of woods caught between busy highways. After dropping downhill and swinging right, the trail soon begins to climb even as it passes under the north- and southbound lanes of the Franconia Notch Parkway.

With civilization now at your back, the trail steps over another brook and climbs through a beech and maple forest that grows on the crooked contours of a bumpy side hill. The steady but sometimes root-bound trail curls north and west, crosses a handful of tiny brooks, and jumps over drainage channels that score the flanks of the mountain. Flattening on the gentle slopes that ease north from the low summit, the trail turns south again and passes the end of the Indian Head Trail that enters on the right just 0.1 mile from the top.

The Mount Pemigewasset Trail ends on the northern end of Indian Head's brow, a broad strip of granite ledge with views across Bog Pond to the wild White Mountain region that holds the Lost River Valley, the distinctive mass of Mount Moosilauke, and the summits of Kinsman Ridge. Most people who arrive on this scenic brow are happy to perch on the ledge, enjoy the southern view, and pose for prize photographs of a hiker on top of the world. Few of those hikers realize that they're missing half the show. Walk to your left as you look off the ledge, push beyond the stunted trees that grow at the end of the brow, and curl around a corner. From the scree slopes of Cannon Mountain to the ski trails of Loon Mountain, the full scope of Franconia Notch swiftly swings into view with the pointed summits of Mounts Flume, Liberty, Lincoln, and Lafayette looming above the trees.

The brow of Indian Head tilts with a modest pitch that is just steep enough for unwatched water bottles to roll over the lip. Especially in wet weather, be extra careful that you don't slip and do the same.

CRAWFORD NOTCH

The colorful history of Crawford Notch culminated in the era when the elite of America traveled by train to vacation at fashionable summer resorts in the cool White Mountain air. Located just north of the notch, the beautifully restored railroad station at Crawford Depot now serves as an information center and repository for memorabilia of those faded glory days, when the impressive Crawford House played host to a stylish crowd. The old resort hotels are mostly gone now, victims of changing times and disastrous fires, but modern travelers who wish to reprise a bit of the past can still find lodgings at the incomparable Mount Washington Hotel, a spectacular survivor in nearby Bretton Woods.

Crawford Notch made hiking history, too. This bold pass that separates the expansive Pemigewasset Wilderness from the majestic Presidential Range is the site of America's oldest mountain trail still in use today. The timeless beauty of the Crawford Path leaves the north end of Crawford Notch, explores a ridge of wind-scoured summits, and dramatically concludes on the highest peak in the northeastern United States. Of course, Crawford Notch has always promised more than high-altitude exploration. Quick family hikes overlooking the pass from Mount Willard or Elephant Head, moderate hikes to falls or ponds, and rugged treks in the Dry River Wilderness or along the Montalban Ridge all serve to round out the region's extensive repertoire.

58 Arethusa Falls Trail

General description: A half-day family hike to watery recreation.
General location: Between Bartlett and Twin Mountain near the southern end of Crawford Notch.
Length: 2.5 miles round trip to the falls; 4.5 miles as a loop hike that includes Frankenstein Cliff.
Difficulty: Moderate.
Elevation gain: 620 feet to the falls; 1,280 feet for the full loop.
Special attractions: New Hampshire's highest falls and views of Crawford Notch from the top of Frankenstein Cliff.
Maps: USGS Crawford Notch and Stairs Mountain quads.
For more information: Saco Ranger District, 33 Kancamagus Highway, Conway, NH 03818, (603) 447-2166.

Key points:
- 0.1 Junction, Bemis Brook Trail.
- 0.5 Bemis Brook Falls via Bemis Brook Trail.
- 0.6 Rejoin Arethusa Falls Trail.
- 1.25 Base of Arethusa Falls.
- 2.35 Junction, Arethusa–Ripley Falls Trail and Frankenstein Cliff Trail.
- 3.15 Top of Frankenstein Cliff.

Arethusa Falls Trail

To Ripley Falls

To Twin Mountain

Frankenstein Cliff

Frankenstein Cliff Trail

Arethusa–Ripley Falls Trail

Arethusa Falls Trail

Bemis Brook

Arethusa Falls

Bemis Brook Falls

Bemis Brook Trail

NORTH

0   0.5   1

MILE

P

302

To North Conway

Finding the trailhead: From the traffic lights at the junction of U.S. Highways 3 and 302 in Twin Mountain, turn east on US 302 and continue to Crawford Notch. The driveway to the Arethusa Falls Trail leaves the right (west) side of the highway 3.2 miles

south of the Willey House site in the middle of Crawford Notch. The large gravel area immediately to the right is for spill-over parking and access to Frankenstein Cliff. Continue 0.2 mile uphill on the paved driveway to reach a smaller parking lot at the Arethusa Falls Trailhead.

The hike: Dropping more than 200 feet in a swath of lacy mist, the plunge of Bemis Brook creates New Hampshire's highest falls and a premier natural wonder. But seasoned hikers understand that there's more to Arethusa Falls than a first-class visual treat. In the hot days of midsummer the sluicing cascades, broad rocks, and tiny pools that emerge from the base of the falls create a perfect spot for cooling your feet, splashing your children, or simply enjoying the pleasures of its backcountry sights and sounds.

A family-friendly trail to watery recreation makes for a popular destination. Hikers of all shapes and sizes seem able to negotiate the 2.5 miles round trip to Arethusa Falls without undue stress, but few show much interest in the

Splashing in the cooling pools of Arethusa Falls.

extra trek to Frankenstein Cliff. If you're up to a vigorous effort after splashing in a cooling pool, a 3.4-mile extension turns an easygoing walk into a moderate loop hike that climbs to views of Crawford Notch from a cliff named for a painter, not a fictional monster.

The scene at the Arethusa Falls Trailhead underscores the family appeal. Directly across a railroad track, next to a picnic table, a shocking-pink snack bar sells soda, ice cream, and T-shirts to hikers who happen by. It's not very woodsy, but this private enterprise is sure to look more inviting at the end of a summer hike.

Just to the left of the snack bar, the Arethusa Falls Trail angles south up a small embankment, parallels the railroad tracks for about 30 yards, and then turns right in a hardwood forest to follow Bemis Brook. About 100 yards upstream, the trail soon divides. To the right, the main Arethusa Falls Trail takes the more gradual route that climbs the surrounding slopes. I turned left instead on the less traveled Bemis Brook Trail, a much more scenic route, which hugs the stream past rapids and riffs before reaching an isolated overlook of enchanting Bemis Brook Falls. Having postponed its climb, the Bemis Brook Trail scrambles 0.1 mile up a very steep slope to catch the main trail. Turn left at the signed junction at the top of the high bank to resume your hike on the Arethusa Falls Trail that rolls more comfortably across the hill, easing to its destination.

About two-thirds of the way to the falls, two small pools in Bemis Brook offer pleasant rest to the weary before the path crosses a feeder stream on a jumble of washed boulders and finally spans Bemis Brook on a log hiker's bridge. The Arethusa Falls Trail ends about one-tenth of a mile farther upstream at the base of Arethusa Falls where it also meets the Arethusa–Ripley Falls Trail at one of the White Mountain's most inviting trail junctions.

After serving time as a spectator below the glistening falls, or maybe risking a brisk swim in a crystal cascade or pool, you can return the way you came or tiptoe across Bemis Brook on the Arethusa–Ripley Falls Trail and head for Frankenstein Cliff. Climbing high up the opposite bank on a path that leads downstream, the Arethusa–Ripley Falls Trail quickly reverses course when it hits the top of the bank and tracks a smaller stream through a gently rolling woodland plateau west of Crawford Notch. Crossing this small stream after another 0.3 mile, the trail eases east, circling back toward the trailhead with views of the wooded summits on the far side of Crawford Notch flickering through the trees. To complete the loop, turn right on the Frankenstein Cliff Trail 1.1 miles from Arethusa Falls. To the left, the Arethusa–Ripley Falls Trail continues 1.1 miles to Ripley Falls and 1.5 miles to the Ethan Pond Trail (Hike 66) that leads to Zealand Notch.

From the Arethusa–Ripley Falls Trail junction, the Frankenstein Cliff Trail rolls up and over another rise to a vista of Mount Washington at the head of the Dry River Valley (Hike 63) before descending briskly to complete its 0.8-mile journey to the top of Frankenstein Cliff. A junior version of Mount Willard (Hike 64), the view from this high perch presents an intimate look at the southern end of Crawford Notch and the White Mountain valley that carries an active railroad track, U.S. Highway 302, and the winding Saco River south and east toward the Gulf of Maine.

Sitting in a clearing at the top of this sheer cliff, you'll also spot Arethusa Falls, the cut of Bemis Brook, and the familiar pink snack bar next to the lot where you parked your car. Follow the blue-blazed path out of the opposite side of the clearing on a ragged, loose, gravelly trail that totally lacks charm. After zigzagging below the base of an impressive wall of rock, the Frankenstein Cliff Trail begins a free-fall descent that passes under an immense railroad trestle that is strictly off limits and should never be explored. Turn right just beyond the trestle and follow a path that parallels the distant highway for 0.3 mile before crossing a brook (where a spur trail leads left to spill-over parking) and returning to the trailhead lot. Remember that gaudy snack bar? It's time for a Ben & Jerry's!

59 Mount Carrigain, Signal Ridge Trail

General description:	A long day hike to an observation tower atop a jagged ridge in the center of the White Mountain National Forest.
General location:	About 7 miles southwest of Crawford Notch, off the Sawyer River Road.
Length:	10.0 miles round trip.
Difficulty:	Difficult.
Elevation gain:	3,300 feet.
Special attractions:	Encyclopedic, panoramic, stunning mountain views; perhaps the most comprehensive of any in the White Mountains.
Maps:	USGS Mount Carrigain quad.
For more information:	Saco Ranger Station, 33 Kancamagus Highway, Conway, NH 03818, (603) 447-2166.

Key points:

0.2 Crossing Whiteface Brook.
1.7 Junction, Carrigain Notch Trail.
4.5 Crest of Signal Ridge.
5.0 Summit fire tower.

Finding the trailhead: The Sawyer River Road departs the west side of U.S. Highway 302, 10.3 miles south of Crawford Depot and 7.6 miles south of the Willey House site in the middle of Crawford Notch. Two miles down this well-marked gravel road look for the Signal Ridge Trailhead on the right (north) side, just before a bridge spanning Whiteface Brook. The parking area is on the left (south), just across the bridge.

Mount Carrigain, Signal Ridge Trail

The hike: If hiking paths were cleared in Crawford Notch in the early 1800s, it's hard to believe that the first reported climb of nearby Carrigain Mountain did not take place for another fifty years. Perhaps settlers spotted the vicious-looking profile of jagged Signal Ridge and decided that conquering this bony crest simply wasn't worth a try. It took a massive logging boom in the last quarter of the nineteenth century to promote further exploration of the Sawyer River Valley and prove that difficult-looking mountains aren't always what they seem.

A century ago most of the trees in this valley were hauled away on a logging railroad, past the town of Livermore, over what is now the Sawyer River Road. Except for a noticeable scarcity of evergreens that continues to the present day, the woods are healthy, the town has disappeared, and we are left with comfortable hiking paths that penetrate the forest along the old logging routes. The Signal Ridge Trail makes abundant use of these well-worn paths, wisely waiting to top the ridge until 0.5 mile from a summit fire tower with what may be the White Mountain's most comprehensive view.

Thirty yards from its start, the Signal Ridge Trail joins a logging grade and follows the northeast side of Whiteface Brook for nearly 0.2 mile before crossing to the opposite side. After a mile or so, the wide path flattens and shies away from the stream, ambling easily to the crossing of Carrigain Brook near the junction with the Carrigain Notch Trail, 1.7 miles from the road. Just beyond this junction, a beaver marsh opens early views of Mount

Lowell's distinctive cliffs, which mark the plunging northeast wall of remote Carrigain Notch.

The trail soon narrows and begins a gradual climb, rapidly becoming moderate as it twists and turns up the base at the side of the extended ridge. Sharply turning left and right in a series of erratic switchbacks, the route enters a reworked, shale-covered section that ends with another overlook of the gorgeous backwoods notch. A mile-long march past files of gleaming birch on the middle slopes of Signal Ridge ends none too soon at a left turn that begins the final 0.6 mile to crest the top of the ridge.

Immediate views from a bare bulge at about the midpoint of the ridge provide incentive for the last 0.5 mile of this journey. A rush of mountain peaks reduces the impact of Carrigain Notch, with Signal Ridge, Crawford Notch, and the distant summit of Mount Washington now dominating the alpine scene. Ahead, a stubby fire tower is plainly evident across a shallow col, standing atop another wooded slope still 500 feet above your head. To reach your destination, bear left at a former cabin site (now a camping spot), and keep a sharp eye on the trail as it snakes up the knoll.

The weather is brisk on the open platform at the top of the tower, but the views are truly superb. Mounts Washington, Chocorua, Tripyramid, and Hancock, the Twins, the Bonds, Montalban Ridge, Franconia Ridge, Garfield Ridge, the southern Presidential Range, Crawford Notch, Carrigain Notch, Zealand Notch, as well as the Sawyer River Valley and most of the Pemigewasset Wilderness are all visible from this most incredible spot.

Distinctive Carrigain Notch as seen from Signal Ridge.

60 Crawford Path, Mizpah Spring Loop

General description:	A gradual day hike to glorious views on the historic Crawford Path, with huts and tent sites for overnight options.
General location:	Off U.S. Highway 302 between Twin Mountain and North Conway, near the north end of Crawford Notch.
Length:	6.4 miles round trip, excluding the excursion to Mount Eisenhower.
Difficulty:	Moderate.
Elevation gain:	2,400 feet.
Special attractions:	Magnificent views of the Presidential Peaks from Mount Pierce, Mount Eisenhower, and their connecting alpine ridge.
Maps:	USGS Crawford Notch and Stairs Mountain quads.
For more information:	Ammonoosuc Ranger Station, 660 Trudeau Road, Bethlehem, NH 03574, (603) 869-2626.

Key points:

0.3	End of Crawford Connector.
1.8	Junction, Crawford Path and Mizpah Cutoff.
3.0	Summit, Mount Pierce (Clinton).
3.9	Mizpah Spring Hut.
4.6	Return to junction, Mizpah Cutoff and Crawford Path.

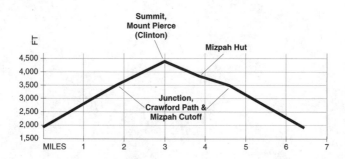

Finding the trailhead: From the traffic lights at the junction of U.S. Highways 3 and 302 in Twin Mountain, follow US 302 east 8.2 miles and turn left onto the Mount Clinton Road. Within 0.1 mile look for the new hiker's parking area on the left. The trailhead for the Crawford Connector is at the far end of the parking lot.

The Crawford Path's original trailhead is on US 302 almost directly across from a small parking area at the Crawford House historic marker, 0.1 mile farther down the road. This trailhead is still active, but hikers are better off using the new facilities off the Mount Clinton Road.

Crawford Path, Mizpah Spring Loop

The view from Mount Eisenhower: Washington, Clay, and Jefferson in the northern Presidentials.

The hike: The USDA Forest Service regards the 1819 Crawford Path as the oldest continuously used mountain trail found in the United States. It's hard to fathom how Abel and Ethan Allen Crawford managed to clear this route from notch to timberline at such an early date. More intriguing, though, is the question of why they wanted to do such a thing. Apparently, the answer was tourism.

The same father-and-son team built the nearby Crawford House in 1828, the first in a series of ill-fated inns that achieved considerable acclaim before burning to the ground. Daniel Webster, Nathaniel Hawthorne, John Greenleaf Whittier, and five United States presidents were guests of these establishments, no doubt drawn in part by advertisements extolling the virtues of a newly improved bridle path that granted access to nearby mountains. By 1870, the path had reverted strictly to foot traffic, and in time most of the large White Mountain resort hotels either were lost to fiery disasters or faded from the scene.

Although local efforts at hospitality ultimately failed, it's safe to say that lack of scenery did not contribute to their fall. Modern-day hikers will find that the marvelous Crawford Path still runs all the way to Mount Washington amid astounding mountain views. The Mizpah Spring Loop explores the southern end of the Crawford Path and leads to impressive vistas from the top of Mount Pierce (also known as Mount Clinton) with a chance to extend the day by walking through extravagant scenery around and about Mount Eisenhower's summit cone.

The 0.3-mile Crawford Connector crosses the Mount Clinton Road, spans Gibbs Brook on a footbridge below a small cascade, and meets the Crawford Path 0.2 mile east of the original trailhead. As is typical of former bridle paths, this is a gradual hike, but don't expect smooth footing on this old, eroded trail as it rises 1.5 miles past refreshing Gibbs Falls and intersects with the Mizpah Cutoff.

Evidently, most people use this route to access the Mizpah Spring Hut and Nauman tent sites that are down the Mizpah Cutoff 0.7 mile to the right. From this junction, the Crawford Path continues straight ahead as the narrower, less-traveled route, angling off toward Mount Pierce with early views of more northerly peaks flickering through the trees. In a little more than a mile, this endearing segment of trail gains significant elevation without seeming to pay a commensurate price. Before you know it, fabulous views of Mounts Eisenhower, Monroe, and Washington greet you just above timberline. Here also is the northern terminus of the scenic Webster Cliff Trail.

Already, the return trip begins with a right (south) turn onto the Webster Cliff Trail scampering 200 yards uphill to open ledges on the summit of Mount Pierce. There are perfectly lovely spots to sun, lunch, and study the sights before briskly descending to the Mizpah Spring Hut, connecting with the Mizpah Cutoff, and finally completing the loop. But we're getting way ahead of ourselves. In good weather, most hikers will have a lot more on their minds than getting back to the trailhead.

From the junction with the Webster Cliff Trail, the extraordinary opportunities of the Crawford Path are plainly within sight. The trail leads onto a winding ridge that rises to the bald summit of Mount Eisenhower, immersing hikers in vistas that are among the most compelling in the White Mountains. As you ramble over ledges and dip into scrub-covered cols, take time to admire Castellated Ridge, Ridge of the Caps, and Mounts Washington, Jefferson, and Clay. Hiker's heaven, or in bad weather, just the reverse. Less

The Mount Washington Hotel preserves a grand tradition.

adventurous souls can avoid Mount Eisenhower's absolute peak by staying on the Crawford Path. All others should climb the mountain's rocky cone on the handy summit loop. Either way, if the weather allows, I highly recommend a jaunt to the far (north) side of Mount Eisenhower, a beguiling world of majestic peaks observed from a graceful col of intersecting paths, a windswept tarn, and fascinating nooks and crannies.

A final word about history to clarify names and (perhaps) stem political debate. A good century before the recent Clinton administration, one of the summits visited on this hike bore the name Mount Clinton. In 1913, that mountain was officially renamed in honor of New Hampshire's very own President Franklin Pierce, a tribute that turned out to be less than universally pleasing. We inherit confusion and paradox—a mountain with two names and a Mount Clinton Road and Mount Clinton Trail that officially provide access to Mount Pierce.

61 Nancy Pond Trail

General description:	An energetic day hike to two mountain ponds on the edge of the Pemigewasset Wilderness.
General location:	Between Twin Mountain and North Conway, 6.5 miles south of Crawford Notch.
Length:	About 8.5 miles round trip.
Difficulty:	Moderate.
Elevation gain:	2,170 feet.
Special attractions:	Pristine ponds, a waterfall, and a stunning wilderness view.
Maps:	USGS Bartlett and Mount Carrigain quads.
For more information:	Saco Ranger District, 33 Kancamagus Highway, Conway, NH 03818, (603) 447-2166.

Key points:

1.5   First crossing of Nancy Brook.

2.5   Nancy Cascades.

3.5   Nancy Pond.

4.25 Outlet, Norcross Pond.

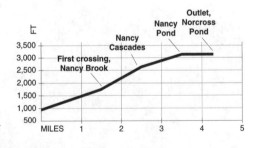

Finding the trailhead: From the traffic lights at the junction of U.S. Highways 3 and 302 in Twin Mountain, turn east on US 302 and drive through Crawford Notch. The Nancy Pond Trailhead leaves from the right (west) side of the highway 9.2 miles south of the information center at Crawford Depot and 6.5 miles south of the Willey House site in the middle of Crawford Notch. A wide gravel area off the shoulder of the highway provides parking for six to eight cars.

Nancy Pond Trail

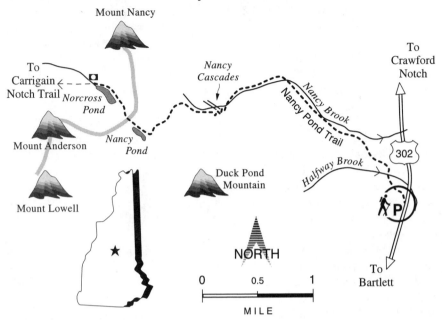

The hike: I misjudged this trail. Most first-time hikers here probably do. A 4-mile jaunt to a waterfall and two secluded pools, the Nancy Pond Trail doesn't scale a mountain peak but still climbs more than 2,100 feet into the high, wooded country that hides behind the western wall of beautiful Crawford Notch. This hike through a rugged watershed is tougher than you think, but worth a concerted effort.

The hike begins calmly enough, as the trail angles northwest on a leaf-covered logging road that more or less parallels US 302. Passing a Forest Service information kiosk after 0.1 mile, the route narrows to a woodland path that curls past a private residence, crosses Halfway Brook, and wanders between hardwood trees within sight of another home. Keep an eye on yellow blazes and handmade arrow signs that guide the trail through a maze of paths and woods roads that crisscross this early section.

With preliminaries over, the Nancy Pond Trail turns away from the highway on another wide logging road and soon converges with Nancy Brook, which rushes by on the right at the bottom of a small ravine. Don't be confused by the blizzard of blazes that appears along this route. Those startling red scars are government survey marks that slant toward the logging road as it tracks the brook upstream and enters the White Mountain National Forest at a cairn of red-painted stones.

Turnouts onto spur paths lead to views of rushing water before the trail angles across a feeder stream and climbs to a crossing of Nancy Brook a little more than 1.5 miles from the trailhead. Use caution as you tiptoe over the rocks that poke above the flow and get ready for a change of pace.

Climbing now on the opposite bank with Nancy Brook on your left, the trail becomes less steady as it hops a small stream and passes the crumpled foundation of an old mill just 0.2 mile beyond the Nancy Brook crossing. Ascending even more briskly into a narrowing watershed, the path dips through a tiny gorge, crosses a clutter of flood-washed stones, and climbs across gritty slopes where rocks and small boulders have slid into the chasm. Nearly 0.8 mile of moderate slogging traverses this rough terrain where bending and broken trees form a canopy over your head as they bow to touch the water.

Re-crossing Nancy Brook on a jumble of slick stones, the trail curls upward less than 100 yards before reaching the tree-lined pool at the foot of Nancy Cascade. The velvety foam of Nancy Brook falling over a sheer headwall is the good news in this ravine. The bad news, of course, is you still have to climb to the top of those lacy falls. A series of steep switchbacks on the south side of the stream climb first to a small lookout near the mid-point of the cascade and then continue upward while great views of the watershed open to the east.

Bunchberries and blueberries line the root-bound trail that meanders west beyond the top of the falls. About six-tenths of a mile of amiable hiking leads through an untouched forest as you track upstream through a fecund region of boggy, wooded wetlands and ascend to a pair of ponds. The northern shore of Nancy Pond is pretty and certainly pleasing. You're likely to spot the print of a moose in the mud at the edge of the water and savor the peaceful solitude of this high mountain pool, but don't even think about ending this hike without visiting Norcross Pond.

The tranquil shores of Norcross Pond.

Tantilizing views of the Pemigewasset Wilderness from the outlet of Norcross Pond.

The waters of Nancy Pond flow east to Crawford Notch and the emergent Saco River. Hike 0.3 mile farther, though, and you'll top a low rise, cross a wilderness boundary, and discover the waters of Norcross Pond that flow west to the Pemigewasset. Surrounded by gentle hills, 7-acre Norcross Pond is a perfect destination. Walk the length of its northern shore, make a quick left turn, and step onto a giant boulder at the pond's northwest end. Sitting on this natural bedrock dam just inches above the water, you can visit with Canada jays, consider the slick-rock sluiceway that feeds the outlet stream, and gaze west to a one-of-a-kind White Mountain panorama. Tumbling over granite boulders and falling down a mountain, the outlet stream accentuates a tantalizing view of the Pemigewasset Wilderness and the distant summits of Franconia Ridge that peer over the shoulders of Mount Guyot and Mount Bond.

Day hikers to Norcross Pond must return the way they came. Backpackers can continue west 2.8 miles on the Nancy Pond Trail to a junction with the Carrigain Notch Trail in the vicinity of Desolation Shelter. See Hikes 59 and 70 for alternate exit routes that approach Desolation Shelter or pass near Carrigain Notch.

62 Rocky Branch, Davis Path, Isolation Trail Loop

General description: An overnight loop along Montalban Ridge to the summit of Mount Isolation, returning through the Rocky Branch Valley.

General location: About 30 miles south of Berlin near the village of Glen.

Length: 19.0 miles.

Difficulty: Moderate.

Elevation gain: 2,800 feet.

Special attractions: Miles of uncrowded trails, unequalled views of the southern Presidential Peaks, and shelters on a river that lures anglers.

Maps: USGS Stairs Mountain quad.

For more information: Saco Ranger Station, 33 Kancamagus Highway, Conway, NH 03818, (603) 447-2166.

Key points:

2.0	Shelter No. 1.
3.8	Stairs Col.
4.2	Spur to top of Stairs.
9.5	Summit, Mount Isolation.
10.3	Junction, Davis Path and Isolation Trail.
12.9	Shelter No. 2.
17.0	Return to Shelter No. 1.

Finding the trailhead: At the junction of U.S. Highway 302 and New Hampshire Route 16, north of North Conway in Glen, continue west on US 302 and turn right (northeast) 1.0 mile later onto Jericho Road. The pavement ends in another mile or so, before the gravel road deadends at the trailhead, 5.2 miles from the highway.

The hike: It doesn't take long in New Hampshire to realize that the old Yankees who named this territory were seldom taken with fits of ironic humor. If this sober bunch labeled a mountain Isolation, they meant to be taken seriously. In spite of the fact that this trailhead is located 6.0 miles from one of northern New Hampshire's busiest intersections, the appellation applied by our ancestors remains as accurate as ever. This remote region is well removed from usual day-trip routes, visited mostly by anglers who enjoy two shelters that border the Rocky Branch River.

The Rocky Branch Trail begins at a locked vehicular gate, crosses two wooden bridges, and continues up a closed forest road for almost half a mile. As the road swings left, an information board signals a turn onto the gentle grade of an old railroad bed used for logging in the last century. With only a minor interruption, the attractive, birch-lined route runs straight as a string for another 1.5 miles before reaching a 40-yard spur path to tent sites with a water view and Rocky Branch Shelter No. 1.

Rocky Branch, Davis Path, Isolation Trail Loop

To Mount
Washington

NORTH

0   0.5   1

MILE

Isolation Trail

Mount
Isolation

Mount
Davis

Rocky Branch Trail

Shelter
No. 2

Rocky Branch Trail

Davis Path

MONTALBAN · RIDGE

Rocky Branch River

Maple
Mountain

Stairs
Mountain

Shelter No. 1

Stairs Col Trail

Mount
Resolution

To Crawford Notch

P

To US 302

FT.

4,500
4,000
3,500
3,000
2,500
2,000
1,500
1,000

Mount
Isolation

Spur to
Stairs

Shelter No. 1

Stairs
Col

MILES   1   2   3   4   5   6   7   8   9   10

A few steps beyond the tent-site spur, a left turn onto Stairs Col Trail begins the clockwise circumnavigation of the loop that includes Mount Isolation. This 1.8-mile connecting path leads directly west, rising out of the Rocky Branch Valley to a col south of Stairs Mountain on the crest of Montalban Ridge. After scrambling to the top of an embankment, the smooth, sunny Stairs Col Trail steadily ascends for more than a mile before it skims the edge of a small, deep ravine and then climbs steeply for 0.5 mile to the flat col below the stony face of Stairs Mountain.

The trail descends slightly after cresting the ridge to meet the Davis Path. Constructed as a bridle trail, this 150-year-old route originates in Crawford Notch and traces the coarse line of Montalban Ridge as it rises proudly to the summit of Mount Washington (see Hike 88). No backyard dobbin would dare to attempt this rugged journey today. Turning right (north) at the trail junction, the Davis Path revisits Stairs Mountain by tightroping along its angular flanks and curving sharply right over jagged boulders to a spur path that leads to a view at the top of the jumbled peak. The Davis Path turns left at the spur junction, gains the top of the evergreen-cloaked ridge, and finally begins a slow descent of the mountain's northern slopes.

The difficult start to the Davis Path in the Stairs Col area rapidly eases into a pleasantly varied ridge walk through sheltering evergreens, ferny glades, wet bogs, and the tops of knolls. The nearly 6 miles of trail that interpose on the way to Mount Isolation immerse the hiker in a remote world of moose tracks, owls, and private glimpses of distant mountain peaks. South of Mount Davis, campsites can be found on top of many of the smaller hills, but reliable water is scarce along the bony ridge.

The Davis Path runs east of the absolute summit of Mount Isolation, crosses a wet area on split logs, and seems for all the world to be descending away from the top. Don't be alarmed! The left turn to the summit path is well marked with a sign and cairn. Standing tall about 5 miles due south of the summit of Mount Washington, the marvelous outlook from Mount Isolation is truly one of a kind. In spectacular low relief on the north and west horizons, the entire chain of the southern Presidential Peaks descends in perfect hierarchy from Mount Washington towering above Boott Spur and Slide Peak to Mounts Monroe, Franklin, Eisenhower, Pierce (Clinton), Jackson, and Webster standing at the edge of Crawford Notch.

When you tear yourself away from the awesome summit, the loop continues north for almost a mile, easing down the mountain with departing

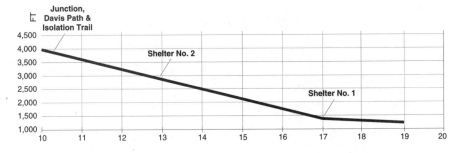

glimpses of Mount Monroe. The moderate path is brushy, muddy, and presents a conundrum about one tenth of a mile before it meets the Isolation Trail. Side paths and unfathomable signs look more like a trail junction than an abandoned site of a hiker's shelter. Solve the riddle by walking a short distance farther to the well-marked right turn onto the east branch of the Isolation Trail.

Any lack of water on the ridge is more than made up for on the sloppy descent back to the Rocky Branch Valley. After wending its way downward through stands of fir, the Isolation Trail encounters the first of several sections where brooks and runoff flood the path. Curving to the southeast for 2.6 miles, the route crosses the infant Rocky Branch stream four times and really dries out only near its merge with the Rocky Branch Trail within sight of Rocky Branch Shelter No. 2.

In the final 6 miles, the route spans the now mature river four more times at crossings that may be difficult and dangerous during high water. Also watch your step where long-since-vanished railroad trestles force scrambled crossings of various tributaries. With these exceptions, the rest of the trail is a veritable jogging path that calmly follows the crisp Rocky Branch waters back to Shelter No. 1, and all the way home to the trailhead.

63 Dry River, Mount Isolation

General description: A backpacking hike that traverses the core of the Presidential Range–Dry River Wilderness.

General location: Between Bartlett and Twin Mountain near the southern end of Crawford Notch.

Length: 17 miles round trip.

Difficulty: Moderate.

Elevation gain: 2,800 feet.

Special attractions: Serene backcountry wilderness, a panoramic mountain view, and alternate access to the southern Presidential Range.

Maps: USGS Stairs Mountain quad.

For more information: Saco Ranger Station, 33 Kancamagus Highway, Conway, NH 03818, (603) 447-2166.

Dry River, Mount Isolation

Mount Pierce

To Lake of the Clouds

To Mount Washington

Isolation Trail

Isolation Trail

Isolation Brook

Mount Isolation

Mount Jackson

Dry River

Davis Path

Mount Davis

PRESIDENTIAL RANGE — DRY

RIVER WILDERNESS AREA

MONTALBAN RIDGE

Dry River Trail

To Bretton Woods

CRAWFORD NOTCH

P

302

To N. Conway

NORTH

0   0.5   1

MILE

Key points:

1.7 River crossing on suspension bridge.
4.9 Junction, Dry River Trail and Isolation Trail.
7.3 Junction, Isolation Trail and Davis Path.
8.5 Summit, Mount Isolation.

Finding the trailhead: From the traffic lights at the junction of U.S. Highways 3 and 302 in Twin Mountain, turn east on US 302 and proceed past Bretton Woods into Crawford Notch. The Dry River Trailhead leaves from the left (east) side of the highway 5.2 miles south of the information center at Crawford Depot, and 2.5 miles south of the Willey House site in the middle of Crawford Notch. Park well off the highway on the wide gravel brim that's provided.

The hike: The core of the Presidential Range–Dry River Wilderness extends north from Crawford Notch roughly parallel to the Crawford Path and Montalban Ridge before ending on the intermediate slopes south of Mount Washington's summit. The Dry River Trail penetrates the center of this wilderness expanse as it follows the Dry River to the far reaches of its watershed and ends at Lakes of the Clouds between Mounts Washington and Monroe. Frankly, this trail may not appeal to the average New Hampshire hiker, but those few self-sufficient souls who seek quiet backpacks in rugged country will regard this hike with pleasure.

The trip to Mount Isolation is just one of several options available in this area. If you enjoy getting off the beaten path, deposit the Dry River Trail in your bank of hiking knowledge for the day you'd like a rough-and-tumble, backdoor approach to the Mizpah Hut, Mount Pierce, Mount Eisenhower, or even Mount Washington.

Soon after reaching the trailhead it becomes clear that "Dry River" absolutely fails to describe the conditions here. In fact, a posted notice warns that this long, deep valley, fed by numerous tributaries, is hazardous in times of heavy snowmelt or unusually heavy rain and is extremely prone to flooding. Washout patterns of forest debris on early sections of trail immediately lend weight to the seriousness of this warning. After my note in Hike 62 about ironic historic names, I need to point out that this un-dry stream began its life more accurately known as the Mount Washington River.

The hike begins on a gully-bottom jeep track that later jumps up to the elevated bed of an old logging railroad, crosses the wilderness boundary,

Crawford Depot, recalls the history of Crawford Notch.

and tracks upstream northwest of the river. As soon as the flow of water clearly comes into view, the trail takes a hard left turn and climbs on a narrow path high up on a bank, in a characteristic detour that promptly returns to the edge of the stream. A second detour rises even higher to a view of mountains and valley framed in maple leaves before returning to cross the river on a wooden suspension bridge, 1.7 miles from the trailhead.

The next 3.2 miles to the junction with the Isolation Trail are marked by vacillations between rocky climbs of steep slopes along the riverbank and straight-as-an-arrow open paths down old logging grades. Constants in this changing mix are supplied by aisles of paper birch and the vigorous rush of the river through a jumble of burnished stone. Past the midpoint of this stretch, the Mount Clinton Trail bears left on its way to the Mizpah Spring Hut, while the Dry River Trail continues right to its rendezvous with Isolation Brook.

A few yards after spanning mossy Isolation Brook, the Isolation Trail bears right parallel to the stream, and the Dry River Trail bears slightly left on its way to the higher peaks. Within 0.25 mile, the Dry River Trail spins out two alternate hikes on the Mount Eisenhower Trail and Dry River Cut-off that angle in different directions to catch the Crawford Path.

Our hike turns northeast with the Isolation Trail, a junior version of Dry River, narrower, less well defined, and tracking a smaller stream. This little-used trail links Dry River with the top of Montalban Ridge and climbs at a moderate pitch as it intercepts the Davis Path, about a mile north of the summit of Mount Isolation. Turn right (south) on the Davis Path's elongated, bumpy ridge, and ignore the eastern half of the Isolation Trail that exits to the left (east) as it heads for the Rocky Branch Valley. From this point all that's left is a short climb to a bare mountain peak with fabulous views of the Presidential Range described in Hike 62.

Backpackers are the most likely people to make use of this moderately difficult route that is long and slow enough to make it questionable as a one-day excursion. Except for the top of Montalban Ridge, water is plentiful throughout the hike, and attractive wilderness campsites are very easy to find.

64 Mount Willard

General description:	An entertaining family hike to blueberry-sprinkled ledges overlooking Crawford Notch. Count on 2.5 hours, round trip, with time to enjoy the view.
General location:	About 9 miles southeast of Twin Mountain, at the north end of Crawford Notch.
Length:	3.2 miles round trip.
Difficulty:	Moderate.
Elevation gain:	900 feet.
Special attractions:	Crawford Depot, a family-friendly trail, and the best view of Crawford Notch.
Maps:	USGS Crawford Notch quad.
For more information:	Ammonoosuc Ranger Station, 660 Trudeau Road, Bethlehem, NH 03574, (603) 869-2626.

Key points:

0.0   Crawford Depot.
0.1   Junction, Avalon Trail and Mount Willard Trail.
0.5   Centennial Pool.
1.6   Outlook ledge.

Finding the trailhead: The Avalon Trailhead is across the railroad tracks, directly behind the Crawford Depot information center, 9.4 miles southeast of Twin Mountain on U.S. Highway 302. Ample parking is provided in the immediate area.

The hike: As U.S. Highway 302 climbs north through Crawford Notch, it commences a sweeping curve toward the east to avoid Mount Willard's massive bulk blocking the head of the pass. A surprisingly simple walk leads to south-facing cliffs near the top of this wooded peak, where blueberries and spectacular views vie for your attention. High above Crawford Notch, Mount Willard's sunny ledges are perfectly positioned for a grandiose vista of the glacial valley that swoops from Mount Webster to Mount Willey and gives rise to the Saco River.

Mount Willard

Before beginning your hike, take a few minutes to peruse the historic memories housed in Crawford Depot. Just across the tracks from the platform of this old station, the Avalon Trail passes through a scruffy clearing and then blends into the woods where it finds a trailhead kiosk. Turn left at this juncture on the Mount Willard Trail, which wanders through the trees to commence its 1.4-mile climb. On the way up the hill, this blue-blazed, well-trod path touches the left bank of a stream and then turns left again at Centennial Pool, a tiny private basin, just big enough for two. Another 0.2 mile of walking leads to a right turn onto the wide remains of a graded carriage road that climbs in slanting vectors to surmount the rest of the slope.

Shortly before reaching the top, look for a spur path to Hitchcock Flume. I found this steep, rough, and stubby detour certainly to be worth the effort, but it's not a place for younger kids or for anyone else in dark or foggy weather. At the end of the short descent, a narrow 10-foot cleft, disguised with vegetation to the lip of its vertical sides. Walk along the rim of this trap to find a perch overlooking the northern end of Crawford Notch, where Silver Cascade tumbles down Mount Jackson to the highway waiting below.

Beyond the spur-path junction the trail runs straight through the arching woods to the sun-drenched open cliff. No doubt company will be here on fair-weather summer days, but the long balcony of rounded ledge grants plenty of elbow room. Spread out a picnic, sample the blueberries, and enjoy the incredible view.

65 Webster-Jackson Trail

General description:	A hard day's hike along the eastern wall of Crawford Notch, crossing the summits of Mounts Webster and Jackson.
General location:	Between North Conway and Twin Mountain at the northern end of Crawford Notch.
Length:	6.5 miles.
Difficulty:	Difficult, but the shorter round trip to Bugle Cliff is moderate, and the walk to and from Elephant Head is easy.
Elevation gain:	2,100 feet.
Special attractions:	Elephant Head, Bugle Cliff, and unobstructed views of the Presidential Peaks from Mount Jackson's barren summit.
Maps:	USGS Crawford Notch quad.
For more information:	Ammonoosuc Ranger Station, 660 Trudeau Road, Bethlehem, NH 03574, (603) 869-2626.

Key points:

0.1 Spur to Elephant Head.

0.6 Outlook at Bugle Cliff.

1.4 Fork in trail near Silver Cascade.

2.4 Junction with Webster Cliff Trail near pinnacle of Mount Webster.

3.7 Summit, Mount Jackson.

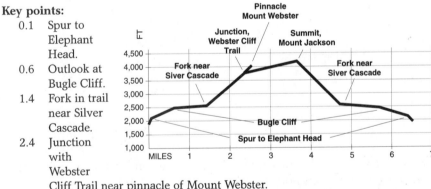

Finding the trailhead: From the traffic lights at the intersection of U.S. Highways 3 and 302 in Twin Mountain, turn east on US 302. Drive 8.6 miles, passing Crawford Depot and Saco Lake, to a hiker's parking lot on the right (west) side of the highway just before entering Crawford Notch. The trailhead is across the road.

The hike: Four distinct destinations allow walks on the Webster-Jackson Trail to be tailored to any hiker. The full circle to the top of Mount Jackson makes for an exacting day, but promises outstanding views of the southern

Webster-Jackson Trail

Presidential Peaks. The difficult ascent that ends on the pinnacle of Mount Webster eliminates an hour of hiking, but still fully examines the eastern wall of Crawford Notch. The moderate trip to Bugle Cliff ends with a compromise: the single best look into the notch, but no long-distance White Mountain view. As a final hiking option, the simple walk to Elephant Head offers a quick introduction to nearby Bretton Woods.

Before leaving your car, look down toward the notch and engage your imagination. With little effort you should recognize the easiest destination: a rounded, quartz-streaked granite brow that nudges the edge of the highway and resembles a pachyderm. Across the road from the parking area, look for a sign for Elephant Head and a less obvious marker for the Webster-Jackson Trail.

The route swings uphill through woods for only a few hundred yards before meeting the 0.2-mile spur that curls to Elephant Head. The Webster-Jackson Trail steadily climbs above Elephant Head Brook and soon turns sharply right parallel to Crawford Notch. Throughout the first half of the outgoing hike, the path waffles between simple strolls and sharp climbs of rock-strewn pitches. At the top of one such steep ascent, about six-tenths of a mile into the hike, a spur path announces your arrival at demanding Bugle Cliff. This scrambling detour drops over the top of a ledge to a rocky (hazardous) aerie with stunning views of surrounding peaks from the rim of Crawford Notch. Be cautious here with children or your not-so-coordinated friends.

Leaving Bugle Cliff, the next 0.5 mile leads to a trail junction in a pretty side-hill ravine, immersed in the churning sounds of nearby Silver Cascade. From the fork, the path straight ahead goes 1.0 mile directly to Mount Webster, while the route of your eventual return steers left, 1.1 miles to Mount Jackson. Continuing on the Webster branch, a short, extremely precipitous descent ends photogenically at a pool and falls, followed by an equally steep clamber up the opposite bank to begin the 0.9-mile climb of Mount Webster's northern flank. When at last you reach the T at the Webster Cliff Trail junction, you'll feel like you've reached the top, but a legitimate mountain pinnacle is still 0.1 mile to the right (south). This craggy observation point looks west to Mounts Field and Willey on the far side of Crawford Notch, and even allows a quick northern glance to Mount Washington, Mount Eisenhower, and related Presidential Peaks.

After retracing your steps back to the T, a boggy 1.3-mile stretch of the Appalachian Trail (Webster Cliff Trail) connects with Jackson's summit. In the worst spots, plank bridges or strategically placed boulders help keep boots out of the muck. Take heart from early Mount Washington views and a close-up look at Mount Jackson from a knoll about two-thirds of the way across. The final climb up the summit cone is short and exceedingly steep. From the nearly bald top, you can site along the Crawford Path as it rides the southern Presidential Peaks to Mount Washington's dominant summit, or scan the silhouette of the Montalban Ridge as it converges from the right. The structure in the foreground is the hut at Mizpah Spring (see Hike 60) conveniently located in a col at the base of rounded Mount Pierce (Clinton).

A few haphazard cairns guide hikers off the peak for the steep departure from Mount Jackson's upper cone. A continuous, mile-long, moderately difficult descent of this branch of the Webster-Jackson Trail crosses three streams, skirts Silver Cascade, and reconnects with its companion path as it returns to the fork in the pretty side-hill ravine, 1.4 miles from the trailhead.

PEMIGEWASSET WILDERNESS AND ZEALAND NOTCH

At the center of the White Mountain National Forest lie 45,000 acres of wilderness, a vast, mountain-rimmed region long avoided by travelers in favor of more hospitable routes through Franconia and Crawford Notch. Bounded on the south by the Kancamagus Highway, the Pemigewasset Wilderness is enclosed to the north by an immense semicircle of mountains less spectacular than the Presidential Peaks, but comprising the core of New Hampshire's alpine country. The Franconia, Garfield, and Zealand ridges, together with the Twin and Willey Mountain ranges, fashion an enormous horseshoe protecting a hiker's paradise of remote, forested valleys and the source of the East Branch of the Pemigewasset River.

Officially declared a wilderness in 1984, motorized or mechanical equipment is no longer permitted in the area, a restriction that in this case has ample historic cause. Within a span of seventy years beginning in the nineteenth century, steam engines and logging railroads devoured this beautiful land, giving rise to disturbing memories that echo in the name of the Desolation Trail. The aspect of these woods is certainly brighter today. The Pemigewasset Wilderness has become New Hampshire's most popular backpacking region, with miles of inviting trails fanning out through isolated valleys, a land once again resplendent in its regenerated hardwood cloak.

Zealand Notch is a special case, in several exciting ways. One of the state's lesser-known roadless notches, Zealand conveniently leads to a broad selection of extended hikes through the Pemigewasset's northeastern back door. Allow plenty of extra time if you plan to travel through Zealand Notch. The compelling attractions of Zealand Falls, Thoreau Falls, and stunning Whitewall Mountain are guaranteed to slow you down.

66 Ethan Pond Trail

General description:	A short family backpack to a shelter at Ethan Pond.
General location:	Off U.S. Highway 302, midway between Twin Mountain and Glen, near the south end of Crawford Notch.
Length:	4.8 miles round trip.
Difficulty:	Moderate.
Elevation gain:	1,400 feet.
Special attractions:	Mountain views, waterfalls, and a backcountry campsite at Ethan Pond on the edge of the Pemigewasset Wilderness.
Maps:	USGS Crawford Notch quad.
For more information:	Ammonoosuc Ranger Station, 660 Trudeau Road, Bethlehem, NH 03574, (603) 869-2626.

Ethan Pond Trail

Key points:

0.2 Start of detour to Ripley Falls.

1.3 Junction, Kedron Flume Trail.

1.6 Junction, Willey Range Trail.

2.4 Ethan Pond.

Finding the trailhead: From the junction of New Hampshire Route 16 and U.S. Highway 302 West in the town of Glen, follow US 302 west 17 miles to the southern end of Crawford Notch State Park. You'll pass other trailheads, but look for a left (west) turn onto a small paved road that is marked by signs for the Appalachian Trail and Ethan Pond. The side road climbs steeply for about one-third of a mile to a parking area at the trailhead. From the opposite direction, the turn off US 302 is about 1.1 miles south of the state-run snack bar at the Willey House site in Crawford Notch.

The hike: Sitting astride the Appalachian Trail, Ethan Pond is a convenient waypoint for long-distance trekkers, and a perfect destination for short family backpacks from nearby Crawford Notch. Although its shelter and tent platforms rest on a hillside set back from the immediate shore, the area's soothing beauty and rich menu of nearby attractions make Ethan Pond an ideal base camp for weekend explorations, or a pleasant day-hiking goal. Located on the northeastern fringe of the Pemigewasset Wilderness, Zealand Notch, Thoreau Falls, Shoal Pond, Mount Willey, and Ripley Falls all comfortably lie within striking distance on an active family hike.

Bouncing up an embankment from the trailhead, the path immediately crosses a railroad track at the end of a trestle bridge opposite the site of Willey House Station. The trail climbs southwest for 0.2 mile, directly challenging the slope, and then pauses on a small plateau where the Arethusa–Ripley Falls Trail diverges to the left. A 0.3-mile detour up the deep ravine of Avalanche Brook will please the entire family with the 100-foot plunge of impressive Ripley Falls.

The main trail continues its gradual advance angling west/southwest with glimpses of Mount Webster on the eastern wall of Crawford Notch. After about half a mile the grade eases significantly as the path swings right (northwest), working its way more gradually behind Mount Willey's protruding slopes. Just beyond the halfway point of the hike, the Kedron Flume Trail branches to the right, dropping precipitously into the notch. From here, the path to Ethan Pond climbs moderately for 0.3 mile to meet the Willey Range Trail, which rises to the summit of Mount Willey on a ragged 1.0-mile route that I consider too steep and difficult for general family use.

The Ethan Pond Trail turns left and rises another 0.25 mile before rolling over the top of the ridge, crossing a brook, and skimming an elevated corner of the Pemigewasset Wilderness on the back side of Crawford Notch. Within another mile, look for a trail marker pointing down a spur path to Ethan Pond, where a shelter and tent platforms perch on an embankment about 100 yards above the northeastern shore.

Campsites at Ethan Pond are scattered among evergreens that rise in graceful tiers from the water's edge and end dramatically beneath Mount Willey's southern cliffs. The mountain recedes into the west where sunsets over the peaceful pond silhouette Mounts Zealand, Guyot, and Bond at the northern edge of the official wilderness. If you can muster the gumption to walk beyond this spot, the incredible wonders of Zealand Notch lie only ninety minutes up the trail. While you're at it, why not take a swim at Thoreau Falls or check for moose at tiny Shoal Pond?

67 Gale River and Bondcliff Trails

General description:	An arduous two-day backpack to high mountain peaks in the heart of the Pemigewasset Wilderness.
General location:	Off U.S. Highway 3 about halfway between Franconia Notch and Twin Mountain.
Length:	19.3 miles round trip.
Difficulty:	Difficult.
Elevation gain:	3,300 feet from lowest to highest point, with additional gains and losses on intervening peaks.
Special attractions:	Spectacular vistas from major summits and a comfortable backcountry campsite overlooking a wilderness scene.
Maps:	USGS South Twin Mountain quad.
For more information:	Pemigewasset Ranger Station, RR#3, Box 15, Route 175, Plymouth, NH 03264, (603) 536-1315.

Key points:
- 1.7 Hiker's bridge over Gale River.
- 4.0 Junction, Garfield Ridge Trail.
- 4.6 Galehead Hut.
- 5.4 Summit, South Twin Mountain.
- 7.4 Junction, Twinway and Bondcliff Trail.
- 8.0 Spur to Guyot Campsite.
- 8.5 Summit, Mount Bond.
- 9.7 Summit, Bondcliff.

Gale River and Bondcliff Trails

To Five Corners, US 3

Gale River Road

FR 25

FR 92

P

Gale River Trail

Haystack Mountain

Flat Top Mountain

Gale River

North Twin

Garfield Ridge Trail

To Mount Lafayette

Mount Garfield

Mount Galehead

Galehead Hut

South Twin

Twinway Trail

To Zealand Notch

Mount Guyot

Guyot Campsite

West Bond

Mount Bond

Bondcliff Trail

Bondcliff

To Wilderness Trail

NORTH

0   0.5   1

MILE

Finding the trailhead: Drive north through Franconia Notch on Interstate 93 and take exit 35 onto U.S. Highway 3, north. In about 4.9 miles you'll come to Five Corners, where a highway sign points left for Trudeau Road or Bethlehem, and a hiker sign for the Gale River Trail points down a gravel road to the right. Turn right on the gravel Gale River Road (Forest Road 25), bear left at a fork in 0.7 mile, and turn right onto FR 92, 1.4 miles from the main highway. The parking lot and trailhead are 0.2 mile on the left, just beyond a crossing of the Gale River.

The hike: Imagine a stony trail that flirts with the edge of a precipice and soars to a mountain peak, a windswept summit of speckled boulders sheltering alpine flowers within their lee, and an isolated pinnacle encircled by successive ranges of mountains that recede into the mists. Imagine Bondcliff, my favorite White Mountain peak.

Hikers will climb other summits on this arduous hike: South Twin, Guyot, and Bond, with short detours available to West Bond and Galehead, too. All of these summits have absolutely stupendous views over seas of mountaintops, but none beckon with the same allure as oft-ignored Bondcliff. Some cautions are in order before beginning this formidable trip. The difficult 0.9-mile segment between Galehead Hut and the top of South Twin is very steep, but don't underestimate the cumulative effect of hardy mountain tramping while carrying an overnight pack. Topographic maps don't accurately convey a sense of the elevation gain and loss encountered on this hike. Some 300 to 600 feet of difficult climbing can be added to your hiking equation with each successive peak, remembering, naturally, that you need to turn around and repeat a reciprocal course. Also be aware that Mounts Guyot and Bondcliff are particularly remote and exposed, requiring extra vigilance for changes in the weather.

The first 3 miles of the hike are rather easy as they track the course of the Gale River, heading south to find its source. Except for a quick glimpse in the first 0.1 mile, hikers won't see the river on half of this early route. After 1.7 miles the trail crosses to the east bank of the stream on a distinctive hiker's bridge, passes rest stops at water's edge, and re-crosses to the west on large boulders after less than another mile. The climbing doesn't begin in earnest until the trail comes to a gravel knoll that rises above the river and looks up at North Twin Mountain at the head of the watershed.

The final segment of the Gale River Trail stiffens greatly in the last 0.3 mile before topping Garfield Ridge. Consider this stretch a useful test. If you're pushing your limits as you climb these moderate slopes, you'll want to reexamine any plans to proceed beyond Galehead Hut.

At the crest of the ridge, turn left (east) on the Garfield Ridge Trail (blazed as part of the Appalachian Trail) for a 0.6-mile link that offers sketchy views down the Gale River Valley and ends within sight of the hut. A comfortable porch with glorious views of South Twin, Galehead, and pointy Mount Garfield makes a natural spot to rest and brace for the worst this route can offer. After leaving the hut, turn onto the Twinway Trail in the direction of South Twin Mountain. The trail dips into a col and offers views of this angular peak. It's a very steep climb to South Twin's summit, and for all but the strongest hikers the 0.9 mile will feel like a whole lot more.

The summit of South Twin feels like the top of the world, the highest point on this journey, where the view includes more mountains than anyone would care to name. Of immediate interest for the remainder of the hike are the nearby summits to the south, grassy Mount Guyot sporting a scar on its flank, with Bond and West Bond obscuring Bondcliff, their neighbor to the south.

The Twinway Trail continues rapidly down a less demanding side of South Twin, commencing a pleasant 2.0-mile walk along an undulating wooded ridge that connects with Guyot Mountain. Climbing muscles catch a break in this mostly flat stretch of trail. Watch for spruce grouse, which prefer to scamper away on the ground rather than use their wings to fly.

With a welcome surprise, the path breaks out of the woods just shy of the junction with the Bondcliff Trail and the open summit of Mount Guyot. The majority of hikers seem to come and go on the Twinway Trail veering over the ridge to the left (east) and descending to the Zealand Hut at the north end of Zealand Notch (see Hike 68). But our hike is more adventurous than that and continues straight on the Bondcliff Trail to enter a delightful alpine zone on Guyot's scoured heights. After providing yet another chance to survey incredible views, the trail quickly drops off Mount Guyot and submerges again into evergreens where another col holds the spur trail to Guyot Campsite. It's almost 2 miles from here to Bondcliff summit, and unless

Bondcliff, looking closer than a mile away.

you're traveling cross-country to the Wilderness Trail (see Hike 70) you're sure to return to this point. If plans, time, and weather permit, it makes sense to set up camp or at least jettison overnight gear before pushing on to the climax of the hike. At the bottom of the spur, six tent platforms, a wonderfully spacious log shelter, and fresh spring water compose a perfect mountain enclave that faces the morning sun.

Continuing south on the Bondcliff Trail, the route quickly passes the 0.5-mile spur to the West Bond summit and begins the ascent of Mount Bond and its intervening knoll. Classic views from Mount Bond's peak swirl out to the horizons of Franconia Ridge, Garfield Ridge, Zealand Notch, Mount Carrigain, Mount Hancock, and all the lesser summits above the Pemigewasset's valleys. Four hundred feet below, the startling countenance of Bondcliff and its winding ribbon of trail look close enough to touch, yet remain more than a rugged mile away. Surrounded by mountains, yet completely exposed, I hope you'll value your time on that peak in the same special way that I do.

68   Mount Hale, Zealand Loop

General description:	A wonderfully varied day hike to a mountaintop, waterfall, and wetlands on the fringe of the Pemigewasset Wilderness.
General location:	South of U.S. Highway 302, between Twin Mountain and Bretton Woods.
Length:	8.7 miles.
Difficulty:	Moderate.
Elevation gain:	2,400 feet.
Special attractions:	Zealand Falls, mountain views, blueberry ledges, ponds, marshes, beaver lodges, and a campground near the trailhead.
Maps:	USGS South Twin Mountain and Crawford Notch quads.
For more information:	Ammonoosuc Ranger Station, 660 Trudeau Road, Bethlehem, NH 03574, (603) 869-2626.

Key points:
- 0.0   Hale Brook Trailhead.
- 0.6   Convergence with Hale Brook.
- 2.2   Summit, Mount Hale.
- 5.0   Zealand Hut near Zealand Falls.
- 7.8   Zealand Trailhead.
- 8.7   Return to Hale Brook Trailhead.

Finding the trailhead: From the traffic lights at the intersection of U.S. Highways 3 and 302 in Twin Mountain, travel east on US 302 for 2.1 miles

Mount Hale, Zealand Loop

South Sugarloaf

To US 302

Hale Brook

Hale Brook Trail

Zealand Road

P

P

Mount Hale

Lend-A-Hand Trail

Zealand Trail

Zealand River

Zealand Pond

Twinway

Hut

Zealand Falls

Whitewall Brook

Ethan Pond Trail

ZEALAND NOTCH

Whitewall Mountain

NORTH

0   0.5   1

MILE

to the entrance to Zealand Campground. Turn right (south) onto Zealand Road, which passes two camping areas before its paved portion ends. Measured from the highway, the Hale Brook Trailhead is 2.4 miles on the right, and the Zealand Trailhead is 3.4 miles, at the end of Zealand Road.

The hike: The Zealand Road provides more than easy access to the northern Pemigewasset Wilderness (see Hike 70). This 3.4-mile link between US 302 and the threshold of Zealand Notch also spawns a circle of paths imbued with such variety that pre-hike planning is clearly in order to make the most of this opportunity. Through-hikers to the Wilderness Trail and patrons of the Zealand Falls Hut generally select an easy walk on the Zealand Trail that tracks the Zealand River from the end of the access road past ponds, marshes, and beaver lodges on a parklike path to the hut. Peak climbers usually opt to get right to the heart of the matter by starting from the Hale Brook Trailhead to ascend directly to the summit of Mount Hale.

Adventurers with less focused plans could choose to begin from either trailhead to rendezvous with the Lend-A-Hand Trail for waterfalls, moose, and walks on blueberry ledges. Still, day hikers may find that one starting point turns out to be clearly better. For a loop that keeps views in front of you as you descend the mountain, offers swimming after your climb, and ends with a downhill glide on the Zealand Road, Hale Brook is the place to begin.

In the first several hundred yards, the Hale Brook Trail spans a small stream and crosses a Nordic ski path, commencing a moderate ascent under lofty maple, beech, and birch. The pitch increases after 0.6 mile as the route slowly converges with Hale Brook's rocky ravine, crossing and later recrossing it about halfway to the peak. The bulge to the left is an angular shoulder, not the true summit of Mount Hale, which remains unseen as the trail diagonals up a sharp slope. Soon a series of switchbacks helps maintain a comfortable pace until the grade naturally eases, and the trail meanders to the top.

Mount Hale's summit may seem odd, a clear circle 30 yards in diameter, edged by tiny evergreens and centered with a giant cairn. As if hesitant to intrude, North Twin, South Twin, Guyot, the Bonds, southerly Mount Hancock, and the summits of Crawford Notch barely poke above the trees.

The Hale Brook Trail ends on the summit, where the Lend-A-Hand Trail takes over to gradually descend a southern ridge. Paradoxically, this extended, temperate path features less reliable footing and segments of steeper pitches than does Hale Brook's rapid ascent. After passing through a flat, emerald

225

Entering the Pemigewasset Wilderness on the Lincoln Woods Trail.

forest of moss, ferns, and evergreens just below the peak, the Lend-A-Hand Trail rock-hops down to airy, open ledges filled with blueberries and pleasing vistas of Whitewall Mountain on the far end of Zealand Notch. In its lower reaches, the path encounters moose habitat and yards of wooden planks that cross wetland muck, beginning near several brook crossings 0.3 mile west of the hut.

The Lend-A-Hand Trail terminates at the Twinway junction near a sluicing stream that previews Zealand Falls. Turn left (east) on the Twinway, which leads 0.1 mile directly to the porch of Zealand Hut. On the opposite side of the trail, about 75 yards below the hut, a side path slips into the woods to refreshing Zealand Falls. Don't expect a gushing torrent. This pleasant cascade allows sunny lunches on comfortable rocks, dangling feet in a slippery stream, and cool dips in tiny pools.

Beyond the front door of the hut, the Twinway drops 0.2 mile down a short, moderately steep slope to intersect with Zealand Trail and Ethan Pond Trail near the south end of Zealand Pond. Bear in mind that this junction is about halfway between Zealand Road and Thoreau Falls. If time permits, it's a great chance to turn right (south) on the Ethan Pond Trail for a scenic traverse of Zealand Notch. If not, a left (north) guides you along the peaceful Zealand Trail through a marvelous assortment of wetlands before it exits at Zealand Road, 1 easy mile uphill from the starting point of the hike.

69 Franconia Brook and Lincoln Brook Trails

General description: A multiple-day hike circling Owl's Head Mountain in the western end of the Pemigewasset Wilderness.

General location: 5 miles east of Lincoln/North Woodstock off the Kancamagus Highway.

Length: 20.0 miles.

Difficulty: Moderate in a 3-mile section; otherwise long but rather easy.

Elevation gain: 2,000 feet.

Special attractions: Wildlife, wetlands, wilderness camping, remote 13 Falls, and views of Franconia Ridge above the Lincoln Brook Valley.

Maps: USGS Mount Osceola and South Twin Mountain quads.

For more information: Pemigewasset Ranger Station, RR#3, Box 15, Route 175, Plymouth, NH 03264, (603) 536-1315.

Key points:
- 0.1   Suspension bridge over East Branch.
- 2.9   Franconia Brook Campsite.
- 8.5   13 Falls.
- 9.3   Top of divide.
- 11.9   Spur to Owl's Head.
- 15.4   South junction, Lincoln Brook and Franconia Brook Trails.

Finding the trailhead: From exit 32 of Interstate 93, follow New Hampshire Route 112 (Kancamagus Highway) east for 5 miles. The Lincoln Woods parking area is on the left (north) just beyond the highway bridge across the East Branch of the Pemigewasset River. The trailhead is at the back of the parking lot, adjacent to the front steps of a USDA Forest Service information center.

The hike: The size of the 160-car Lincoln Woods parking area is a clue to the immense popularity of this easily accessible trailhead. Attracted for decades by the "wilderness" label, long-distance hikers flock to the Lincoln Woods and Wilderness core trails that serve as pedestrian expressways into the backcountry. Such traffic should not necessarily keep you away. Long, easy trails quickly disperse visitors into 45,000 acres of marvelous backpacking territory and along a variety of routes that radiate into the mountainous rim of the wilderness. The popularity is well deserved. Just don't expect to enjoy it alone.

The Lincoln Woods Trail (formerly a portion of the Wilderness Trail) leaves the information center via a suspension bridge that spans the East Branch of the Pemigewasset River. On the far side, turn right for the 3-mile walk to the Franconia Brook Campsites. Embedded railroad ties are the only obstacles on this long, flat access route as it bears north along the river and passes an oxbow with a beautiful view.

Franconia Brook and Lincoln Brook Trails

In the last 0.1 mile before crossing the bridge over Franconia Brook, look for a ranger tent and information sign explaining the layout of the Franconia Brook Campsites. Sixteen tent platforms, scattered in the woods to the left, provide a handy staging area for hikes into a wilderness that officially begins just on the opposite bank of the stream.

On the far side of the bridge, the Franconia Brook Trail immediately departs up a short embankment on the left and continues to track northerly on another old railroad grade. No longer an expressway, the Franconia Brook Trail remains a major secondary route that rushes 5 miles along the east side of Franconia Brook and Owl's Head Mountain on its way to the upper junction with the Lincoln Brook Trail near the campsite at 13 Falls. This easy walking route makes several routine brook crossings, veers right around a beaver bog, and obtains a nice view of Mount Flume near the southern end of Franconia Ridge. Passing the return leg of the Lincoln Brook Trail in a little less than 2 miles, the path continues beside ponds, marshes, and dense woods, where fresh moose prints speckle wetland mud beneath the lower slopes of Bondcliff Mountain.

As the Franconia Brook Trail gradually bends left around the northern flank of Owl's Head, a sharp drop into Twin Brook's steep ravine signals imminent arrival at 13 Falls. A beautiful series of falls on Franconia Brook makes a stay in this area more than just a logical stopping point on the northern end of this hike. A short distance up a spur path to the right, the established campsite features six tent platforms, communal fire pit, and centralized ropes for food storage, a necessary precaution in black bear country.

The Lincoln Brook Trail traces the highlights of 13 Falls as it angles left from the trail junction and crosses a stream where plummeting water spreads over a bedrock ledge. As the trail works uphill between two forks of the brook, the series of falls on the left fascinates with their variety: a vigorous flow cascading into a pool circled by a dark, wooded glade; a granite spigot funneling meekly into a basin of polished stone; and a sidelong jet swirling into a cauldron framed with autumn gold. All too quickly the trail leaves this medley of falls and begins the rugged, 3-mile stretch that earns this hike its moderate rating.

Now on the Pemigewasset version of a back-road byway, the route climbs about 700 feet in the next 0.75 mile, ascends the low divide that separates the drainages of Franconia and Lincoln Brooks, and discovers views of Mount Garfield to the north and Franconia Ridge to the west. The trail is wet in spots, but a new, well-marked bypass avoids ankle-deep mud that was once the hiker's lot.

The return trip commences with an unmistakable descent south along Lincoln Brook plunging through an angular valley carved between Owl's Head and Franconia Ridge. At the level of the brook, a large stone cairn in a small clearing at about the midpoint of the Lincoln Brook Trail marks a detour to the top of Owl's Head Mountain.

The detour to Owl's Head is a difficult, steep ascent over the loose footing and slippery rocks of a very precarious slide and is not recommended for the average hiker. Almost everyone who does make this two-hour, up-and-back climb parks their pack near the trail junction, giving the local red squirrels plenty of time to chew all the way through to their lunch. Avoid problem squirrels and steep terrain by carrying your pack up the Owl's Head path as far as comfort allows. You don't need to go far to obtain beautiful views of Mounts Lincoln and Lafayette on Franconia Ridge and a perfect perspective on the Lincoln Brook Valley spilling down the divide between you and 13 Falls.

The Owl's Head cairn also signals the resumption of easy hiking as the last 3.5 miles of the Lincoln Brook Trail rejoins a gentle logging grade along the western bank of Lincoln Brook. The peaceful walk slowly hooks left beside the stream, bearing east and northeast before re-crossing Lincoln Brook about 0.5 mile before spanning Franconia Brook, and 1 mile before ending at the southern junction with the Franconia Brook Trail. Be leery of these stream crossings at times of high water, and bear right at the final trail junction for the long, easy amble back to the trailhead.

70 Pemigewasset Traverse

General description:	A multiple-day hike from Lincoln Woods to Zealand Notch through the heart of the Pemigewasset Wilderness. Best accomplished as a one-way trip leaving cars at either end.
General location:	5 miles east of Lincoln/North Woodstock off the Kancamagus Highway.
Length:	18.0 miles one way.
Difficulty:	Moderate.
Elevation gain:	1,000 feet.
Special attractions:	Shoal Pond, Thoreau Falls, superb wilderness camping, and dazzling Zealand Notch.
Maps:	USGS South Twin Mountain, Crawford Notch, Mount Carrigain, and Mount Osceola quads; also maps from the USDA Forest Service.
For more information:	Pemigewasset Ranger Station, RR#3, Box 15, Route 175, Plymouth, NH 03264, (603) 536-1315.

Key points:

0.1	Suspension bridge over East Branch.
2.9	Franconia Brook Campsite.
5.4	180-foot swinging bridge.
8.9	Stillwater Junction.
12.1	Shoal Pond.
12.8	Junction, Ethan Pond Trail.

Pemigewasset Traverse

13.3   Junction, Thoreau Falls Trail.
15.5   Zealand Pond.
18.0   Zealand Road.

Finding the trailhead: See Hike 69 for access to the Lincoln Woods Trail on the southern end of the Pemigewasset Traverse. The northerly terminus is the same as the Mount Hale, Zealand Loop, described in Hike 68.

The hike: A number of trails bisect the vast Pemigewasset Wilderness by running from the Kancamagus Highway to U.S. Highways 3 and 302 on the far side of towering summits to the north. In fact, there are at least three obvious routes that penetrate the heart of the state's original wilderness and gracefully exit through delightful Zealand Notch. Of these three, Bondcliff Trail attains the most glorious views outside the Presidential Peaks (see Hike 67) but is by far the most strenuous hike, reserved for backpackers who are willing to tackle an additional 2,500 feet of difficult elevation gain. Thoreau Falls Trail provides less variety and is unusually hard to follow in a rough-and-tumble stretch south of the vigorous falls. I favor instead the Shoal Pond Trail, which maintains a basically level walk, yet offers a wonderful change of pace on a backwoods route with the untrammeled aura of a much less traveled path.

The first 3-mile segment of the Pemigewasset Traverse is the same as the start of Hike 69. The easy access of the Lincoln Woods Trail runs north on a railroad grade beside the East Branch of the Pemigewasset River to a wilderness boundary near the Franconia Brook Campsites. Rather than diverging left on the Franconia Brook Trail, however, the traverse hike continues straight ahead, bearing east with the river for the full length of the Wilderness Trail to Stillwater Junction. It's an intriguing 6-mile walk.

Muted sounds of the unseen river accompany the first 0.75 mile of the green-canopied Wilderness Trail as it follows the course of a narrow spur of an old logging railroad. A bend in the East Branch approaches briefly, rushing by 40 feet below the level of the track that crosses Cedar Brook and passes the junction with the Bondcliff Trail another mile down the line. A bit beyond Camp 16, site of an old logging encampment where tenting is no longer permitted, a footbridge spans Black Brook next to the massive wooden joinery of an antique railroad trestle, an engaging slice of history that should be inspected only from below.

Near its midpoint, the Wilderness Trail literally swings to the south side of the river on a 180-foot suspension bridge that deposits you at the junction with the Cedar Brook Trail. Turning left, still parallel to the stream, the Wilderness Trail continues its eastern journey as a broad, fir-lined path that drifts close to the river and meets the Thoreau Falls Trail at an intersection that seems to join two parallel paths. Take the high road (right) for the final 2.6 miles to Stillwater Junction where the Wilderness Trail ends, and Carrigain, Norcross, and Shoal Pond Brooks join to create the East Branch of the Pemigewasset River.

Desolation Shelter and tent sites are located 0.6 mile from Stillwater Junction down an easy detour on the Carrigain Notch Trail. Desolation is a logical stopover if you plan to be out more than one night, but unruly bears

Secluded Shoal Pond in the Pemigewasset Wilderness.

have caused problems in the past. Keep your eyes open for warnings that may be posted at various trailheads, or remember to check with the USDA Forest Service for current information before you set out.

Heading north from Stillwater Junction, don't judge the Shoal Pond Trail by its first easy mile up yet another railroad grade. After "The Pool" (a great swimming hole with natural waterslide and campsite), the trail slowly transforms into a wet, woodsy, grassy path through forest, marsh, and bog and makes four stream crossings before finding its way to Shoal Pond. Wet feet are the price you pay for a great backcountry feel and a chance to camp near a berry-lined lake with wonderfully stark mountain views.

Shoal Pond is 0.7 mile south of the junction with the Ethan Pond Trail, a link in the Appalachian Trail. Potential campsites are plentiful in this area, far removed from the Forest Protection Areas that envelop earlier portions of the hike. A 2-mile detour to the right (east) onto the Ethan Pond Trail leads to a shelter and tent sites at picturesque Ethan Pond (see Hike 66). A left turn (west) continues the traverse that passes several riverfront campsites, spans the North Fork on a wooden bridge, and leads 0.5 mile to the northern junction with the Thoreau Falls Trail. Be sure not to miss the nearby view from the top of Thoreau Falls, where a beautiful fan of water cascades more than 100 feet from a high ledge with distant mountain views.

Any good entertainment saves the best for last, and the Pemigewasset Traverse is no exception. An easy fifteen minutes beyond the Thoreau Falls junction, gleaming human-sized boulders tumble in a jagged slide beneath the heights of Whitewall Mountain in Zealand Notch. The carefully crafted Ethan Pond Trail advances through the field of rock clinging to the mountain's slope. A dearth of vegetation opens vistas north past Zeacliff's western wall to Zealand Hut at the far end of the notch, and south to lofty peaks rising from the wilderness interior. These are memorable images to carry home, as you withdraw from the notch on the Zealand Trail 2.5 miles from the end of Zealand Road.

KANCAMAGUS HIGHWAY

The Kancamagus Highway breaks New Hampshire's tradition of north–south orientation with a 34.5-mile east–west link between Interstate 93 and New Hampshire Route 16 through the heart of the scenic White Mountains. From the Pemigewasset River in Lincoln, this USDA Forest Service Scenic Byway rises to its height near Mount Kancamagus and descends beside the Swift River on a breathtakingly beautiful drive that joins the Saco River just south of Conway village.

In a region better suited to old farm roads and logging trails, the Kancamagus Highway is a relative newcomer that became the present thoroughfare by expanding upon local routes in 1959. This twisting mountain road is still no place for drivers in a hurry. Steep grades, hairpin turns, vacation traffic, scenic outlooks, and fabulous mountain terrain set a pace better geared to laid-back summer fun. Campgrounds, picnic areas, historic sites, wandering moose, and Swift River swimming holes round out the list of family attractions on this perennially popular route.

For those who wander on foot, the Kancamagus Highway is equally attractive. Whether backpacker, experienced trekker, or extended family group, leg-stretching walks to Sabbaday Falls, overnight visits to Sawyer Pond, classic climbs of Mount Chocorua, and heady ascents of the Hancock peaks always assure that there's plenty of hiking to do.

71 Mount Chocorua, Champney Brook Trail

General description: A two-hour family outing to a scenic falls, or an optional day hike to the summit of Mount Chocorua.

General location: 10 miles west of Conway on the Kancamagus Highway.

Length: 3.0 miles to the falls and back; 7.25 miles round trip to the summit.

Difficulty: Easy to the falls; moderate to the summit.

Elevation gain: 700 feet to the falls; 2,200 feet to the summit.

Special attractions: Mountain views atop a glistening falls, and panoramic vistas from a legendary summit.

Maps: USGS Mount Chocorua quad.

For more information: Saco Ranger Station, 33 Kancamagus Highway, Conway, NH 03818, (603) 447-2166.

Key points:
0.25 Convergence with Champney Brook.
1.5 Champney Falls.
3.0 Junction, Piper Trail.
3.6 Summit, Mount Chocorua.

Mount Chocorua, Champney Brook Trail

Finding the trailhead: The large parking area for the Champney Falls Trailhead is situated on the southern side of the Kancamagus Highway. From the west, it's 24.3 miles east of exit 32 on Interstate 93. From the east, it's 10.4 miles west of the junction of New Hampshire Routes 16 and 112 (Kancamagus Highway).

The hike: Originating from the magnificent Kancamagus Highway, the Champney Brook Trail ascends the gradual, northern facet of Mount Chocorua's jutting peak. From this bearing, it may be difficult to recognize Chocorua as the same mountain that asserts itself so boldly when seen from Route 16. Compared to the southern approach on the Liberty Trail (Hike 32), the Champney Brook route is more scenic in its lower reaches, less difficult near the summit, but far more heavily traveled.

There are ample reasons for this trail's popularity. As an appealing family hike, the route explores delicate cascades and reveals a wonderful alpine vista from boulders at the head of Champney Falls. For more energetic hikers, the optional second half of the journey leads to an alluring peak with extensive mountain views. One caution is in order if the falls are your principal destination. Dry spells or midsummer conditions can reduce the water flow to levels that may cause disappointment. Check the volume of the stream early in the hike and plan your trip accordingly.

From the parking area, the trail promptly crosses a minor stream (maybe just a dry bed) on a log bridge and proceeds for about a quarter of a mile before converging with Champney Brook. Over the next mile, the courses of both trail and stream run roughly parallel, except for an interlude when the path rises on a duff-coated embankment well above the flow. After returning to the stream, the gravel path continues a gradual, rolling ascent through hardwoods that surround this walk with a blaze of colors in the fall.

The spur trail to Pitcher and Champney Falls departs to the left at a junction where the primary trail enters a Forest Protection Area. The 0.4-mile detour loop begins by descending quickly, passing above a small pool, and climbing to a lookout on immense boulders shading the mountain stream. A succession of stone stairs leads past Champney Falls, more than 200 feet of fragile cascades spilling through a random progression of boulders and stratified ledge. When water levels permit, most hikers enjoy scurrying about at the head of the falls on broad outcroppings of rock, cantilevered platforms with memorable views of northern mountains framed by the valley.

The falls loop rejoins the main trail 2.1 miles from the summit of Mount Chocorua and 1.5 miles from the highway. Beyond this junction, the trail is more rocky and less sedate but maintains a moderate pace. A clear view to the north precedes the first of seven switchbacks that climb to the intersection with the Middle Sister Trail on a flat ridge between the peaks of Chocorua and Middle Sister Mountains. Bear right for 0.1 mile until the Champney Brook Trail terminates at its junction with the Piper Trail only 0.6 mile from the summit. The final leg of the hike is a delightful jaunt that follows the yellow blazes of the Piper Trail on a weaving course over and around craggy ledges enveloped in mountain views.

The outlook from the sculptured top of Mount Chocorua is legendary, but its enjoyment is rarely a solo activity. On warm summer days you're likely to find clusters of hikers lounging on the smooth summit rock, basking in the sun or lunching in the lee of a friendly crag. If you happen to savor this experience during sultry midsummer weather, keep in mind that the Swift River flows near the trailhead, another popular destination that waits to cool you on your return.

72 Hancock Notch Trail, Hancock Loop

General description: A comfortable day trip to the connected summits of Mount Hancock's north and south peaks. Good campsites for an overnight stay.

General location: 10 miles east of Lincoln/North Woodstock on the Kancamagus Highway.

Length: 9.8 miles round trip.

Difficulty: Moderate.

Elevation gain: 2,300 feet.

Special attractions: Sweeping views of Signal Ridge and the Sawyer River Valley, easy walking to pleasant campsites, and a stream that disappears.

Maps: USGS Mount Osceola and Mount Carrigain quads.

For more information: Saco Ranger Station, 33 Kancamagus Highway, Conway, NH 03818, (603) 447-2166.

Key points:

0.5   Brook crossing.
1.7   Junction, Cedar Brook Trail.
3.6   Fork, Hancock Loop Trail.
4.1   Summit, South Peak.
5.4   Summit, North Peak.
6.2   Return to fork.
8.1   Return to junction, Cedar Brook Trail.

Finding the trailhead: The Hancock Overlook parking area is on New Hampshire Route 112 (Kancamagus Highway) about 10.5 miles east of Interstate 93, exit 32. It's on the south side of the road, immediately east of the hairpin right turn where traffic is supposed to slow to 20 miles per hour, and a sign warns of parking in 600 feet. A path leaves the far end of the parking lot and returns to the hairpin turn for what is clearly the most hazardous portion of the hike. The trailhead is across the highway at the very apex of the curve.

The hike: A number of trails run south from the Kancamagus Highway to access peaks more readily reached from the Lakes Region or Waterville Valley. The Hancock Notch hike is one of the energetic few that runs north from the road to a collection of unique New Hampshire views. From the summit of

Hancock Notch Trail, Hancock Loop

NORTH

0   0.5   1

MILE

North Peak

Mount Hancock

Hancock Loop Trail

South Peak

Cedar Brook Trail

Hancock Notch Trail

Hancock Notch Trail

Mount Huntington

North Fork

Hancock Notch Trail

To Lincoln, N. Woodstock

P

Kancamagus Highway

To Conway

112

Mount Hancock's North Peak, even newcomers to the region will easily identify the stark profile of Mount Carrigain atop bumptious Signal Ridge and enjoy the bird's-eye view of the encompassing forests of the Sawyer River Valley that spread southeast from the adjacent Pemigewasset Wilderness.

The Hancock Notch Trail descends off the roadway, jumps a small sluice box, and rambles along a former railroad bed graded into the side of a hill. The course slants easily over hardwood-covered slopes, interrupted only by the crossing of a pretty brook at about the half-mile mark. The river genealogy of a substantial portion of the White Mountains is soon revealed when the trail meets the North Fork of the Hancock Branch of the East Branch of the Pemigewasset River. The trail parallels the waterway through flat groves of evergreens, while possible campsites appear across the pleasant stream.

The left turn onto the Cedar Brook Trail may be a little confusing, since a sign only notes the 1.7-mile distance back to the original trailhead. You won't go astray if you keep in mind that from this point on, Cedar Brook is the wider, more heavily traveled route. Turn north across a brook that almost flows through the trail junction. The ensuing path rises easily up a small slope and rapidly rejoins the North Fork at a crossing where the river delicately tumbles over ledges. If water levels are not too high, this crossing signals entry into an amusing 0.5-mile segment of low-lying trail that abounds with stream crossings and campsites. The fifth and last crossing is passed where the path spills into a boulder-strewn course 150 yards south of the junction with the Hancock Loop Trail.

Bearing right at this junction, the Hancock Loop Trail crosses the stream yet again and begins a moderate 1-mile climb to reach the loop that connects Mount Hancock's summits. At the tangent where the prongs of the loop depart, the North Peak peers down through the trees, and hikers face a dilemma of how to begin this 2.6-mile alpine circuit. Between a steep 0.8-mile struggle to the North Peak or a similar 0.5-mile climb up the south, the shorter route sounds easier, and leaves the best views to last.

The trail to South Peak forges moderately ahead and soon veers right, directly up the mountain, a test of stamina. I found it helpful to stop, catch my breath, and frequently gauge my progress against the expanding view of the opposing peak. Watch your footing on loose stones and gravel near the top of this wearying ascent.

There are no views from the wooded South Peak, but a spur trail passes 30 yards directly across the top to find impressive outlooks over the Sawyer River Valley and distinctive Mount Chocorua. This tiny niche is a great place to pause before returning to South Peak and discovering a view of Mount Carrigain, dead ahead as the loop trail departs the summit.

The forgiving 1.3-mile hike along the ridge connecting the Hancock summits features the warm smell of evergreens percolating in the heat of the sun, the cheer of Canada jays, and good views of massive Arrow Slide plunging down the flank of North Peak. A large portion of the energy saved by climbing South Peak first is expended on this longer but less stressful effort to top out for a second time. Once atop North Peak, follow a sign along a short path to boulders with outstanding 180-degree views. From here views sweep from the tower on Mount Carrigain's summit, down the fractious line of Signal

Ridge, beyond South Peak and the Sawyer River Valley to Mount Chocorua, Mount Tripyramid, and the lesser-known mountains of Waterville Valley.

After you've had your fill of lunch and marvelous views, the trip down North Peak begins slowly, gains momentum, and confirms the wisdom of starting at the southern end. The upper third of the descent negotiates long stretches of loose shale on an unstable gravel base. The middle third is equivalent to the steepest portions of the south side trail. And the bottom third moderates only slightly. Eventually, this travail ends near one of the White Mountains' more puzzling sights. At a crossing just before a sharp ascent near the starting point of the loop, a gurgling stream flows down the mountain on the left. To the right, the stream is gone. Something to ponder as you cross a damp patch of sand and begin your hike back to the trailhead.

73   Sawyer Pond Trail

General description:	A gentle backpack to a shelter or campsite on the wooded shore of Sawyer Pond.
General location:	About 12 miles west of Conway off the Kancamagus Highway.
Length:	A little under 9 miles round trip.
Difficulty:	Moderate because of distance, but the walking is easy.
Elevation gain:	About 700 feet from trailhead to pond; an additional 300 feet gained and lost on Birch Hill.
Special attractions:	Waterfront camping on a picturesque pond with fish, loons, and owls.
Maps:	USGS Bartlett, Mount Chocorua, and Mount Carrigain quads.
For more information:	Saco Ranger Station, 33 Kancamagus Highway, Conway, NH 03818, (603) 447-2166.

Key points:
  0.05   Wade Swift River.
  1.8   Height of Birch Hill.
  2.6   Head of Rob Brook.
  4.5   Shore of Sawyer Pond.

Finding the trailhead: The dirt access road for the Sawyer Pond Trail is on the north side of New Hampshire Route 112 (Kancamagus Highway), 13.3 miles west of its junction with Route 16 and about 1 mile west of Johnson Campground. The 0.2-mile access road ends at the trailhead parking area.

The hike: Many lakes in the White Mountains are in danger of being appreciated to death. While camping is now prohibited at beautiful Greeley Ponds (Hike 43) and spectacular Spaulding Lake (Hike 85), the increasingly rare opportunity to backpack to a camp at water's edge remains at idyllic Sawyer Pond.

Sawyer Pond Trail

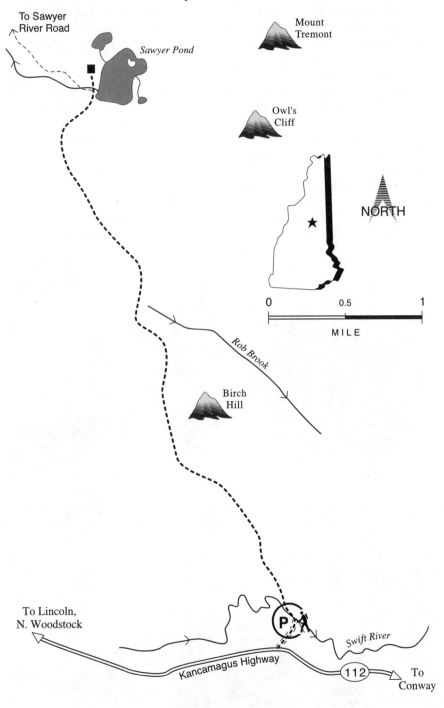

To Sawyer
River Road

Sawyer Pond

Mount
Tremont

Owl's
Cliff

NORTH

Rob Brook

Birch
Hill

0   0.5   1

MILE

To Lincoln,
N. Woodstock

P

Swift River

Kancamagus Highway

112

To
Conway

A three-sided log shelter for eight sits directly on the pond's western bank, near five tent platforms hiding on the pine-studded hillside above. From the comfort of a camp at any of these sites, the world is narrowly defined by Owl Cliff and Tremont Mountain on the opposite shore. Sawyer Pond is a peaceful, sometimes mystical spot, when the last rays of the setting sun gleam in Owl Cliff's rocky eye.

On this route, hikers are forced to make a basic decision only 50 yards beyond the trailhead. The Sawyer Pond Trail crosses the Swift River at a 25-foot wide ford. In summer, the icy water is usually only calf deep and can be readily waded. But high water makes this crossing dangerous and requires a change of plans. Check in advance with the Saco Ranger Station if you're considering an early-season hike.

The Sawyer Pond Trail is fairly level by White Mountain standards. The path ascends easily through sparse fir forest for the first 1.5 miles, where clearings provide glimpses of nearby mountains and browse for deer and moose. Gradually the woods become dense, and the trail climbs gently to cross a gravel road. After rolling up and down the western slopes of aptly

The eye of Owl Cliff, overlooking Sawyer Pond.

named Birch Hill, the route angles across an older logging road and descends to a wet area at the head of Rob Brook where the trail becomes noticeably rougher. Soon the path makes a long, easy ascent up and along an extended low ridge, turns left, and leisurely wanders down to the environs of Sawyer Pond.

The trail crosses the outlet brook near a junction with a path that provides alternate access from the Sawyer River Road located farther to the north and west (see Hike 59). Continue straight along the western shore, past inconspicuous tent platforms, to find the comfortable shelter that sits at the water's edge.

The beauty of Sawyer Pond won't be lost on day hikers, but those who linger for the evening will discover its special charms. At dusk, hungry fish roil the water. Swallows dive for insects above the nearby shore. The call of a loon echoes off Tremont Mountain, and a mournful hoot penetrates the forest as light fades in Owl Cliff's eye.

74 Sabbaday Falls

General description: A short family stroll to a glistening falls on beautiful Sabbaday Brook.
General location: 16 miles west of Conway on the Kancamagus Highway.
Length: 0.8 mile round trip.
Difficulty: Easy.
Elevation gain: 200 feet.
Special attractions: Close-up views of unique falls with swirling pools, water spouts, and an angular, rocky chasm.
Maps: USGS Mount Tripyramid quad.
For more information: Saco Ranger Station, 33 Kancamagus Highway, Conway, NH 03818, (603) 447-2166.

Key points:
0.1 Bank of Sabbaday Brook.
0.3 Base of falls.
0.5 Top of falls.

Finding the trailhead: From the junction of New Hampshire Routes 16 and 112 south of Conway, follow Route 112 (Kancamagus Highway) 15.5 miles west to the Sabbaday Falls parking area on the left (south) side of the road. Sabbaday Falls is near the midpoint of the Kancamagus Highway and can also be reached from Interstate 93 at Lincoln/North Woodstock over the more mountainous western half of the road.

The hike: Scads of tourists pass within yards of this trailhead without ever walking beyond sight of their cars to discover the spectacular gem of a falls that waits only minutes up the trail.

Sabbaday Falls

To
Lincoln,
N. Woodstock

Swift River

Kancamagus Highway   112

To
Conway

Sabbaday Brook Trail

Sabbaday
Falls

Sabbaday Brook

NORTH

0   0.25   0.5

MILE

A broad path enters the woods tracking south from the parking lot at a very gentle grade. Along the first 0.1 mile amidst gray birch and small maple trees, the sound of rushing water gradually builds until the path meets Sabbaday Brook. For almost a quarter of a mile, the trail parallels the channel of this transparent mountain stream as it noisily flows north over a scoured, rocky bottom.

At the first trail junction, the main path continues straight through the woods to the top of the falls and beyond. Turn left, down a small incline to the lowest pool and displays explaining the geologic creation of fascinating Sabbaday Falls. The walk ascends the side of the falls with the aid of 60 or 70 steps, natural wood railings, and a footbridge spanning a narrow gorge.

At the top of the falls, the entire stream of Sabbaday Brook sluices through a narrow funnel of rock before dropping 15 feet into the shallow depths of the first small upper pool. Glistening sheets of water flow smoothly over polished granite into bedrock basins with bulbous shapes and burnished textures reminiscent of modern sculpture. Swirling water spirals into a pothole smoothly worn into solid granite, then spouts up and out to drop 30 feet to the middle pool below. Suddenly, the character of the falls drastically changes. The stream cascades at an improbable angle into a stark, perpendicular gorge, sharply cleft into 50-foot walls of solid rock, before the show ends, quietly again, in a pool at the base of the falls.

These swirling waters can be as mesmerizing as the flames of an open fire. When the reverie ends in the refreshing mists, return from the top of the falls on a casual path that leads back to the easy main trail.

North Conway

Mention North Conway and most people think of traffic, outlet shopping, and a large collection of motels that holds a horde of travelers. But old traditions survive. A gateway to the White Mountain National Forest, this prominent north-country town remains a center of backcountry travel that provides equipment, wilderness rescue, and mountain guides to New Hampshire and the world.

Adventurous hiking isn't far from the sidewalks of North Conway. Rising above the town to the north, a family-friendly trail leads to a fire tower on the summit of Kearsarge North. To the west the rugged Moat Mountains show off their stunning cliffs to shoppers in outlet malls but hide a natural swimming hole at a falls called Diana's Baths. Drive a mere handful of miles from the center of downtown and you can hike to a mountaintop cabin with a view of Mount Washington or camp at a backcountry waterfront site just a short stroll from your car.

75 North and South Doublehead, The Old Path and Ski Trail

General description: A half-day loop to a double peak with an overnight cabin and mountain views.
General location: About 8 miles north of North Conway.
Length: 3.9 miles.
Difficulty: Moderate.
Elevation gain: 1,573 feet.
Special attractions: A mountaintop log cabin and White Mountain views.
Maps: USGS Jackson quad.
For more information: Saco Ranger District, 33 Kancamagus Highway, Conway, NH 03818, (603) 447-2166.

Key points:
0.6 Junction, Ski Trail and Old Path.
1.8 Cabin at North Doublehead summit.
2.1 Trail junction in col.
2.3 Summit, South Doublehead.
3.3 Return to junction, Old Path and Ski Trail.

North and South Doublehead, The Old Path and Ski Trail

Finding the trailhead: Driving north on New Hampshire Route 16 north of Glen and North Conway, turn right onto Route 16A at a highway directional sign for routes 16A and 16B in the Town of Jackson. Cross the Jackson covered bridge and turn right onto 16B 0.5 mile later in the center of Jackson Village. Bear right after crossing a second bridge 1.7 miles from the village and right again onto Dundee Road after another 0.2 miles. Trailhead parking for three or four cars is on the left 0.5 mile south on Dundee Road.

The hike: Three trails lead to these twin peaks that stand above Jackson Village. The most popular route combines two trails that meet on the northern summit where a cozy cabin commands a view of Mount Washington and the rugged Carter Range. Impromptu hikers will enjoy the climb and the White Mountain panorama, but you'll have to make plans in advance to use the mountaintop cabin. Contact the Saco Ranger Station, which distributes the key, collects the fee of $20 per day, and encourages reservations.

When you think of the Doublehead Ski Trail, don't think of sunny, open slopes in resorts like Waterville Valley. A throwback to another era, the Doublehead version of a ski trail is a 20-foot wide corridor coated with ferns and goldenrod that winds up the wooded slopes of North Doublehead Mountain. A sign for this old-fashioned trail is nailed to a tall stump next to the gravel woods road that leads from the parking lot. Follow this lane into the woods for nearly 100 yards before turning onto a forest path that veers off to the right and ambles toward the mountain.

After warming up on the lower slopes for nearly six-tenths of a mile, the Doublehead Ski Trail intersects the original footpath that leads to the north peak. Bear left at this signed junction 1.2 miles below the summit, and save the Old Path that diverges right for your later rapid return. The most gradual of the three routes that climb the Doublehead peaks, the Ski Trail slowly angles north beyond the Old Path junction, maintains a moderate pace, and begins an indirect, looping traverse of the mountain's western slopes that actually circles back to the south to reach the northern summit. The soft mound of South Doublehead appears among the treetops during this ascent, as the broad swath of the Ski Trail swerves through a lengthy series of wide twists and turns, finally drifts to the right, and pops onto North Doublehead's summit near the door of a log cabin.

Set amidst low evergreens directly on the mountain peak, North Doublehead's comfortable cabin offers a common room, bunk space for eight, and a wood-burning stove that warms hikers who have made reservations. If you haven't brought a key, you'll have to be content to sit on a flat boulder just outside the cabin wall. Settled onto this natural perch, you can still view the White Mountain peaks on the crest of Montalban Ridge, the soaring flanks of Mount Washington folded into deep ravines, and a special perspective on Carter Notch, the obvious, low divide huddled between the steep wall of Wildcat Mountain and the sweep of Carter Dome.

Don't leave North Doublehead Mountain without checking the eastern view. Just beyond the spruce trees at the opposite end of the cabin, a small outcrop overlooks Mountain Pond (Hike 77) and the broad selection of lakes and mountains that garnish western Maine.

A room with a view on North Doublehead's peak.

Near the front door of the cabin, signs point to South Doublehead and the two other trails that explore the rest of the mountain. To resume your loop hike, walk rapidly downhill on the duff-covered Old Path and pass a detour on the right that leads to a western view. After falling nearly three-tenths of a mile below the northern summit, the Old Path arrives at an odd junction on the floor of the Doublehead col where the New Path continues straight ahead and the Old Path turns right. You'll return to this point later, turning west on the Old Path and descending 0.6 mile to reconnect with the Ski Trail near the bottom of the slope. For now, though, continue straight on the New Path for an easy stroll that follows a brushy ridge and climbs less than a quarter of a mile to South Doublehead's peak.

Approaching the southern summit, a wide outcrop on the right offers the best view of the day, a stunning panorama from Kearsarge North to distant Carter Dome. Just 0.1 mile beyond this ledgy vista, the New Path turns right, descending to Dundee Road and ending at a second trailhead about half a mile from your car. To complete your Doublehead climb, though, ignore this descent and turn left instead onto a 0.2-mile extension of trail that leads to South Doublehead's peak.

From the second clearing on the mountaintop marked with a small cairn, you can walk to the summit's southernmost outcrop and discover different views. That's Kezar Lake in the middle distance introducing western Maine, while closer at hand that's Kearsarge North (Hike 76) with its stubby fire tower rising as a natural barrier between you and North Conway.

Hiking an easy ridgeline is better than hiking a road. To avoid the New Path descent that ends at the second trailhead 0.5 mile from your car, back-track to the Doublehead col and follow the Old Path home.

76 Mount Kearsarge North

General description:	A four- to five-hour family hike to fire-tower views.
General location:	Just north of North Conway near the Maine/New Hampshire border.
Length:	6.0 miles round trip.
Difficulty:	Moderate.
Elevation gain:	2,568 feet.
Special attractions:	Fine north-country views from the last remaining fire lookout in the White Mountain National Forest.
Maps:	USGS North Conway East quad.
For more information:	Saco Ranger District, 33 Kancamagus Highway, Conway, NH 03818, (603) 447-2166.

Key points:
  0.5   Enter White Mountain National Forest.
  1.3   Viewpoint ledges.

Mount Kearsarge North

2.9	Sharp right turn.
3.0	Fire tower at summit.

Finding the trailhead:
From the junction of River Road with New Hampshire Route 16 and US Highway 302 in North Conway (near the Eastern Slope Inn), drive north on Route 16 and US 302 for 1.8 miles to the state rest stop that has a view of Mount Washington on the left (west) side of the road. Cross a set of railroad tracks and turn right onto Hurricane Mountain Road 0.2 mile beyond the rest stop. Hurricane Mountain Road intersects Kearsarge Road after 1.0 mile. Park in the gravel area marked with a hiker's sign on the left side of Hurricane Mountain Road 0.4 mile beyond the junction with Kearsarge Road.

The hike: I might be slightly biased, but you shouldn't confuse Kearsarge North with the "real" Mount Kearsarge that rises to views of central New Hampshire from its base in my hometown (see Hikes 24 and 25). Also known as Mount Pequawket, this other pretender to the Kearsarge name rises instead near the border of Maine within sight of North Conway. The subject of a friendly rivalry over which summit rightfully claims a distinguished naval ship as its famous namesake, Kearsarge North has nevertheless become noteworthy on its own as a comfortably challenging family hike that ends with superb views from the last remaining fire lookout in the White Mountain National Forest.

The lumpy profiles of Kearsarge North and its neighbor, Bartlett Mountain, are on constant display to customers of the malls of North Conway. Poking up from the highest point of this mountainous silhouette, the distinctive Kearsarge fire tower stands against the sky and entices active vacationers to come and take a hike. A reliable path up the southern slopes that face the bustling town, the Kearsarge North Trail has become a popular choice for hikers who want a natural break from the rigors of outlet shopping.

Skipping through a muddy patch in a thicket by the side of the road, the trail quickly skims past a house and a summer cottage as the early section eases uphill through a forest of mixed hardwoods. The path narrows and picks up the pace after the first 0.5 mile where it veers to the right and officially enters the White Mountain National Forest. Ascending in fits and starts, the trail soon works its way to the crest of a broad ridge extending south from the mountain's summit and passes through a string of clearings

Fire tower and picnic ledges on Mount Kearsarge North.

250

formed by slabs of granite ledge about halfway to the top. Look back over your shoulder between the pitch pine and blueberries that grow in these sunny patches to the Moat Mountain Range (Hike 78), the stark face of Cathedral Ledge, and the very tip of Mount Chocorua rising to the south.

Reentering the woods on the left near the top of the last clearing, the trail swings northwest traversing an easy slope and then slowly turns north again on a rocky and rugged path that climbs sharply at times. Gradually circling back to the east, you're likely to spot steep slopes dropping away to your left, but you probably won't realize that the trail has topped an east–west ridge that connects the Kearsarge and Bartlett summits.

The incredibly rapid end to this hike begins with a sharp turn to the right followed by a 0.1-mile hop over rocks surrounded by mountain azalea. Popping onto the bald summit, hikers flock to the stubby tower that sits at the very peak. Built in 1951 to replace the original lookout that opened in 1909, the well-preserved Kearsarge North tower is listed on the register of National Historic Fire Lookouts and features a glass-enclosed observation room circled by a walk-around deck. Climb a few steps to the top of the tower for unobstructed views of Wildcat Ridge, the Presidential Peaks, and the Mount Washington Valley, or turn your gaze a little more south for a second look at The Moats and the vertical face of Cathedral Ledge beyond the Saco River. Among these mountain scenes, though, my favorite view from this comfortable room is the view that makes it unique. Looking east from the top of the tower, you're able to stare at a huge expanse of rolling terrain where the forests, farms, and small lakes that pepper western Maine recede to the far horizon.

77 Mountain Pond Trail

General description:	A relaxing spin around a White Mountain pond with access to waterfront camping.
General location:	About 10 miles north of North Conway.
Length:	2.8 miles.
Difficulty:	Easy.
Elevation gain:	Less than 100 feet.
Special attractions:	Backcountry scenery, wildlife, and solitary camping.
Maps:	USGS Chatham quad.
For more information:	Evans Notch Visitor Center, 18 Mayville Road, Bethel, ME 04217-4400, (207) 824-2134.

Key points:

0.4 Circle junction.
1.25 Shelter near northeast shore of pond.
2.4 Return to circle junction.

Mountain Pond Trail

No outlet

Shelter

Mountain Pond Trail

Mountain Pond

17

NORTH

0   0.5   1

△ To
East Branch Road

MILE

Finding the trailhead: From the state highway rest stop that offers a view of Mount Washington just north of North Conway, drive 2.0 miles north on New Hampshire Route 16 and turn right onto Town Hall Road. Pass directly across Route 16A after 0.1 mile, continue east on Town Hall Road (sometimes shown as Slippery Rock Road) for 2.5 miles, and then bear left onto East Branch Road. Drive north on East Branch Road and bear right at a fork onto Forest Road 17 after 3.4 miles. Trailhead parking is on the right after 0.7 mile.

The hike: If you've ever camped in a national park, you might have considered a walk-in tent site. Usually stationed not far from a road, these designated sites are designed to give the public the illusion of backcountry camping. If the thought of tenting in these make-believe sites carried a certain appeal, you're bound to love Mountain Pond. For only a little more effort than hiking to a walk-in campground, a quick circle of this wilderness pond finds waterfront locations where the solitude and wildlife couldn't be any more real.

By the time you pull into the lot and park at Mountain Pond, you're certainly going to realize that even this trailhead is rather remote. Gather your gear in the silent woods not far from the Maine border and follow a gravel path that slides between boulders at the edge of a small clearing. Engulfed by evergreens, a broad, flat trail skims the edge of a marsh and passes a spur to the right that leads to a beaver pond. Rising slightly with the forest floor, the 0.4-mile access trail soon arrives at a woodland junction where it meets the 2.0-mile shoreline path that circles the wilderness pond.

To the right, the southern half of the circular trail offers better mountain views but a rockier, rougher hike. Campers should turn left, instead, on the northern half of the trail for a smoother path to waterfront sites and the shortest route to a log shelter near the northeast end of the pond.

Leading left from the junction, the northern half of the Mountain Pond Trail quickly passes another fork where a right turn ends at a stony clearing beneath trees along the shore. Don't stop here. Follow the yellow-blazed trail that wends its way further left, crosses a wetland on wooden planks, and eases closer to shore for your first clear glimpse of the glistening water. As you walk through the woods above the shore, you'll easily spot the best site directly on the water about halfway down the north side of this comma-shaped pond. Look for a fire ring in the soft duff of the tall evergreens that shade this idyllic glade and catch the mountain breezes that waft across the pond. Less than a mile from your car, this spacious waterfront site is a great spot to watch for moose, spy on the twilight antics of local loons and beavers, or simply commune with nature.

A crude Adirondack shelter sits about 50 yards back from the water near the northeast end of the pond. It's a welcome haven in a heavy rain, but tent sites along the shore will hold more appeal for the average hiker. Look for grassy patches beside the trail as the path traces close to shore and approaches the end of the pond.

At one time a trail extended east beyond the end of Mountain Pond, but that path has been discontinued. When the water ends, turn right, instead, and complete the circular trail that quickly swings back to the west and follows the southern shore. Numerous rocks and wet spots make this section

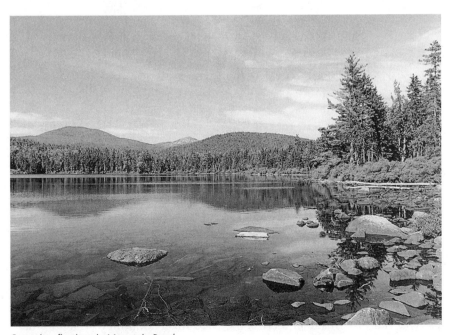

Summit reflections in Mountain Pond.

of trail much rougher underfoot, but views of the nearby mountains make up for the extra effort. As you work your way back to your car, look first for the rounded summits of North and South Doublehead (Hike 75) to the west beyond the pond. As you near the hike's conclusion, look north instead where distinctive Baldface Mountain (Hike 92) pops into scaly view high above the wooded mounds of Chandler, Sable, and Eastman Mountains that reflect in the quiet water.

78 North Moat Mountain

General description: A demanding climb above tree line to 360-degree views.

General location: 3 miles west of North Conway.

Length: 8.9 miles round trip.

Difficulty: Difficult.

Elevation gain: 2,650 feet.

Special attractions: Red Ridge, Diana's Baths, and sweeping mountain views.

Maps: USGS North Conway West quad.

For more information: Saco Ranger District, 33 Kancamagus Highway, Conway, NH 03818, (603) 447-2166.

Key points:
0.6   Diana's Baths.
1.3   Streamside junction, Moat Mountain and Red Ridge Trails.
3.4   Top of unnamed peak on Red Ridge.
4.5   Summit, North Moat Mountain.
6.4   Bank of Lucy Brook.
8.3   Return to Diana's Baths.

Finding the trailhead: Beginning at the junction of River Road with New Hampshire Route 16 and U.S. Highway 302 in North Conway (the traffic light just north of the Eastern Slopes Inn), turn west onto River Road. Pass under a railroad trestle and cross the Saco River. Continue straight where West Side Drive carries most traffic to the left and bear right where Old

North Moat Mountain

West Side Drive angles left toward Cathedral Ledge. A new Forest Service parking area that serves Diana's Baths is on the left side of River Road 2.3 miles from the traffic light on Route 16.

The hike: A sharply chiseled ridgeline that parallels Main Street west of North Conway, the Moat Mountain Range displays a scruffy, thread-bare look thanks to a blend of bald rock and stunted trees that covers its upper reaches. Rising more than a thousand feet on the eastern flanks of this rugged ridge, the stark walls of Cathedral Ledge and White Horse Ledge make the

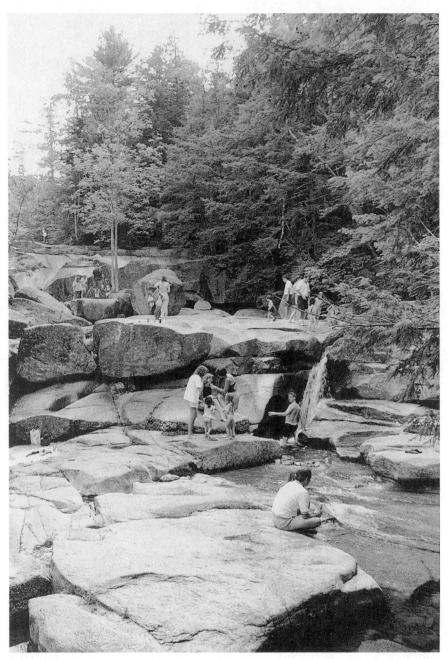

Beating the heat at Diana's Baths.

Moats even more imposing. Little wonder that few hikers venture beyond Diana's Baths, a popular swimming hole, just 0.6 mile from a trailhead at the north end of the range.

The 9.2-mile Moat Mountain Trail passes over five summits and traces the crest of this bony ridge for the full length of the range. End-to-end hikes are grueling and require hikers to station a car at the far end of their trek. There is no easy approach to this region, but there is a better way. The loop hike described here climbs the soaring, exposed heights of beautiful Red Ridge, intercepts the crest near mid-range, returns over North Moat Mountain (the highest peak in the chain), and treats hikers to Diana's Baths at both ends of their journey.

The north end of the Moat Mountain Trail departs a large parking lot designed for swarms of swimmers who come to splash in Diana's Baths. Slide downhill on a duff-covered path that winds through evergreens and loops through a glade of birch and beech before crossing a plank bridge. Turn right onto a gravel lane just beyond the bridge, and 30 yards later you'll spot Diana's Baths on your left where trail signs point straight ahead to North Moat and Red Ridge.

Early on a summer morning, you might be able to enjoy the baths alone. Make the most of your hassle-free chance to explore these gentle falls where a mountain stream tumbles over a series of broad ledges smoothed over eons by water. Potholes and small pools swirl with crystal-clear water that is sure to attract crowds of people in the heat of the afternoon.

Your hike resumes on the gravel lane that now swings left by a small stream, climbs uphill, and rises along Lucy Brook, which fills Diana's Baths. Quickly flattening above the falls and dwindling to a forest trail, this easy, 0.7-mile section arrives at the junction of the Red Ridge and Moat Mountain Trails on the banks of Lucy Brook 1.3 miles from the trailhead and 3.15 miles from the summit of North Moat Mountain.

To begin the loop toward Red Ridge, turn left at this streamside junction onto the Red Ridge Trail and tiptoe across the brook. A sometimes stony path angles away from the water but stays nearly level as it rolls south on easy grades to a junction with the Red Ridge Link Trail, a detour to the left that climbs more than a half a mile to the cliffs of White Horse Ledge.

After another jaunt of 0.7 mile over easy, rolling terrain, the Red Ridge Trail slowly descends to cross a gravel woods road and continues an additional 0.5 mile before meeting Moat Brook. Track uphill for a few hundred yards with the bleached-stone channel of Moat Brook on your left before crossing the water at a point where the trail confronts a serious challenge. Preparing to climb 2,000 feet, the Red Ridge Trail follows a wooden arrow as it loops to the left and then charges up a steep slope sparsely covered with pine. After less than two-tenths of a mile, a stony ledge reveals emerging views if you turn northeast and scan a panorama across the valley of Lucy Brook.

Beyond a last gravelly outlook, the trail becomes less severe as it shoots up faces of granite ledge and then suddenly moderates on the lower end of Red Ridge. Don't be fooled though. As southeast views open toward Mount

Kearsarge North, your climb has just begun. Time after time for a solid mile you'll swear you're near the crest, until you reach the top of a bald rise and another bulge looms dead ahead. Enjoy the journey on Red Ridge, a long extension of Moat Mountain high above timberline. It's the best part of the hike. Stick out your hand on these breezy heights and blueberries fall in your palm as you pass through clusters of low brush and gaze at distant views. Far to the north, Mount Washington and Wildcat Mountain form the sides of Pinkham Notch while swinging south the scene includes the rounded Carter Range and the gradually sloping western flank of nearby Cathedral Ledge.

The Red Ridge Trail ends at the upper junction with the Moat Mountain Trail on top of an unnamed peak about a tenth of a mile southeast of North Moat Mountain. Turn right at this elevated junction for a 5.0-mile trek that bounces along the northern half of the Moat Mountain ridge and returns to Diana's Baths. As you drop into the first col, surrounding rows of ever-greens make this early portion of the Moat Mountain Trail seem tamer than Red Ridge, but a challenging series of rocky scrambles lies in wait ahead. Anticipation increases along with expanding views as the path clambers over a series of knolls that slow progress with deep drops and steep hand-hold climbs.

The challenging trail gives you a break as it climbs the small, bare summit of North Moat Mountain, a 360-degree lookout that collects sensational views. Look for Mount Chocorua near the Kancamagus Highway and the rounded mounds of neighboring summits in the Pemigewasset Wilderness among the countless White Mountain peaks that ripple off to the north and west in unending, misty rows.

Part of the eastern panorama from the crest of Red Ridge.

The wooded ridge that wriggles north from the top of North Moat Mountain tracks the route of your return. Follow the cairns off the summit cone and locate a path down northern slopes that are only slightly less abrupt than the rugged south face. When the trail levels along the ridge, it sweeps past scrub that will soak your clothes if you're hiking after a rain and enters a flat bedrock clearing with a glimpse of Mount Kearsarge North. Rapid descents on long inclines of granite ledge finally lead the trail to a gravel-strewn clearing. Turn sharply left as you enter this gravelly glade, then leave the mountain's shoulder, and descend for the next mile at a much more moderate pace.

The Moat Mountain Trail eventually finds Lucy Brook hidden among tall trees at the base of a steep slope. Turn right on the south bank of the brook for a pleasant streamside stroll. After about a mile of easy walking, the path crosses to the north bank and soon meets the Red Ridge Trail at the junction where the loop began 1.3 miles from the trailhead. Retrace your steps past Diana's Baths to make it back to your car.

PRESIDENTIAL PEAKS

Washington, Adams, Jefferson, Monroe, Madison. For alpine hiking enthusiasts, it doesn't get any better than this. Other summits may bear the names of former presidents, but these mammoth peaks are the five highest mountains in all of New England and the epitome of New Hampshire hiking. Once you've roamed the Presidential Peaks, a profusion of classic images refuses to leave your mind: giant cairns in misty cols, plummeting headwalls, deep ravines, broad lawns of delicate flowers, barren summits reflected in windswept pools, and immense vistas under billowing clouds caught on a mountain peak.

Clustered to the north and west of Pinkham Notch, and ringed by a network of highways, the northern Presidential Peaks are surrounded by a wealth of easily accessible trails. This section of the hiker's guide presents an array of super routes that approach these summits from the north, west, and east. You'll even find a hike that traverses the range, and one that absorbs the majesty of the region from a substantially lower plane. Check the Crawford Notch section for additional treks to these fabulous summits on longer routes originating from the south.

Before you set out, though, do yourself a favor. Read the "Fundamentals" section in the Introduction to this guide. Pay particular attention to how to prepare for the challenging weather that's likely to be encountered in this region of arctic peaks.

---

79 Mount Jefferson, Caps Ridge Trail

General description:	A challenging six-hour round trip to the third-highest White Mountain peak.
General location:	About midway between Berlin and North Conway, near Bretton Woods.
Length:	5.3 miles round trip, including the loop to the Monticello Lawn.
Difficulty:	Difficult.
Elevation gain:	2,700 feet.
Special attractions:	Alpine vegetation on the Monticello Lawn, a look into the Great Gulf's abyss, and high-altitude views of the Presidential Peaks.
Maps:	USGS Mount Washington 7.5 x 15.
For more information:	Ammonoosuc Ranger Station, 660 Trudeau Road, Bethlehem, NH 03574, (603) 869-2626.

Mount Jefferson, Caps Ridge Trail

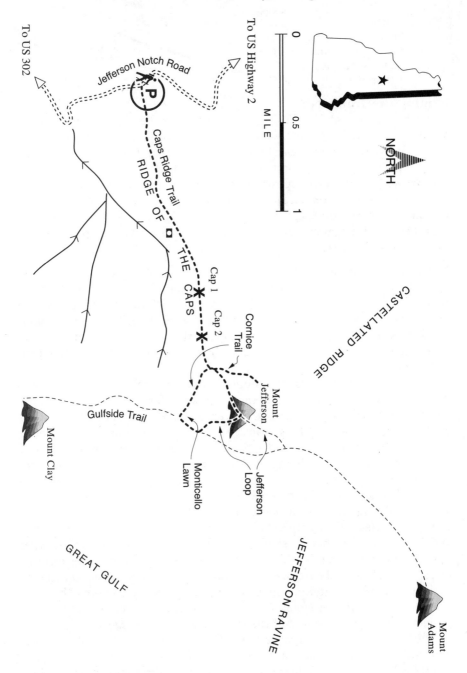

Key points:
  1.5 Cap 1.
  1.9 Cap 2.
  2.1 Junction Cornice Trail for detour to Monticello Lawn.
  2.5 Summit, Mount Jefferson.

Finding the trailhead:
From the junction of U.S. Highways 3 and 302 at the traffic lights in Twin Mountain, follow US 302 for 4.4 miles east and turn left onto Base Road just beyond Fabyans. Continue east on Base Road another 4.4 miles and turn left again at a junction with an unmarked dirt road, within sight of a sign for the Cog Railway and directly opposite a stop sign at the end of the Clinton Road.

You are now on Jefferson Notch Road, the highest state-maintained highway in New Hampshire. This narrow dirt thoroughfare twists and turns for 3.2 miles to the height of land in Jefferson Notch and the large parking area for the Caps Ridge Trailhead.

The hike: With a trailhead elevation of just over 3,000 feet, the Caps Ridge Trail attains the summit of a major Presidential Peak with less elevation gain than any other path. It is also the shortest White Mountain route to timberline. Regrettably, direct mountain routes that sound this good often conceal a truth that is less appealing. In fact, this is a difficult and challenging climb that turns back many hikers who only focus on the elevation gain and distance statistics.

The Ridge of the Caps is the mountainous spine that runs westerly from the summit of Mount Jefferson to the height of Jefferson Notch. The "Caps" are two large areas of bulging rock that act as huge steps in the steep ascent of the ridge. Negotiating these caps requires the use of hands and feet to clamber over rocks and up short faces of slab. Detour routes are available at some spots that look nearly impossible, but the precarious footing and constant exposure on long stretches of trail above timberline limit this hike to a fair-weather adventure for hikers in good condition.

The trail originates from one of the most scenic parking lots in New Hampshire, elegantly set amidst fir trees in the shadow of Mounts Jefferson and Clay. The route begins slowly, crossing several boggy areas but after only 0.2 mile becomes a rocky, moderately difficult path rising through birch and fir. The trail eases a bit, but climbs moderately again, reaching an outlook on boulders after 0.9 mile. From the top of these boulders, there are fine views of Jefferson Notch and Bretton Woods, as well as an excellent preview of the next segment of the route rising over the caps.

The hard work begins in earnest about halfway between the outlook boulders and the first cap, where a steep climb carries the trail above timberline. From this point, as the route traverses both caps and ascends the steep ridge to the base of Mount Jefferson's summit cone, hikers enjoy an astonishing kaleidoscope of changing mountain views. As the first cap falls behind, the lurking summit of Mount Washington emerges from behind Mount Clay, the Lakes of the Clouds Hut appears on a distant slope, and the yawning abyss of the Great Gulf slowly opens below. Eventually, from Jefferson's summit, Mount Clay shrinks to a small knoll on the low ridge that stretches to Mount Washington, and summits to the north and east rise out of obscurity on the opposite side of the range.

As the Ridge of the Caps become less distinct, the trail bears right to commence a rock-hopping ascent of Mount Jefferson across a mountain of crumpled gray rock. It's a long trudge up this summit cone, but the easing of the slope in the last 0.25 mile offers some relief. Immense stone cairns in a narrow col show the way to the jagged peak and countless miles of mountain scenes. From the vantage of this summit even jaded mountaineers are sure to take home a lasting image of Mounts Washington and Adams, the only parts of the visible world that rise higher than this vantage point.

Having come this far, it would be a shame to leave without examining the alpine vegetation that spreads across the Monticello Lawn, a broad plateau on Mount Jefferson's southern flank. For a pleasant interlude on this nearly level expanse of grass, rock, Labrador tea, and mountain azalea, walk toward Mount Washington on the Jefferson Loop Trail that soon intersects with the Gulfside Trail in the middle of this astounding lawn. A right turn onto the gently manicured Gulfside Trail results in an effortless stroll in the heart of delicate alpine beauty. After 0.2 mile, another right turn at a cairn and sign for the Cornice Trail leads back over rough stones and krummholz 0.5 mile to the Ridge of the Caps. Altogether, this short loop tacks only 0.3 mile onto the expedition.

Across the Great Gulf, Mount Washington from Jefferson's summit.

80 Cherry Mountain Trail

General description:	A half-day hike to a pair of peaks with unique White Mountain views.
General location:	Between Twin Mountain and Jefferson, about 10 miles west of Mount Washington.
Length:	5.4 miles round trip.
Difficulty:	Moderate.
Elevation gain:	1,500 feet.
Special attractions:	A lightly traveled trail and all-encompassing, private views of the Presidential Range.
Maps:	USGS Bethlehem 7.5 x 15; USGS Mount Washington 7.5 x 15.
For more information:	Ammonoosuc Ranger District, 660 Trudeau Road, Bethlehem, NH 03574, (603) 869-2626.

Key points:

0.25 Clearing of former logging yard.
1.3 Brook crossing.
1.7 T junction.
1.9 Summit, Mount Martha.
2.7 Summit, Owl's Head.

Finding the trailhead: From the traffic lights at the junction of U.S. Highways 3 and 302 in Twin Mountain, drive 2.0 miles north on US 3 and then turn right onto New Hampshire Route 115. Continue north on Route 115 for 1.9 miles. A gravel parking lot is located on the right directly across the highway from the intersection with Lennon Road.

The hike: Cherry Mountain, Mount Martha, and Owl's Head aren't names that usually come to mind when you think of Presidential Peaks, but these less-than-4,000-foot summits 10 miles west of Mount Washington are part of the same range. Like most hikers intent on conquering higher peaks, I passed this trailhead countless times before I finally stopped. Had I known what vistas waited at the end of this little-used trail, I'd have climbed these summits sooner.

Names of summits and trails can be confusing in this region. The highest peak on multiple-topped Cherry Mountain is known as Mount Martha but may also be labeled as Cherry Mountain on some hiking maps. Shown as a lower summit to the north, Owl's Head is also really part of Cherry Mountain. Oddly enough, the Cherry Mountain Trail doesn't cross Mount Martha, but comes within 0.2 mile of the mountain's highest peak, continues east, and ends at another trailhead on a different access road (Forest Road 14). To add to the confusion, the trail that links Mount Martha and Owl's Head is named Martha's Mile, in spite of the fact that the trail isn't nearly a mile long.

Cherry Mountain Trail

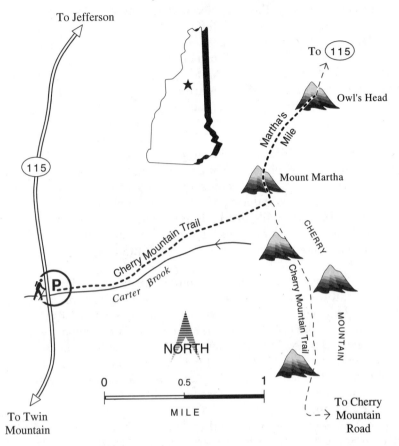

To Jefferson

To 115

Owl's Head

Martha's Mile

115

Mount Martha

Cherry Mountain Trail

CHERRY

Cherry Mountain Trail

MOUNTAIN

Carter Brook

P.

NORTH

To Cherry
Mountain
Road

0   0.5   1

MILE

To Twin
Mountain

From the trailhead parking lot on Route 115, follow a worn path that leads uphill 20 yards to a sign that announces the Cherry Mountain Trail. Centered in the grass-covered swath of a former logging road, the trail rises steadily through thick woods and brush that hide a mountain stream gurgling off to your right. After about a quarter of a mile, the path eases into an old logging yard that is now rapidly filling with poplars and evergreens. Ignore a four-wheel-drive track that diverges to the right near the end of this overgrown clearing, and resume your steady climb on a footpath that rises along the crest of a low, broad ridge.

The path climbs more quickly as trailside brush disappears in a patch of hemlock and birch, but the grade soon eases when brush and woods close in again. About 1.3 miles from its start, the trail skips over a small brook and soon begins a noticeably steeper 0.3-mile ascent that ends at a T junction in a clearing near the peak. To the right, the Cherry Mountain Trail continues south and east to Cherry Mountain Road (FR 14). For an easy 0.2-mile ramble to the summit of Mount Martha, turn left instead onto a wide spur path that follows a logging road now also used by moose.

A convenient boulder gives you a lift on Mount Martha's wooded peak and provides an enticing outlook to the heart of the Presidential Range. You can chart the course of the cog railway that chugs to Mount Washington's top, or pinpoint the summits of Jefferson, Adams, Madison, and Monroe, New Hampshire's next four highest peaks. For a glimpse of Cannon Mountain, Franconia Notch, and the Kinsman Peaks, pass between the footings of a now-removed fire tower to an outcrop that looks to the south and west from the opposite side of Mount Martha.

To extend your hike and also discover the best views of the day, turn north (hard right as you're walking uphill) at the point where the logging road enters the small clearing on Mount Martha's summit. After several paces, trail signs for Martha's Mile suggest a distance of 0.8 mile and a time of forty minutes to reach the top of Owl's Head. While the distance is probably right, you shouldn't be discouraged by this estimate of hiking time that is greatly overstated. Wandering off the summit on the soft duff of an evergreen forest, Martha's Mile descends about 400 feet to the bottom of a narrow col. Trout lily, trillium, ferns, and moss line this pleasant path before a couple of hand-hold scrambles quickly carry the trail to the top of Owl's Head peak.

Break out lunch or a trail snack about 50 yards short of the Owl's Head top where an open granite ledge offers a sweeping panorama. In one extraordinary glance, you can scan a mountainous scene that extends from the height of Mount Webster overlooking Crawford Notch, past Mounts Clinton and Eisenhower to the state's highest peaks, beyond the ribbon of highway that tracks the Jefferson Highlands, and on to the flanks of Mount Waumbek and the edge of the Pilot Range. Best of all, this exceptional view will probably be enjoyed in the absence of other hikers.

Be careful not to overshoot the Owl's Head summit. The Owl's Head Trail continues over the peak and ends at another trailhead a few miles north on Route 115. Better to turn around just beyond the viewpoint ledge and retrace your steps back to your car at the Cherry Mountain Trailhead.

81 Edmands Path

General description: A one-day hike to a windswept col between Mount Eisenhower and Mount Monroe.

General location: Off U.S. Highway 302 between Twin Mountain and North Conway.

Length: 3.0 miles to the crest of the ridge.

Difficulty: Moderate.

Elevation gain: 2,400 feet.

Special attractions: Alpine flowers, scenic crags, and exceptional mountain views.

Maps: USGS Crawford Notch and Stairs Mountain quads; also Mount Washington 7.5 x 15.

For more information: Ammonoosuc Ranger District, 660 Trudeau Road, Bethlehem, NH 03574, (603) 869-2626.

Key points:

0.4 Crossing Abenaki Brook.

0.7 Left turn off logging road.

2.2 Stone gateway.

2.4 Stream crossing at base of falls.

3.0 Junction, Mount Eisenhower Loop Trail.

3.4 Summit, Mount Eisenhower via Loop Trail detour.

4.8 Summit, Mount Monroe.

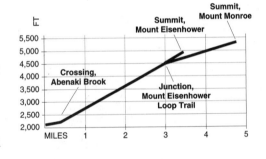

Finding the trailhead: From the traffic lights at the junction of U.S. Highways 3 and 302 in Twin Mountain, follow US 302 east 8.2 miles and turn left onto Mount Clinton Road. Trailhead parking for Edmands Path is on the right after 2.3 miles.

The hike: The popular expression "Been there; done that!" generally makes me cringe. Shunning trails that you've already hiked simply doesn't leave room for old friends like the Edmands Path. I've hiked this trail when leaden skies spit snow in early November and lounged on its crags when the summer sun lured crowds to lunch alfresco. A moderate path to a beautiful col in the heart of the White Mountains, the Edmands Path reveals new facets of mountain travel each time you pass this way. Don't settle for just one visit.

Dating from 1909, the carefully crafted Edmands Path affords a steady, comfortable trail that remains one of the easiest routes to the Presidential Peaks. The amount of care bestowed on the trail in the first 20 yards gives a hint of things to come. Stroll across the plank ramp that introduces the trailhead, walk up a flight of wooden steps, and check trail signs near a kiosk a few feet into the woods. Passing beneath tall beech, maple, and black birch trees, the well-tended Edmands Path remains level for 0.1 mile as it crosses a brook on hand-hewn logs and then rises into the forest.

Edmands Path

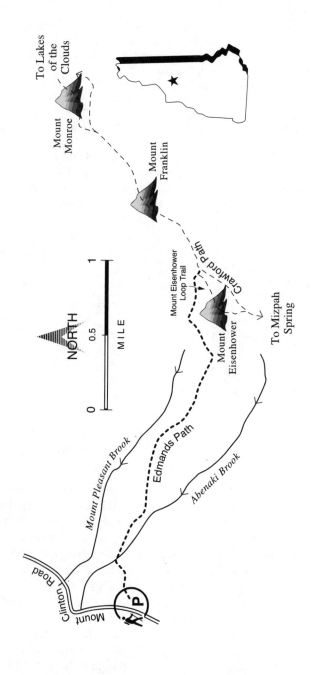

After spanning a second brook, level walking leads the trail to a birch-railed hiker's bridge that crosses the vigorous flow of Abenaki Brook. Turn right on the opposite bank and saunter along a logging road that follows the flow upstream. The sound of the brook slowly recedes over the next 0.25 mile, before the trail angles left onto a woodland hiking path. As you ease through the forest, note the special care that was used in building the drainage channels that keep the trail dry. When the path begins a steady ascent that never becomes taxing, also note the half-round, spaced grooves on the edge of granite steps, a sure sign that someone with a hammer and chisel split the stones by hand.

Winding upwards through several jogs, the trail briefly slackens its pace, climbs through a 5-yard zigzag, and swings left as summits to the north and west pop into view between the trees. Be patient for another 0.25 mile as you ascend the hand-laid path, curl right onto stone steps, and pass through a gate that looks a bit like a gap in a pasture wall. Now bearing northeast on the massive flanks of Mount Eisenhower, the trail crosses a mountain stream at the base of a 20-foot falls (where footing can be slippery), levels for a time, and breaks into open views just 0.2 mile above the gate.

As you peer across the stunted tops of low evergreens, the spectacle of this moderate hike has only just begun. To your left, Ammonoosuc Ravine sweeps west to Bretton Woods, the unmistakable Caps Ridge Trail (Hike 79) rises to Jefferson's heights, and the bulging slope of Mount Monroe hides the northeast's tallest peak that soon slides into view. To your right, delicate ferns and mosses thrive at your feet, while the ragged pitch of Mount Eisenhower towers above your head. As mountainous scenes unfold over

Trail junction on the Crawford Path near the summit of Mount Monroe.

the course of the next 0.5 mile, the trail follows a hand-crafted path that skirts the mountain's flanks, maintains a level course, and then gently curls to the top of an alpine ridge.

Rolling onto the windswept crest that separates Ammonoosuc Ravine from the Dry River Valley, Edmands Path ends just below a small pool at a high-altitude junction with the Mount Eisenhower Loop Trail. Turn right to climb more than 300 feet up this rocky switchback trail that passes over the broad summit of spectacular Mount Eisenhower and continues down the other side on the way to Mizpah Spring (Hike 60). To descend into the col, turn left instead, and follow a well-worn track that intercepts the Crawford Path after only 50 yards. From this picturesque alpine junction you'll be able to spot a carved sign stuck into a stone cairn less than 0.2 mile away at the low point on the ridge between Mount Eisenhower and Mount Monroe.

Before tackling the obvious trail that weaves like a gravelly ribbon more than a mile up Mount Monroe, hang out in this mellow col. Surrounded by alpine flowers, hikers are free to discover an ever-changing world of rocky ledges and distant views. Wander from crag to crag. Identify delicate blooms. Savor the passing scene in this quiet alpine zone as clouds play tag with barren peaks and the sun glints on woodlands that blanket the valleys below.

82 King Ravine: The Air Line, Short Line, and King Ravine Trails

General description:	A one-day hike through a glacial cirque to the Presidential Peaks.
General location:	About 8 miles west of Gorham.
Length:	4.5 miles to the summit of Mount Adams.
Difficulty:	Strenuous.
Elevation gain:	4,465 feet.
Special attractions:	Boulder fields, ice caves, a steep headwall climb, and terrific alpine views.
Maps:	USGS Mount Washington 7.5 x 15.
For more information:	Androscoggin Ranger District, 300 Glen Road, Gorham, NH 03581-1399, (603) 466-2713.

Key points:
- 0.8 Right turn onto Short Line.
- 1.3 Convergence with Randolph Path.
- 1.7 Departure of Randolph Path.
- 2.7 Mossy Falls near junction with King Ravine Trail.
- 3.1 Split, Subway or Elevated.
- 3.4 Base of headwall.
- 3.9 Junction, King Ravine Trail and Air Line.
- 4.5 Summit, Mount Adams.

King Ravine; The Air Line, Short Line, and King Ravine Trails • Lowe's Path, the Gray Knob Trail, the Randolph Path, and Edmands Col

To Gorham

To Jefferson

Appalachia

To Jefferson

P 83

P 82

2

Lowe's Path

The Link

Short Line

Randolph Path

Air Line

King Randolph Path Ravine

Short Line

KING RAVINE Trail

Log cabin

Crag Camp

Mossy Falls

GRAY KNOB

Lowe's Path

Madison Hut

Mt. Madison

Randolph Path

Gray Knob Trail

THE PERCH

Mount Sam Adams

Mount Quincy Adams

CASTLE RAVINE

Gulfside Trail

Mount Adams

EDMANDS COL

JEFFERSON RAVINE

Mount Jefferson

NORTH

0   0.5   1

MILE

Finding the trailhead: Same as Hike 84.

The hike: A massive glacial cirque carved into the northern flanks of the Presidential Range, King Ravine lives up to the lofty standards of its regal name. Swooping down from the overhanging crags that top Durand Ridge, the nearly vertical headwall of this monstrous mountain bowl descends to a field of toppled boulders, each bigger than a house. Regrettably, the headwall portion of this strenuous route looks less like a hiking path than a paint-blazed obstacle course. Leading from the Appalachia parking lot to an elevated plateau between Mounts Madison and Adams, this legendary hike is best left to mountain-goat wannabes. Everyone else should turn the page.

A maze of trails departs the Appalachia parking lot, a convenient stop on the hiker's shuttle and a natural meeting place for hikers exploring the Presidentials. Cross the B & M Railroad tracks along with the rest of the crowd and take heed of the sobering sign that warns you about the dangers of White Mountain weather. After only 30 yards, you'll probably have the trail to yourself as you fork right on the Air Line 4.3 miles from Mount Adams.

Stay left where The Link departs to the right 0.2 mile closer to Mount Adams, and ascend on the Air Line over easy grades through a sun-dappled hardwood forest. Hopping over two small brooks, the Air Line crosses the Beechwood Way and rises a little more steeply to reach a junction with the Short Line Trail 0.8 mile from the trailhead.

Turn right on the Short Line as the Air Line branches left to ascend the heights of Durand Ridge. Easing a bit as it angles across a northwestern slope, the Short Line converges with the Randolph Path after only 0.5 mile. Follow this double route that slithers uphill 0.4 mile on a wet and muddy track, but bear left at the next junction where the Randolph Path diverges right on its way to Mount Washington. Stay the course on the Short Line as rocks in the trail become larger, evergreens mix with birch, and Cold Brook's torrent rushes by in an unseen gully to your right.

The moderate effort on the Short Line includes a 100-yard stretch that resembles a brook, but the trail makes up for the sloppy going with a picture-perfect view of a crook in a mountain stream. Tarry here in a woodland glade, or pitch a tent if you're so inclined. The mood of this hike is about to change.

The Short Line ends at the King Ravine Trail, which angles up from Lowe's Path and enters on the right. Bear left on this cross-grained route just below Mossy Falls where Cold Brook spews out from between giant boulders and the towering walls of King Ravine first command your attention. Slow and steady is your only option as the King Ravine Trail clambers over boulders and slithers past gnarled trees that obscure the headwall's size. A quick scramble to the top of a rock grants a better view of the wall and a good look at Crag Camp (see Hike 83), a superb hut on a distant rim that you'll want to visit on another day.

After a rugged 0.1 mile, the King Ravine Trail breaks into the open at the junction with the Chemin Des Dames Trail, another route that reconnects to the Air Line via the cirque's eastern wall. Continue your course on the floor of the bowl for only 10 more yards and the King Ravine Trail splits in two. Take either the Subway, a tortuous path to the right that weaves over, under, around, and through a mammoth jumble of house-sized boulders, or bear left on the Elevated, an easier route that avoids all the fun and struggle. Both branches reunite at the head of the boulder field 150 yards to the south, where the King Ravine Trail pauses for another brief sojourn in the woods. Beyond the junction with the Great Gully Trail, you face another option as you walk through this stunted forest. Scramble to your right on the Ice Caves Loop where water-dripping boulders keep temperatures almost frosty, or turn left on the primary trail that quickly exits the woods.

For average hikers a difficult but exhilarating outing is about to turn nasty. If the weather is bad or you're not prepared to cling to vertical rocks, turn back now. You're about to climb more than 1,000 feet in less than 0.5 mile.

Descending Mount Adams towards Mount Madison's summit and the Hut at Madison Spring.

On this very strenuous headwall stretch of the King Ravine Trail, you'll be happy when the boulders you hug are only human-sized. The one thing worse than ascending this route is trying to get back down. You really shouldn't begin this headwall climb unless you're sure you're going to finish.

At some point as you climb this wall, you'll slowly begin to realize that you can walk without clutching rock. Looking ahead, the King Ravine Trail leads through a giant chute that thrusts to the top of the rim between overhanging boulders. With the dangerous scramble behind you, the massive curve of the headwall has become only a harmless frame for glorious mountain views. When the trail ends at the Air Line on the upper slopes of Mount Adams, you're on top of an alpine world. To the right is the summit of Mount Adams still 0.6 mile away. To the left is the hut at Madison Spring in the Madison/Adams col and the rocky mound of Mount Madison that you can top in less than a mile.

Turn right on the Air Line at the crest of Durand Ridge. Continue on to the Mount Adams summit, or walk just 200 feet to a junction with the Gulfside Trail. From this point the Madison Hut, trails to Mount Madison, and the upper end of the Valley Way, a safe route of return (Hike 84), are just twenty minutes away.

North Country views from the Hut at Madison Spring.

83 Lowe's Path, the Gray Knob Trail, the Randolph Path, and Edmands Col

See Map on Page 271

General description: A one-day walk to an alpine col with optional stays at cabins or shelters and excursions to nearby peaks.

General location: About 10 miles west of Gorham.

Length: 5.1 miles.

Difficulty: Moderate.

Elevation gain: 3,572 feet.

Special attractions: Superb alpine views and a choice of overnight cabins near the lip of King Ravine.

Maps: USGS Mount Washington 7.5 x 15.

For more information: Androscoggin Ranger District, 300 Glen Road, Gorham, NH 03581-1399, (603) 466-2713.

Key points:

2.4 The Log Cabin.

3.2 Gray Knob cabin.

3.6 Crag Camp via Grey Knob Trail.

5.1 Edmands Col.

Finding the trailhead: Lowe's Path leaves U.S. Highway 2 on its south side 5.05 miles east of the junction of US 2 and New Hampshire Route 115. Parking is not available at the trailhead. A gas station and convenience store diagonally across the highway provide parking for a small fee.

Lowe's Path is also 2.0 miles west of the Appalachia Trailhead (see Hike 84). Some may prefer to park at Appalachia and begin their hike on The Link Trail which connects to Lowe's Path.

The hike: Built in 1875 to 1876 as a route to Mount Adams, Lowe's Path has been overshadowed in recent years by a wealth of more convenient trails that climb the impressive northern slopes of the Presidential Range from the Appalachia Trailhead. In spite of its fading glory, though, Lowe's Path holds a few surprises. On its way to a stunning alpine zone, this venerable mountain trail wanders past a broad range of overnight accommodations that can't be matched anywhere else in all of the White Mountains.

Preserving a proud tradition, the Randolph Mountain Club maintains more than 100 miles of local hiking trails and a string of four backcountry camps clustered near Nowell Ridge, which rises to Mount Adams. Alone or in combination, Crag Camp, Gray Knob, the Perch, and the Log Cabin give hikers a rare chance to wander for several glorious days through New

A mellow welcome to Crag Camp.

England's highest peaks. As you hike the soaring summits of Mount Jefferson and Mount Adams, you can spend nights in a crude shelter, a heated two-story cabin, or a modern hut on the very lip of majestic King Ravine. Guests at each of the Randolph camps should expect to be self-sufficient, and of course you'll need to pack out whatever you packed in. Caretakers collect an overnight fee. Reservations are not accepted.

From a sign that sports a hiker's logo by the side of US 2, follow a jeep track into the woods for about 80 yards and then bear right where a larger sign notes the history of Lowe's Path. Quickly crossing a railroad bed and ducking power lines, the trail warms you gradually over the next 1.5 miles. Slabbing uphill, crossing a brook, and turning sharply left at a flight of stone steps, Lowe's Path soon meets The Link, an alternate route that connects to the Appalachia Trailhead 2.7 miles to the east.

After passing the junction with the King Ravine Trail that angles off to the left (east) on its way to Mossy Falls (see Hike 82), Lowe's Path gives hikers a brief struggle during the next moderate mile as it climbs to the Log Cabin. Located near the junction with the Cabin-Cascades Trail 2.5 miles from the trailhead, the nearly enclosed Log Cabin provides only basic shelter but serves as a welcome rest stop before tackling a challenging climb.

Beyond the Log Cabin, Lowe's Path negotiates the toughest stretch of the day. Crossing the Randolph Path (an alternate route of return), the moderate trail flirts with being difficult for 0.7 mile as it struggles through steep woodlands and breaks for a brief moment into a small patch of scrub with a clear view of Castellated Ridge descending from Jefferson's peak. Topping another bulge just 200 yards later, Lowe's Path meets the Quay, a shortcut trail that leads to the Gray Knob cabin after only 100 yards and makes connections to Crag Camp just 0.4 mile beyond. Turn left on the Quay and make a mental note of the junction with the Gray Knob Trail that departs to the right (south) about halfway to the Gray Knob cabin.

Tucked into evergreen woods, the two-story Gray Knob cabin is favored by winter hikers. When warmed by a wood stove, the kitchen area, sitting room, and sleeping loft are cozy by any standards but confining in warm weather. For the crown jewel of summer huts, descend another 0.4 mile east on the Gray Knob Trail to amazing Crag Camp. Reconstructed in 1993 to replace cabins that stood on this site since 1909, unheated Crag Camp has space for 20 overnight guests in three separate bunkrooms, a kitchen with tile counters, and a large wall of windows with a world-class mountain view. Set near the edge of a precipice, the deck and dining area of this singular mountain retreat look across the plunging depths of massive King Ravine to Mount Madison and Mount Adams to the east and southeast.

To resume your hike to Edmands Col, backtrack past Gray Knob and turn left (south) on the Gray Knob Trail where it diverges from the Quay. At the next junction, continue straight on the Gray Knob Trail as it crosses Lowe's Path, which now departs for a 1.6-mile climb of Mount Adams. Flanking Nowell Ridge, your steps on the Gray Knob Trail soon nudge above timberline on a track that is never truly steep, but extremely rocky and rough.

Before you pass the path to the Perch that diverges to the right, you're likely to spot the gleam of its roof about 300 feet below. Unless the weather is closing in, there's no practical reason to descend to that rugged shelter astride the Randolph Path. Continue instead on the Gray Knob Trail that finds a steady pace as it skirts the flanks of Mount Adams, swings southwest amidst constant views, and ends at the Randolph Path, which rises up to meet you high above a deep cleft known as Castle Ravine.

In a realm of black rock tripe and colorful map lichens, the Israel Ridge Trail enters from the right and stays with the Randolph Path for only 150 yards before diverging left again for the summit of Mount Adams. Edging the rim of Castle Ravine and easing across a mountain of rocks high above timberline, the Randolph Path comes to its scenic end just 0.6 mile later at the junction with the Gulfside Trail in the heart of Edmands Col.

Not to be confused with Edmands Path that leads to another ridge about 5 miles farther south, Edmands Col stands on a narrow crest between Mount Jefferson and Mount Adams, high above the deep gulfs of Jefferson and Castle Ravines. Befitting the memory of the trail builder, J. Rayner Edmands, hiking options from his namesake col are almost without limit. To the north, the Gulfside Trail connects to a web of paths that explore Mount Adams' summit and continue on to Madison Spring, Star Lake, and the Parapet (see Hike 84). To the south, the Mount Jefferson Loop Trail climbs to Mount Jefferson's summit in only 0.6 mile, while the Gulfside Trail avoids the heights and tracks Monticello Lawn, a vast terrace of alpine flowers overlooking the Great Gulf and Mount Washington beyond.

Crag Camp, near the lip of King Ravine.

Hiking north from Edmands Col toward Mounts Adams and Madison.

To return home, backtrack to Edmands Col and retrace your steps on the Randolph Path to its junction with the Gray Knob Trail. Unless you're staying at Crag Camp or the Gray Knob cabin, turn left on the Randolph Path. This quick descent passes the Perch and rejoins Lowe's Path only about two-tenths of a mile above the Log Cabin.

84 Mount Madison, Valley Way Trail

General description:	A long day trip or overnight backpack to an elevated col at the base of Mounts Madison and Adams. One of the most protected White Mountain routes to high altitude.
General location:	About 8 miles west of Gorham.
Length:	7.6 miles round trip to the Madison/Adams col.
Difficulty:	Moderate.
Elevation gain:	3,500 feet.
Special attractions:	Alpine flowers, Star Lake, towering summits, and the White Mountain's most magnificent view.
Maps:	USGS Mount Washington 7.5 x 15.
For more information:	Androscoggin Ranger District, 300 Glen Road, Gorham, NH 03581-1399, (603) 466-2713.

Mount Madison, Valley Way Trail

To Gorham

To Lancaster

NORTH

0   0.5   1

MILE

DURAND RIDGE

Snyder Brook

GORDON RIDGE

Watson Path

Tent platforms

Madison Hut

Mount Madison

Star Lake

The Parapet

Mount Sam Adams

Mount Quincy Adams

Mount Adams

MADISON GULF

Key points:
- 2.4 Junction, Watson Path.
- 3.8 Hut at Madison Spring.
- 4.1 Star Lake and the Parapet via detour.
- 4.2 Summit, Mount Madison.

Finding the trailhead: Follow New Hampshire Route 16 north through Pinkham Notch to the town of Gorham and turn left (west) on U.S. Highway 2. The large Appalachia Trailhead parking area is on the left (south) side of the highway about 6 miles west of Gorham. The Appalachia parking area is also a scheduled stop on the Hiker Shuttle.

The hike: Hikers planning their first venture into the Presidential Peaks might well consider the Valley Way Trail. A maze of historic paths ascends from US 2 along various ravines and ridges to the northern fringe of the Mount Washington Range. Other trails may be more scenic or carry a bit more panache, but the Valley Way is a direct, moderate, weather-resistant route that ends within yards of reliable shelter at the AMC Madison Hut. In bad weather, this relatively safe trail is also an ideal escape route from the exposed northern summits. If you need more incentive to select this hike, consider, too, that the most magnificent view in all the White Mountains waits at the end of the path.

Mount Madison and Star Lake.

Approaching Madison Hut below Mount Madison's summit.

The trail itself is by no means dull. Crossing railroad tracks and ducking under power lines, the route quickly leaves civilization at the trailhead, as a selection of side paths almost immediately lends variety to the hike. Short detours lead to small waterfalls, while other trails branch to more exposed mountain routes where cabins and shelters provide overnight accommodations (see Hikes 83 and 86). Large hardwoods dot the forest in the course of the next 0.5 mile, before the Fallsway loop branches left to visit a series of falls and sliding steps, rejoining the Valley Way in 0.1 mile.

After a short meander along Snyder Brook, the Valley Way climbs quickly uphill at the junction with the Brookside Trail and crosses the Randolph Path 2.4 miles below the Madison Hut. Over the next mile, the trail gradually climbs the lower slopes of Durand Ridge and enters the upper reaches of the narrowly constricted watershed. As the trail slices across a side hill, the grade increases, the route enters a Forest Protection Area, views open north to the city of Berlin, and the Watson Path bears left on its difficult journey directly to the summit of Mount Madison.

A cursory look at a topographic map will convince you that the Valley Way should become quite steep sooner than it really does. In fact, the moderate climb continues well into the higher segments of this elevated mountain valley. It's not until you pass a side path to tent platforms that the trail becomes vertical, rocky, and rough on the final 0.5 mile of the hike.

In one form or another, there has been a stone hut for overnight shelter at Madison Springs since 1888, taking advantage of a superb location in an awe-inspiring col nestled beneath massive peaks. To the northeast, the solitary dome of Mount Madison rises 600 feet above the hut, while to the southwest, Mount Adams and its subordinate family of peaks reach almost 1,000 feet above the col. Even hikers without evening reservations are welcome to find daytime respite, words of advice, or a warm drink at the present stone structure, completed in 1941. After settling in at the hut or taking a break, hikers can top out on the nearby peak of their choice in less than one hour.

The best reward of this hike is saved for last on an easy, ten-minute, 0.25-mile stroll beyond the door of the hut. Just over the low ridge behind the shelter awaits tiny Star Lake, huddled on a rocky plain at the foot of Mount Adams, along with a breathtaking view from a precipice of boulders known as the Parapet. From this vantage on the lip of the White Mountain world, the immense forms of both neighboring mountains plummet into the bottomless space of Madison Gulf and gaping Jefferson Ravine. To the south across the huge emptiness of the Great Gulf abyss, the ribbon of the auto road snakes its way to the summit of Mount Washington, and east, across Pinkham Notch, miniature ski slopes appear below the rugged Wildcat Ridge. The view is truly spectacular. Once you've seen it, you'll likely return again.

85 Great Gulf Trail, Spaulding Lake

General description: A short backpack or extended day hike beneath towering summits of the Presidential Peaks in the heart of Great Gulf Wilderness.

General location: Between North Conway and Berlin about 4 miles north of Pinkham Notch.

Length: 13.0 miles round trip.

Difficulty: Moderate.

Elevation gain: 3,000 feet.

Special attractions: Beautiful walks beside a stream, fabulous alpine views, a tiny lake under mountain walls, and remote wilderness campsites.

Maps: USGS Carter Dome quad and Mount Washington 7.5 x 15; also Great Gulf Wilderness map and brochure available from the address below.

For more information: Androscoggin Ranger Station, 300 Glen Road, Gorham, NH 03581-1399, (603) 466-2713.

Key points:

    0.1   Bridge over Peabody River.
    1.4   Wilderness boundary.
    2.5   The Bluff.
    4.0   Crossing of Chandler Brook.
    6.5   Spaulding Lake.

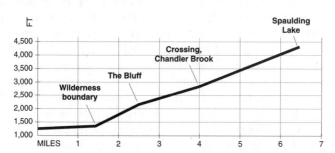

Finding the trailhead: From North Conway, follow New Hampshire Route 16 north through Glen, Jackson, and Pinkham Notch. Parking for the Great Gulf Trail is on the left, past the entrance to the Mount Washington Auto Road, 4.2 miles north of the AMC Pinkham Notch Visitor Center. The trailhead is at the far (northern) end of the parking/turnaround area.

The hike: You don't have to climb a mountain to enjoy the glamour of the Presidential Peaks. Surrounded by magical alpine scenes, the Great Gulf Trail tracks the West Branch of the Peabody River as it arches far below the spectacular summits of Mounts Washington, Jefferson, Madison, and Adams in a breathtaking display of classic wilderness beauty. Mind you, this hike is not

Great Gulf Trail, Spaulding Lake

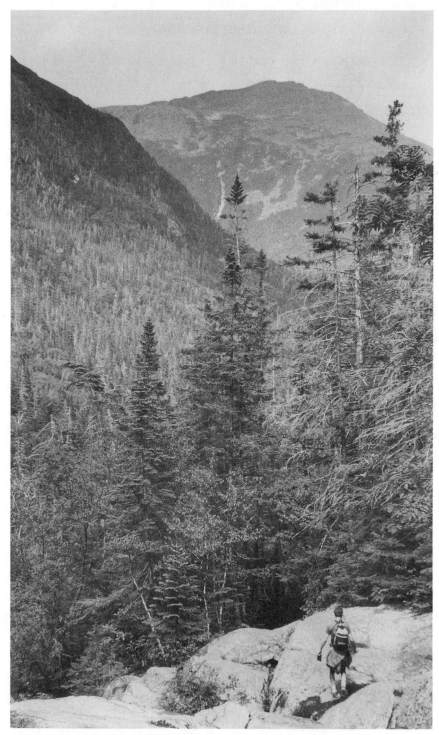

Adrift in the Great Gulf, shadowed by Mount Adams.

flat, but spreading the elevation gain over 6.5 miles makes this journey into the heart of the Great Gulf Wilderness more woodland walk than alpine assault.

The destination of this hike is Spaulding Lake in the palm of the Great Gulf, one of three immense glacial cirques contained within the 5,500-acre Great Gulf Wilderness. Bounded on the north by Mount Madison's Osgood Ridge, on the south by Mount Washington's Chandler Ridge, and on the west by the high ridge connecting the summits of Mounts Jefferson, Adams, and Clay, this entire valley is within a Forest Protection Area. Camping is prohibited within 200 feet of any trail or above the Sphinx Trail junction. These regulations effectively preclude camping anywhere in the vicinity of Spaulding Lake, but a number of attractive designated tent sites scattered along the West Branch of the Peabody River make the Great Gulf a busy paradise for knowledgeable backcountry hikers.

From the trailhead, an old paved road leads 100 yards or so to an elaborate wooden suspension bridge across the Peabody River. On the opposite bank, the trail turns left, parallel to the stream, traverses the barely perceptible grade of a cross-country ski trail, and runs 1.4 miles to the wilderness boundary. Not until it passes the junction with the Osgood Trail does the route fully lose its ski-trail character, as it begins a moderate climb along the riverbank. Look for a nice rest stop where the trail touches the boulder-filled river, before it swings right to make a brief, angular ascent on stone steps to a parallel ridge.

The first inspiring views of the day come about 2.5 miles into the hike, as the trail passes an overflow campsite near the top of a gravel knoll called The Bluff. This quick but impressive look portends better views to come, as Mounts Washington, Jefferson, Adams, and Madison sweep from west to north in a tight arc.

Just beyond this campsite, the Great Gulf Trail turns left at the junction with the Osgood Cutoff and promptly descends an embankment to cross Parapet Brook on a short section of the Appalachian Trail. The path immediately ascends the opposite bank of the brook to an attractive ridgetop tent site, passes the east junction with the Madison Gulf Trail, and descends yet another embankment to cross the Peabody River on a small suspension bridge. The Appalachian Trail departs left with the Madison Gulf Trail, as your route settles into a mile-long jaunt along the southern bank of the river on the way to Chandler Brook. Although not difficult, this stretch of trail is slow going with poor footing between rocks and tree roots and passes another designated campsite at about the halfway point of the hike.

Chandler Brook is crossed about 4 miles from the trailhead, followed quickly by the junction with the Wamsutta and Six Husbands Trails. Immersed in a genuine backcountry atmosphere, the next 0.75 mile of trail now passes three of the most appealing campsites found in the Great Gulf Wilderness. Nestled in the shadows of Mounts Madison and Adams and hard by the flow of the river, these sites make perfect base camps for day hikes, whiling away the hours, or catching sun on midstream boulders.

The final 1.3-mile leg from the last campsite to Spaulding Lake requires a more vigorous ascent but rewards the traveler with the gulf's most startling

Mount Adams and Madison tower above Spaulding Lake.

scenes. On either side of the Sphinx Trail junction, two short ascents make up the steepest portions of the hike corresponding with falls and cascades on the parallel course of the river. The first climb leads to a marvelous midstream outlook toward Mount Adams across the top of a plunging cascade. The second begins beneath a sparkling falls that fans out on the dark ledges of its wide granite base.

Tiny Spaulding Lake is reached by a last, moderate ascent along the elevated floor of the gulf. Pristine waters reflect the headwalls of Mounts Clay and Washington rising 1,200 feet. The trail continues up that imposing wall, but I prefer to stop here to enjoy a quiet lunch by the side of the rocky shore. There is much here to attract the eye, but the ultimate view back down the Great Gulf may be the White Mountain's most memorable scene. Months later you'll still recall the crystal pool of Spaulding Lake reflecting the twin sentinel summits of Mounts Madison and Adams, protecting their wilderness valley.

86 Presidential Traverse

General description:	A multiple-day grand tour of the Presidential Peaks.
General location:	Between Crawford Notch and U.S. Highway 2 near the town of Randolph.
Length:	13.5 miles to more than 17.5 miles, one way, depending upon choice of route.
Difficulty:	Moderate to difficult depending upon route.
Elevation gain:	2,700 feet to 3,800 feet, but substantially greater with climbs to optional summits.
Special attractions:	The ultimate White Mountain hike: mountain views, alpine gardens, and prolonged days of exploration above timberline.
Maps:	USGS Mount Washington 7.5 x 15.
For more information:	Androscoggin Ranger Station, 300 Glen Road, Gorham, NH 03581-1399, (603) 466-2713.

Key points:

- 0.0 Lakes of the Clouds Hut.
- 1.4 Junction, Crawford Path and Westside Trail.
- 1.8 Junction, Westside Trail and Gulfside Trail.
- 4.6 Edmands Col.
- 6.8 Hut at Madison Spring.

Skirting Star Lake on the way to Mount Madison's peak.

Presidential Traverse

NORTH

0   1   2
MILE

Log Cabin

Crag Camp

Gray Knob

The Perch

To US 2

Valley Way

Madison Hut

Mount Madison

Star Lake

Mount Adams

JEFFERSON RAVINE

Mount Jefferson

MONTICELLO LAWN

GREAT GULF

Gulfside Trail

Mount Clay

Cog Railway

Westside Tr.

Mount Washington

To Base Road, US 302

Ammonoosuc Ravine Tr.

To Pinkham Notch

TUCKERMAN RAVINE

Lakes of the Clouds Hut

Mount Monroe

Davis Path

Mount Franklin

Boott Spur Trail

Mount Eisenhower

Crawford Path

Boott Spur

Mount Pierce

To US 302

Mizpah Hut

Finding the trailhead: The high-altitude trails at the core of this traverse can be reached by various routes. See Hikes 60, 62, 63, 79, 81, 83, 84, 87, and 88 for directions to a few of the trailheads that can make this journey possible.

The hike: The Presidential Traverse is more theoretical concept than specific hike. There are dozens of approaches to the fantastic realm of the Mount Washington Range, but the general idea of this ultimate hike is to maintain elevation for the bulk of the trip, luxuriating in the splendid reward of one or more full days above timberline. A broad array of overnight shelters can turn this concept into sensational reality, even for hikers of average ability. As usual, of course, there is always a catch.

In this case the catch revolves around weather and luck. Most reservations for AMC overnight shelters need to be made weeks (or months) in advance, forcing a gamble that the weather will permit completion of the hike. Even in midsummer, the odds on really fine weather are a long shot, easily surpassed by the strong possibility of genuinely severe conditions. Approaching this hike with a firm resolve to conquer the weather and complete the traverse can get you into serious trouble. Avoid danger and aggravation by philosophically planning this trip, resolved only to enjoy whatever experience the vagaries of weather allow.

The heart of this hike traverses the 7 miles of stunning alpine scenery that stretches between Mount Monroe and Mount Madison, passing optional excursions to the summits of Mounts Washington, Clay, Jefferson, and Adams. This incredible landscape, well above timberline, visits a collection of memorable highlights among the best the White Mountains offer. Fragile alpine vegetation on the Monticello Lawn, mountain reflections in delicate Star Lake, mind-boggling views over gaping Great Gulf, mists on a moonscape near Lakes of the Clouds, and the scoured bowl of Tuckerman Ravine. A graded path for much of its length, the Gulfside Trail passes most of these sights, avoiding climbs of summit cones in favor of less strenuous grades on the shoulders of the towering peaks. However, even without including the detour loops that pass over the mountaintops, some of this route can be rocky and rough, crossing miles of exposed ridge highly vulnerable to sudden changes in weather. It's not a hike to be taken lightly, or by anyone who is unprepared.

By no coincidence, the core of the Presidential Traverse lies exactly between the Appalachian Mountain Club (AMC) huts at Lakes of the Clouds and Madison Springs. By far the most comfortable way to complete the traverse along the Crawford Path, Westside Trail, and Gulfside Trail is to sandwich a glorious day above timberline between overnight visits at each of these huts. If this is your plan, the Valley Way (Hike 84) and Ammonoosuc Ravine trails (Hike 87) offer perfect ingress and egress at either end. The early June to mid-September season for these two high-mountain huts is very limited, compressed even more by questionable weather at the beginning and end of the summer. Early planning and reservations are an absolute must, especially in July and August.

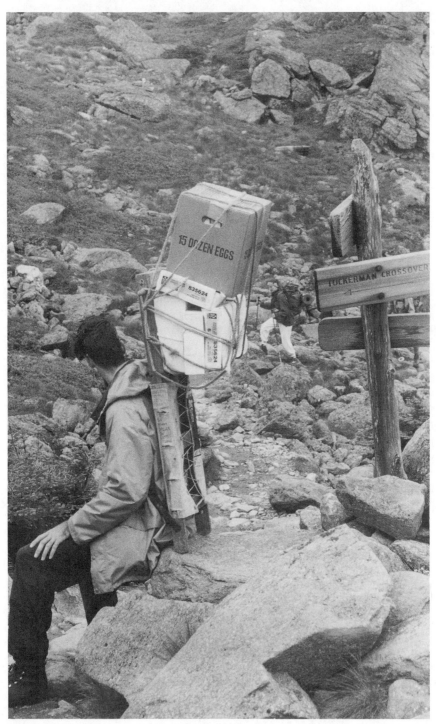

Supplies wait for traffic to clear near Lakes of the Clouds.

Lakes of the Clouds Hut.

For those lucky enough to be able to spend more than a weekend in the mountains, it's easy to prolong a hike by beginning in Crawford Notch and ascending the gradual Crawford Path to the hut at Mizpah Spring (see Hike 60). This extension adds Mounts Clinton (Pierce), Eisenhower, Franklin, and Monroe to the itinerary and makes for almost two full days of marvelous high-altitude hiking.

Forest Protection Areas prohibit summertime camping above timberline, making it difficult to complete the traverse without conforming to the regimen of a hut. If you're prepared to go it alone, though, other options can be found. For a few really self-reliant types, the Randolph Mountain Club (RMC) operates the Log Cabin, the Perch, Crag Camp, and Gray Knob on the northwestern slopes of Mount Madison (see Hike 83). These facilities range from open shelter to basic cabin with stove, are open to the public at modest fees, and provide good overnight alternatives on the northern end of the trip. Backpackers can also find less costly accommodations in separate facilities at Lakes of the Clouds, and truly independent hikers can locate tent platforms at Mizpah Spring, the Perch, and a short way down the Valley Way Trail from the hut at Madison Spring.

87 Mount Washington, Ammonoosuc Ravine Trail

General description:	A long day hike to Mount Washington's alpine zone on a reliable southwestern approach to the Presidential Peaks. This trail is also a direct route to the hut at Lakes of the Clouds.
General location:	About midway between Berlin and North Conway near Bretton Woods and Crawford Notch.
Length:	9.0 miles round trip to the summit.
Difficulty:	Moderate, but shading toward difficult.
Elevation gain:	3,800 feet to the summit of Mount Washington.
Special attractions:	Waterfalls and pools along the Ammonoosuc River, glittering cascades on alpine slopes, and spectacular mountain views.
Maps:	USGS Mount Washington 7.5 x 15.
For more information:	Androscoggin Ranger Station, 300 Glen Road, Gorham, NH 03581-1399, (603) 466-2713.

Key points:

1.0 Ammonoosuc River.
2.1 Gem Pool.
2.35 Spur path to The Gorge.
3.1 Lakes of the Clouds Hut.
3.6 Summit, Mount Monroe via side trail.
4.5 Summit, Mount Washington.

Finding the trailhead: Same as Hike 79, but do not turn left onto Jefferson Notch Road. Continue straight instead on Base Road for 1.0 mile to a large USDA Forest Service parking area on the right. If you arrive at a parking lot for the cog railway, you've driven about half a mile too far.

The hike: The Ammonoosuc Ravine Trail is the most direct western route to the alpine splendor that cloaks Mount Washington's shoulders. Recent groundwork has tamed the ascent of the ravine's headwall, resulting in a trail that is nearly the equivalent of the Valley Way (Hike 84), a moderate

Mount Washington, Ammonoosuc Ravine Trail

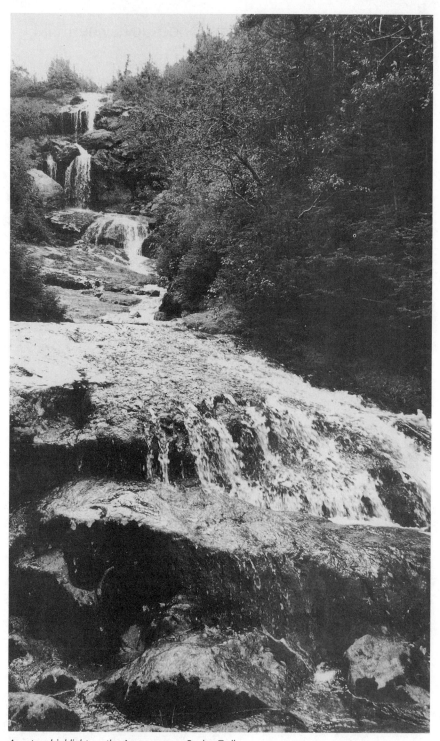

A watery highlight on the Ammonoosuc Ravine Trail.

path and reliable escape route from exposed mountain summits. Ammonoosuc Ravine also embraces one of the most enchanting water-laced trails to be found in all the White Mountains.

Hikers and cog railway customers no longer share parking facilities. An added section of muddy, root-bound trail departs the east end of the new hiker's parking lot and works easily uphill parallel to the railway access road. After about a quarter of a mile, the path descends to cross a mossy brook, and the sound and unmistakable coal-smoke smell of steam engines become constant companions as the path skirts the railway base station. By the end of the first mile, though, the old route converges with the new trail on the banks of the Ammonoosuc River, with rushing waters that mask all sound but the occasional toot of a locomotive whistle.

The trail bears right along the river, following still-active water pipes to their catchment pool about 100 yards upstream. Leaving this last evidence of human ingenuity, the next mile becomes a classic White Mountain walk through birch, fir, ferns, and moss ascending upriver in concert with a distant ridge that defines the northern boundary of the ravine. Directly ahead, watch for glimpses of the concave sweep of the unavoidable headwall, scarred by a vertical ribbon of rock marking the course of a stream. At this point in the journey, this disconcerting sight offers little clue to the delightful surprises awaiting.

Arrival at the base of the steep ascent is announced by delicate Gem Pool, filled by a narrow cascade, and fronted by a small amphitheater of rock where hikers snack and assess the challenge of the effort to come. To the left of the pool, steplike stones pull the trail sharply upward to the first distant views down the ravine. From these initial heights, the distinctive red roof of the Mount Washington Hotel appears in the valley, and the sound of the cog railway is heard again over the crest of the northern ridge.

The trail maintains its steep, steplike qualities for 0.25 mile above the pool, where the slope markedly increases and a short side path leads to The Gorge, a mandatory detour. You really don't want to miss the astounding sight of two parallel streams, separated by a bulbous ridge, crashing down a ravine into a black pool of chiseled rock.

Back on the main trail, the next 0.2 mile is aerobically challenging. Tremendous trail improvements have greatly reduced the difficulty of this route by providing footing that is generally solid and secure, but it helps to be in shape. Nearing the top of the headwall, the trail crosses the first stream that emptied into The Gorge and angles across the slope. The trail climbs pitched slabs along the side of the second stream, and turns sharply right across the flow of the water on flat ledges near the top of the falls. The hardest part is over. You've earned the wonderful views that expand from the edge where the stream plunges over the brink.

Typical of the region, the top of the steep headwall is not the top of the ravine. The upper bowl is scooped much more gently out of the terrain, making the last 0.5 mile a gradual ascent in the breathtaking alpine zone. It's an enchanting, watery walk, with remarkable beauty all around. A foamy, white stream hops down the slope in multiple cascades over mossy rocks.

Everywhere, seepage moistens protruding ledges, nourishing tiny alpine flowers hiding under a dense cover of stunted evergreens. Wide-angle mountain vistas open in all directions until, finally, a chimney rises above the ridge as the Ammonoosuc Ravine Trail ends at the Lakes of the Clouds Hut.

The last 1.4 miles of the Crawford Path link Lakes of the Clouds to the summit of Mount Washington, gaining another 1,200 feet, mostly in the final struggle up the rocky summit cone. Hike it if you must, especially in clear weather, but don't feel compelled, particularly if persistent clouds threaten to obscure the view. A fascinating alpine world is found well below the dominant peak. Visit the shallow lakes just up the wind-scoured ridge, explore the Bigelow Lawn via the Crawford and Davis Paths, find eastern views from the top of Tuckerman Ravine, tour the alpine gardens east of the summit, or gain an unforgettable view from the top of the large hill that stands just west of the hut. Nine hundred feet lower than Mount Washington, and only 300 feet above the hut, what appears from this angle as only a hill is really Mount Monroe, the fourth highest peak in New England, and a great way to end your hike.

88 Mount Washington: Boott Spur and Davis Path

General description:	An ascent of the highest peak in the Northeast from the Pinkham Notch Trailhead. Count on a very full day.
General location:	About midway between North Conway and Berlin.
Length:	Almost 11 miles round trip to the summit or 7.8 miles round trip to the top of Tuckerman Ravine.
Difficulty:	Strenuous.
Elevation gain:	Nearly 4,300 feet to the summit of Mount Washington.
Special attractions:	Crystal Cascade and unsurpassed views of Huntington Ravine, Tuckerman Ravine, the Mount Washington Valley, and the surrounding Presidential Peaks.
Maps:	USGS Mount Washington 7.5 x 15.
For more information:	Androscoggin Ranger Station, 300 Glen Road, Gorham, NH 03581-1399, (603) 466-2713.

Key points:

0.4 Fork, Boott Spur and Tuckerman Ravine Trails near Crystal Cascade.
2.1 Spur to bird's-eye view.
2.4 Split rock.
3.3 Junction, Boott Spur and Davis Path.
3.9 Bigelow Lawn.
4.2 Tuckerman Junction.
5.4 Hermit Lake Shelters.
7.8 Return to trailhead via Tuckerman Ravine.

Mount Washington: Boott Spur and Davis Path

Finding the trailhead: From North Conway, follow New Hampshire Route 16 north through the towns of Glen and Jackson. Park at the Pinkham Notch Visitor Center, 11.7 miles north of the junction of U.S. Highway 302 and Route 16 in Glen. The trailhead is just past the courtyard formed by the two main structures, directly behind the building that holds the Trading Post.

The hike: If there is a spiritual center of New Hampshire hiking, a place that physically embodies the traditions of high peak exploration, in short, a mecca of alpine enthusiasm, then Pinkham Notch is it. Its reputation is well deserved. Trails that radiate from behind these walls immerse the hiker in spectacular scenery on the way to the highest summit in the northeastern United States. Food, clothing, lodging, equipment, advice, maps, outdoor educational programs, current weather forecasts, telephones, hot showers, reservations, shuttle buses, mountain rescue, parking, and a place to rest and meet others are all available here. This recitation should explain why a hike from this trailhead is included in a comprehensive guide to New Hampshire hiking.

By definition, meccas attract lots of people, and Pinkham is no exception. The description of this hike really portrays two routes to high altitude, ascending Boott Spur and descending Tuckerman Ravine. In reality, you can complete the loop as described, or ascend and descend on either route you choose. The Tuckerman Ravine Trail is long, steep, and difficult, and usually busy. The Boott Spur route is longer, also steep and difficult, and rated strenuous due to a particular hand-hold climb of rock crevice that the average hiker may wish to avoid. On the other hand, it's the very dearth of other hikers on the Boott Spur Trail that some find appealing.

Both trails depart Pinkham Notch on a common gravel path, cross a stream on a large wooden bridge, and climb steeply to a beautiful outlook on Crystal Cascade less than half a mile from the trailhead. Within 200 yards of the cascade, where the Tuckerman Ravine Trail turns hard right, the Boott Spur Trail departs to the left, forsaking the broad lane for a narrow woodland path that climbs quickly and soon encounters a risky scramble up a crevice in a 20-foot-high group of boulders.

During the next 1.5 miles, the Boott Spur Trail negotiates a rugged and rocky journey through the woods, rising steeply over a succession of ridges. Views expand from the Wildcat Ridge, to Huntington Ravine, and finally, down a short spur trail on the right, to a bird's-eye view of Tuckerman Ravine.

300

From this perch, look for the summit of Mount Washington, Lion Head on the ravine's north wall, and sometimes a steady stream of hikers passing Hermit Lake Shelter as they approach the headwall of the glacial cirque.

The trail breaks above timberline 0.2 mile beyond the Tuckerman overview and promptly turns left across the face of a slope with commanding views of Pinkham Notch and the Mount Washington Valley. Turning back up the slope near Split Rock, 2.5 miles from the trailhead, the route ascends sharply up a knob, appearing later from above like a giant ship's prow that juts from the mountainside. At this point, the trail ahead looks easy, curling high on a gravelly path just to the right of the prominent peak. But this view lacks perspective and scale. You're still more than 900 vertical, heart-pounding feet below the top of Boott Spur.

The Boott Spur Trail terminates at the Davis Path on the far side of the Boott Spur summit. Turn right (northwest) on an easy trail heavily marked with cairns toward Bigelow Lawn on the plateau above Tuckerman Ravine. This 1.4-mile section of the Davis Path connecting Boott Spur Trail to Crawford Path is a remarkable highlight after hours of difficult climbing. Cairns, ghostly in the frequent fogs, guide the way over rock-strewn lawns and fields of black and green boulders stained by lichen and moss. This is an imaginary answer to the Scottish Highlands, where you can enjoy the views if weather permits, or simply wander about on a web of mist-shrouded trails connecting the nearby Lakes of the Clouds Hut (see Hike 87) and Tuckerman Junction with the Davis Path.

Use discretion if you choose to complete the last 0.6 mile from the Crawford Path junction to the summit of Mount Washington. Having gotten this far, most people make the effort to ascend the additional 700 feet, even though the peak may be covered by impenetrable cloud. Aside from a weather station, there are also tourists, motor vehicles, and a snack bar at the top. On a rare clear day, though, the experience will be worth the climb, when the whole world spreads entirely beneath your gaze.

To return via the Tuckerman Ravine Trail, walk east on either the Southside Trail or the Tuckerman Crossover. Both of these short links leave the Davis Path south of its junction with the Crawford Path and lead to Tuckerman Junction. From this major intersection, it looks as if it's only a matter of following a gravel path over the headwall all the way back to the trailhead.

In fact, the Tuckerman Ravine Trail eases just north of the headwall, which presents a vertical face well below the rim of the ridge. The trail is unrelenting, but dangerous only in those few places where water spills over the edge of dizzying drops. Descending into the ravine, you gain wonderful perspectives on Boott Spur and Lion Head, prominences that grandly top the north and south rims of the cirque.

The Hermit Lake Shelter is primarily a facility for skiers who flock here in the early spring to test their skills by climbing as high as they dare before plunging down the precarious face of Tuckerman's headwall. As hikers approach the shelter in their descent to the floor of the ravine, the trail takes on a groomed look with rock stairs to accommodate skiers and permanent storage lockers for stretchers and avalanche probes. The last 2.4 miles from

the shelter back to the trailhead tracks a wide path designed to accommodate snow machines that haul away the skiers who climbed too high.

Wisely or not, people of all sizes, shapes, ages, and conditioning levels
attempt the Tuckerman Ravine Trail. With proper footwear and adequate
clothing (that many often don't have), most risk nothing more than blisters,
sore muscles, and a day they may regret. If you're not in reasonably good
condition, however, you should understand that the climb of the headwall
to the top of Tuckerman Ravine will be nothing short of grueling.

CARTER RANGE

From Mount Moriah to Wildcat Ridge, the under-appreciated Carter Range forms the eastern wall of Pinkham Notch, an effective barrier discouraging all but pedestrian access to the Wild River Valley hidden on the other side. It takes a real effort to drive into the heart of this region. You'll need to circle well north or south of the Baldface Mountains and weave in and out of Maine just to reach the back door in the vicinity of Evans Notch. Impediments like these are regarded as good news by many hikers, who enjoy this opportunity to ditch the crowds and do some serious backcountry trekking.

The Carter-Moriah, Nineteen Mile Brook, and Wild River Trails triangulate this inviting area. Each hike is enjoyable in its own right as an independent day trip to a marvelous peak, a stunning notch, or a secluded river valley, but backpackers are encouraged to connect these points with long-distance explorations. Huts and shelters dot the Appalachian Trail along the crest of the Carter Range, linked, in turn, by a variety of paths to campsites and other shelters sited near the Wild River. Pack a map and compass when you travel in this region and you'll find no lack of adventurous hiking options.

A perfect view of Presidential Peaks.

89 Imp Trail Loop

General description: A half-day family hike to an exposed cliff with perfect Presidential Range views.

General location: About 4.5 miles south of Gorham, just north of Pinkham Notch.

Length: 6.5 miles for the entire loop; 4.5 miles for the round trip on the northern prong.

Difficulty: Moderate.

Elevation gain: 1,900 feet.

Special attractions: Good family exercise and an absolutely superlative view of the Presidential Peaks.

Maps: USGS Carter Dome quad.

For more information: Androscoggin Ranger Station, 300 Glen Road, Gorham, NH 03581-1399, (603) 466-2713.

Key points:

0.0   North Trailhead.
0.8   Crossing, Imp Brook.
2.2   Imp Face.
3.4   Junction, North Carter Trail.
6.5   South Trailhead.

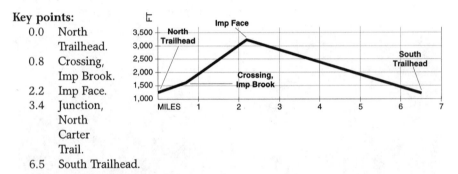

Finding the trailhead: Follow New Hampshire Route 16 north from North Conway to Pinkham Notch. Take note of your mileage as you drive by the Pinkham Notch Visitor Center. Pass Wildcat ski area, the Mount Washington Auto Road, and Camp Dodge before arriving at the southern prong of the Imp Trail loop on the right (east) side of the road, 4.9 miles later. The other prong of the trailhead is 0.2 mile farther north. Park well off the highway at either location.

The hike: Tired of the same old hikes? Need something to lift your spirits? The Imp Trail loop may be just what the doctor ordered. The view of the Presidential Peaks at the midpoint of this circuit is guaranteed to rekindle the ardor of any hiking enthusiast. This one is really special!

The prongs of this loop meet Route 16 about two-tenths of a mile apart, and both are a little more difficult than most hikers probably expect. The southern prong is longer, less scenic, and more gradual. Some might even call it tedious. I prefer the northern route that sandwiches good entertainment between a few sharp uphill pitches.

The northern leg climbs directly away from the highway to immediately overlook Imp Brook. The first third of the ascent flows along under tall hemlocks high on a bank above the stream before easing down to cross a

Imp Trail Loop

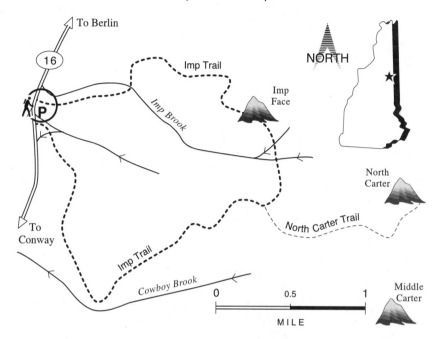

tributary near a pool and beautiful cascade. In 50 more yards, the trail crosses Imp Brook and departs on a long, looping climb that avoids the steepest grades on the lower part of the hill.

As the sounds of the brook fade, there's a promise of views through the treetops at your back, then a restful stroll on a mostly flat, hardwood-covered ridge. Linger here awhile with the trillium and trout lily, and make the most of this chance to catch your breath. Soon enough, the trail begins another curling ascent and pauses yet again for a final respite with views north toward Gorham and the summit of Mount Surprise.

The last push crosses a small brook at the bottom of stone stairs overlooking a rough ravine. The steepest pitch comes early in the final stretch of this assault, as the trail swings back to the right and vigorously climbs to your unmistakable goal.

No doubt other hikers will be nestled among boulders on the edge of this incredible cliff, with absolutely the world's most idyllic view of the northern Presidential Peaks. One after another, from south to north, and top to valley bottom, the highest summits in the Northeast stand majestically to the fore. Here are Mounts Washington, Clay, Jefferson, Adams, and Madison, with views straight up the gut of the Great Gulf and all the way through Pinkham Notch on the floor of the Mount Washington Valley. Perfect!

Those tired of exploration can return the way they came. I was intrigued by the boisterous cascade of Imp Brook billowing down from North Carter Mountain a little farther down the trail. To descend the south prong, continue beyond the bare cliffs and drop quickly to an overlook of Imp Brook

Ravine and a private glimpse of Boott Spur that still appears on the right. The trail maintains a fairly even keel as it circles below the headwall rim and meets the North Carter Trail 1.2 miles from the Carter-Moriah Trail (see Hike 90) and 3.1 miles from Route 16. From this junction it's all downhill with scenic glances directly at Mount Washington. Turn right (north) at the highway. Your car is just around the corner.

90   Carter-Moriah Trail

General description: A rugged day hike to the summit of Mount Moriah. For backpackers, a northern link to Wild River and the Carter Range.

General location: About 6 miles south of Berlin, near the town of Gorham.

Length: 9.0 miles round trip.

Difficulty: Pushing the outer limits of moderate.

Elevation gain: 3,200 feet.

Special attractions: Impressive views of the Carter Range, the Presidential Peaks across Pinkham Notch, and the Androscoggin River.

Maps: USGS Berlin and Carter Dome quads.

For more information: Androscoggin Ranger Station, 300 Glen Road, Gorham, NH 03581-1399, (603) 466-2713.

Key points:

0.1   Top of steep bluff.
2.0   Summit, Mount Surprise.
2.2   Viewpoint ledges.
4.5   Summit, Mount Moriah.

Finding the trailhead: Follow New Hampshire Route 16 north to its junction with U.S. Highway 2 in Gorham. Turn right (east) onto US 2, travel 0.5 mile across a river and a railroad track, and turn right again (southwest) onto Bangor Road. This road deadends in a residential area in another 0.5 mile. Parking is provided on the left within sight of a sign that marks the trailhead.

The hike: While driving through photogenic Pinkham Notch, Mount Washington rivets travelers' attention with stunning landscapes of barren elevations and stark ravines. Distracted by this famous view to the west, most people barely notice the Carter Range that ruggedly carries the Appalachian Trail on the opposite side of the road. So near yet so far from the heavily traveled Presidential Peaks, the Carter Range–Wild River area appeals to long-distance hikers and day-trippers who are looking for a path less traveled.

Carter-Moriah Trail

To Maine

Town of Gorham

2

16

Peabody River

NORTH

Pea Brook

Carter-Moriah Trail

To Pinkham Notch

Mount Surprise

Stoney Brook

Kenduskeag Trail

Mount Moriah

0   0.5   1

MILE

Moriah Brook Trail

Imp Shelter

To Carter Notch

To Wild River

The Carter-Moriah Trail can certainly be enjoyed as a day hike but may also serve as northern access to the large backcountry area wedged between Route 16 and the Maine border. Spanning the territory from Mount Moriah to the trailheads of Hikes 91 and 93 are miles of connecting paths with huts, shelters, and tent sites scattered along the Wild River and Appalachian Trail. For backpackers equipped with a good map and a sense of adventure, this hike to the top of Mount Moriah can literally be just the beginning.

In the first 70 yards, the trail quickly climbs a steep bluff to escape a residential neighborhood near the trailhead. Over the next 2 miles, the route assumes a more gradual course through woods of birch and maple, meanders sideways up a beech-covered slope, and ascends ledges ringed in blueberries. The low prominence of Mount Surprise unexpectedly ushers in initial views of the majestic summit of Mount Washington across the valley of the Peabody River.

The trail descends 0.1 mile down the back side of Mount Surprise and climbs vigorously up steeper slabs that open even more extensive vistas north and west to Mount Washington and the town of Gorham. From these exposed ledges, views include part of the watershed of the Peabody River's West Branch as it snakes beneath the feet of Mounts Madison, Adams, and Jefferson, curls out from behind Chandler Ridge, and sinuously emerges from the glacial cirque known as the Great Gulf.

Technically, the second half of the hike follows the top of a ridge that extends northwest from Mount Moriah's peak. Maps show elevation contours dropping away to either side, but hikers have little chance to appreciate this topography as they struggle along the trail. The route clambers over short, steep rocks, dips into birch-filled glades, crosses wet areas, bobs and weaves, bounces up and down, and sways from side to side on an erratic scramble through the woods. Finally, on a narrow, overgrown, rocky stretch, the trail approaches a hump that must be the summit. It's not. Before long, a bare rock on top of a small knoll offers a tantalizing glimpse of the softly rounded peak ahead. It's really closer than it looks, but you won't reach your goal until you enter a region of stunted evergreens and find the spur path that detours 50 yards to the top.

If you meet the junction with the Kenduskeag Trail, you've gone a few yards too far and begun the next 2-mile leg of the Carter-Moriah Trail, which leads to a shelter near the summit of Imp Mountain. Backpackers can continue along the crest of the Carter Range all the way to Carter Dome (Hike 91), or choose the option of turning south on the Moriah Brook Trail for connections to Wild River (Hike 93).

Day-trippers will find their turnaround point on Moriah's hard-won peak, a small, bouldered summit whose impressive views are a great ending to a long day. The town of Gorham and city of Berlin lie to the north with the Androscoggin River turning boldly east into the sprawling space of Maine. To the southwest, clouds gathering on the Presidential Peaks merely serve as backdrops for the ragged crests of the Carter and Wildcat Mountains, formidable barriers that stand in the foreground, protecting these unspoiled acres from the clamor of Pinkham Notch.

91 Nineteen Mile Brook Trail

General description:	A full day's hike to Carter Dome, Mount Hight, and beguiling Carter Notch.
General location:	About 11 miles south of Berlin, near the north end of Pinkham Notch.
Length:	10.0 miles round trip.
Difficulty:	Moderate..
Elevation gain:	3,300 feet.
Special attractions:	Presidential views from the top of Mount Hight, and the unique environs of Carter Notch.
Maps:	USGS Carter Dome quad.
For more information:	Androscoggin Ranger Station, 300 Glen Road, Gorham, NH 03581-1399, (603) 466-2713.

Key points:

1.0	Dam and bench.
1.8	Left turn onto Carter Dome Trail.
3.7	Zeta Pass.
4.9	Summit, Carter Dome.
6.4	Hut and ponds in Carter Notch.
6.5	Junction, Wildcat Ridge Trail.
10.0	Return to trailhead.

Finding the trailhead: Follow New Hampshire Route 16 north through Pinkham Notch. The trailhead parking area is on the right (east) side of the highway exactly 1.0 mile north of the entrance to the Mount Washington auto road.

The hike: If you envision a "notch" as a narrow pass between chiseled mountains, with overhanging cliffs and stark boulders reflecting in pools near an old stone hut, then Carter is the notch for you. The highly versatile Nineteen Mile Brook Trail leads to overnight stays in Carter Notch, facilitates day trips to nearby mountains, and connects to cross-country jaunts along Carter Ridge and the valley of the scenic Wild River. The hike described here is a one-day loop that hits the highlights of the area, panoramic views from Mount Hight, and the beauty of the rugged notch.

Nineteen Mile Brook Trail

Within 50 yards of its rocky start, Nineteen Mile Brook becomes a well-mannered trail, groomed and pitched to give cross-country skiers a sensible glide as they return from visits to the hut. To the right, an especially charming stream is chock-full of glacial erratics that encourage endless varieties of small pools and tiny cascades. About a mile up the V-shaped valley the trail passes a small dam and spectator bench before the path narrows and the footing becomes less secure.

The path to Carter Dome diverges left 1.8 miles from Route 16, and 2 miles from the Carter Notch Hut farther up the trail. The section of trail between Carter Notch and Carter Dome is very vertical indeed. As a result, hikers intent upon summit views usually avoid this difficult climb by ascending the 2.9-mile alternate route that swings east through Zeta Pass. To begin the more gradual loop, turn left on the Carter Dome Trail and follow it along a small brook as it rises out of the valley. The path crosses the brook twice, passing campsites along the way, before it weaves the final mile to the top of the ridge with the rounded summits of Mount Hight and Carter Dome plainly visible on the way.

Trail mileage is usually a close estimation, but a pair of signs at Zeta Pass that stand 20 feet apart differ by 0.3 mile in stated distance to the same destination. Even though two trails leave the pass on a common route, the signs are actually correct. The Carter-Moriah Trail soon angles left and climbs

Carter Lake in rugged Carter Notch.

to the summit of Mount Hight, tacking on the extra distance required to achieve good views of the Presidential Range. The Carter Dome Trail only skirts the flanks of the mountain, and looks out toward the Peabody River before both routes rejoin in the shallow col on the far side of Mount Hight. After the Black Angel Trail departs to descend to the Wild River (Hike 93), the next 0.4 mile on the two Carter trails may seem anti-climactic as they amiably roll through stunted fir trees to Carter Dome's rounded peak. Views are a bit restricted, but a stroll on the spreading summit should yield entertaining results.

The Carter Dome Trail ends at the summit of Carter Dome. Take the Carter-Moriah Trail 1.5 miles down the mountain to arrive at the Carter Notch Hut. About two-thirds of the way to the bottom, a 30-yard spur climbs to a fantastic overlook of the notch. Looking down on the roof of the hut and the sheer cliffs across the way, hikers can get an inkling of how precipitous the rest of this trail will be. Go slowly and pick your footsteps carefully, descending from rock to rock.

The Carter-Moriah Trail ends 0.1 mile north of the hut at the junction with the Nineteen Mile Brook Trail on the shore of the larger Carter Lake. Whether you plan to spend the night or not, Carter Notch is a marvelous place to snoop around rocky shores, gasp at magnificent cliffs, and be thankful that you weren't around when those house-sized hunks of granite crashed to the valley floor. A steep, low ridge traps the Carter Lakes in the notch and separates them from the trailhead. When it's time to leave, climb to the high point north of the lakes where the Wildcat Ridge Trail exits to circle above the Wildcat Cliffs. From this junction, the Nineteen Mile Brook Trail moderately descends for about half a mile before easing into a comfortable 3-mile ramble back to your car.

92 Baldface Circle Trail

General description:	A one-day hike to three summits arrayed on a rugged ridge.
General location:	Near the Maine border, about halfway between Berlin and North Conway.
Length:	9.8 miles.
Difficulty:	Difficult.
Elevation gain:	3,060 feet.
Special attractions:	Miles of trail above tree line and a circle of mountain views.
Maps:	USGS Chatham and Wild River quads.
For more information:	Evans Notch Visitor Center, 18 Mayville Road, Bethel, ME 04217-4400, (207) 824-2134.

Baldface Circle Trail

North Baldface Mountain

South Baldface Mountain

Eagle Crag

Baldface Circle Trail

Bicknell Ridge Trail

Eagle Cascade Link

Baldface Circle Trail

Charles Brook

Shelter

NORTH

MILE

0   0.5   1

113

P

To Fryeburg Maine

To Evans Notch

Key points:

- 0.7   Circle Junction.
- 0.9   Brook crossing.
- 2.5   Baldface Shelter.
- 2.6   Face of giant steps.
- 3.7   Summit, South Baldface.
- 4.5   Col.
- 4.9   Summit, North Baldface.
- 5.6   Junction, Bicknell Ridge Trail.
- 6.1   Eagle Crag.
- 9.1   Return to Circle Junction.

Finding the trailhead: Beginning just south of Conway, drive east on New Hampshire Route 113 as it joins U.S. Highway 302 and approaches Fryeburg, Maine. On the outskirts of Fryeburg, turn left (north) on Route 113 and follow its various twists and turns through farmland intervale as it weaves back and forth across the Maine/New Hampshire border and rises into the foothills of North Chatham, New Hampshire. A Forest Service parking lot for the Baldface Circle Trail is on the right (east) side of Route 113, 14.5 miles north of US 302 and 0.15 mile north of the access road to the AMC Cold Water Campground.

The hike: Good things come in small packages, and challenging alpine adventures can be found below 4,000 feet. Cherished by knowledgeable New Hampshire hikers but ignored by baggers of peaks, the three summits on Baldface Ridge yield a classic White Mountain climb. Arrayed in a tight semicircle that stretches above treeline for nearly three miles, the Eagle Crag, North Baldface, and South Baldface summits provide alpine flowers, stunning views, and a short climb on a face of rock guaranteed to give you a chill in the middle of a summer day.

The access path to the circular trail that traverses these alpine peaks skitters up an embankment on the west side of Route 113 about 80 yards north of the parking lot. The rocky but nearly level path curls through an immature forest for 0.7 mile before arriving at Circle Junction where a spur path to Emerald Pool detours to the right. After resting on the banks of this mountain stream, backtrack to Circle Junction and resume your hike by turning left on the Baldface Circle Trail, a route that returns to Circle Junction 8.4 miles later on the opposite end of the looping trail that lies straight ahead.

Easy hiking prevails for another 0.2 mile as the Baldface Circle Trail begins its circumnavigation. Hopping a small brook, the trail curls slightly south before passing the Slippery Brook Trail 1.6 miles from Baldface Shelter. Just beyond this junction, the yellow-blazed Baldface Circle Trail jumps to the top of a ridge where it turns right and flattens again on the traces of an old woods road. A scenic spur to Chandler Gorge wanders off to the left and returns farther up the slope, as the main trail begins a long, steady ascent that ends at the Baldface Shelter, a crude Adirondack hut tucked into a small clearing.

Leaving a perfect staging area for forays onto the ridge, the trail slips behind the Baldface Shelter and angles across the face of a granite ledge. After ducking into the woods, the trail then suddenly pops onto the bottom of a second slope that reveals a startling scene. Beyond a steep 70-yard pitch of sharply angled granite, tiers of stratified outcrop rock rise to an upper ridge, forming a cliff of giant steps. Yellow blazes mark a route up this disconcerting face, which is hazardous in wet weather but challenging even on sunny days when water seeping between rocks makes your footing somewhat precarious. Search for tiny ridges or fissures in a stony surface to complete a series of handhold scrambles up these chest-high pieces of rock.

Once you've conquered the giant steps, you're on top of a mountain shoulder where cairns mark a well-defined trail that ascends at a reasonable pace to the summit that looms ahead. Topping an intervening knoll on the climb to the first peak, the great semicircle of this elevated route comes clearly into view: the 0.5-mile climb up the windswept slopes of South Baldface mountain; the jagged ridgetop crossing to the North Baldface peak; the line of the crest that quickly descends to the ledges of Eagle Crag; and the gradual return that slowly flows into a wooded valley.

Enjoy the next 3.0 miles of exquisite mountain hiking. From the top of South Baldface, identify views of Mountain Pond and the Doublehead peaks to the south, Mount Washington to the west, and the open door of Evans Notch, a gap to the northeast. Drop into a deep col, climb the steep and rugged knobs that lead to the next summit, and bask in the 360-degree views of North Baldface Mountain. Savor a unique panorama that includes the long eastern flank of the Moriah/Carter Range and trails that wander for endless miles in the beautiful Wild River Valley (see Hike 93).

Go easy on the steep descent as you leave North Baldface Mountain. This rapid plunge isn't as tough as the climb up Baldface Ridge, but a large number of slick rocks and impossibly large steps may force some hikers to sit and scoot to accomplish the long drops. Dipping in and out of the woods after leaving the summit cone, the Baldface Circle Trail struggles through a series of ups and downs as it approaches Eagle Crag, where peregrine falcons (not eagles) may be cruising on the thermals.

On the final long, open crest that slopes to Eagle Crag, hikers face a major decision. Most turn right about half a mile before reaching the third summit for a rapid descent on the Bicknell Ridge Trail that reconnects with the Baldface Circle Trail 0.7 mile from Circle Junction. Purists who want to finish what they've begun should continue on the Baldface Circle Trail for

Leaving a circle of views on North Baldface Mountain.

another 0.3 mile to a high-altitude crossroads at the Eagle Link and Meader Trail junction. To visit Eagle Crag, walk 0.2 mile north on the Meader Trail to the ledge that's in plain sight before backtracking to the crossroad and turning east for your descent.

The Baldface Circle Trail is undeniably steep as it drops down from Eagle Crag. Pick your steps carefully over boulders and scattered rocks made slick by runoff water. The challenging part ends, though, as quickly as it begins as the trail tapers downhill and follows a small brook that it crosses and re-crosses twice. After the Eagle Cascade Trail merges from the right, a wet and muddy path traverses nearly level ground and tiptoes over dry stones to cross a mid-sized stream. The Bicknell Ridge Trail also reappears on the right as you near the end of the circle. Follow the joined paths across another stream that tumbles beside the trail until both paths turn south for a final brook crossing just 0.1 mile from Circle Junction.

93 Wild River

General description:	A triangular day hike or short backpack into the Blue Brook and Wild River Valleys.
General location:	Near the Maine border, about 8 miles southeast of Gorham.
Length:	7.75 miles.
Difficulty:	Moderate.
Elevation gain:	1,100 feet.
Special attractions:	The Wild River, a view from the Basin's rim, and a plunging stream with pretty cascades in the woodsy Blue Brook Valley.
Maps:	USGS Wild River quad.
For more information:	Evans Notch Ranger Station, 18 Mayville Road, Bethel, ME 04217-4400 (207) 824-2134.

Key points:

- 0.4   Junction, Moriah Brook Trail.
- 2.7   Spider Bridge.
- 4.0   Top of ridge.
- 5.0   Blue Brook Shelter.
- 5.5   Rim Junction.
- 5.6   View from basin rim.
- 7.75 Return to trailhead.

Finding the trailhead: You can't get there from here! First, you've got to go to Maine.

Follow New Hampshire Route 16 north to the intersection with U.S. Highway 2 in Gorham. Turn right (east) and drive 11 miles through the Androscoggin River Valley past Shelburne, New Hampshire, to the town of Gilead, Maine. You won't actually see Gilead, but the sign is just before the highway bridge that crosses the Wild River. On the far side of the bridge, turn right onto Route 113 and follow the river south 3 miles to a fork at a gravel road. Turn right onto the gravel road (Forest Road 12) and stay with the river 5.5 miles to a hiker's parking lot at the Wild River Campground. You're back in New Hampshire and a few yards from the trailhead.

The hike: This entry-level hike introduces the territory of the Wild River, an out-of-the-way region of sculptured valleys and random foothills east of Pinkham Notch, just west of the Maine border. Attaining elevations of only 2,300 feet, this low-level ramble often avoids the late spring snows that

Wild River

To ME 113

FR 12

NORTH

Wild River
Campground

P

To
Mount
Moriah

Moriah Brook Trail

Basin Trail

Wild River

Wild River Trail

0   0.5   1

MILE

Rim
Junction

The
Basin

Spider
Bridge

Black Angel Trail

Blue Brook

Blue Brook
Shelter

Ragged
Jacket

To Spruce
Brook Shelter

Cedar Brook

Mount
Meader

blanket nearby peaks and sports instead early blooming flowers that carpet the forest floor. A simple, triangular walk upstream, across a hilly divide, and back to the trailhead beside the intricacies of Blue Brook, this delightful five-hour outing can be enjoyed as a moderate day trip or as a superb backpack for families with older children. Veteran hikers can move on to more distant adventures in the far reaches of the Wild River watershed, all the way to the alluring summits of the lofty Carter Range.

Beginning on the opposite side of a small stream across the access road, the Wild River Trail loops behind the Wild River Campground on a duff-covered riverbank cloaked with fir trees, birch, and trillium. The path joins a gravel forest road for the longest leg of the journey, running straight up an easy grade near sights and sounds of whitewater that come and go on the right. Within 0.4 mile, the trail passes the intersection with Moriah Brook Trail, connecting to Hike 90. After a mile or so, the road shrinks to a narrower path as it briefly converges with the banks of the Wild River. Deer and moose leave tracks in the upper portions of this first leg, where a sharply defined valley slowly forces the route ever closer to the stream. Eventually, a gradual flattening of the terrain signals the approach to Spider Bridge, a major trail junction 2.7 miles from the campground.

Illogically, the next leg of the triangle continues straight ahead on the Black Angel Trail where the Wild River Trail departs to the right. (Long-distance hikers can cross Spider Bridge on the Wild River Trail and go 0.9 mile to the Spruce Brook Shelter, 4.3 miles to the Ketchum Pond Shelter, and 7 miles through Perkins Notch to connections with Hike 91.) The course of this shorter hike begins to make more sense as the Black Angel Trail soon turns east, ascending away from the river, on a 2.3-mile walk to Blue Brook Shelter on the far side of the divide. For a time, the long, gradual rise travels a well-disguised logging road high above the deep cut of Cedar Brook among wildflowers and spacious hardwoods. On the opposite side of the hill, a sharp descent opens good views of the Blue Brook Valley and the top of the Basin's rim.

The well-maintained Blue Brook Shelter is the perfect destination for a great family overnight, hunkered at a convergence of trails within yards of a brook and close to surrounding hills. A fire ring and benches are aligned along the open side, just a few steps from signs that point down a cut-off link back to the Wild River Campground. Take this shortcut trail if you're in a hurry when it's time to leave, but you'll miss a lot of fun. For a highlight of the hike, continue instead on the Black Angel Trail in the direction of Cold River Campground on an easy 0.5-mile climb to the intersection known as Rim Junction. From here a 0.1-mile detour on the Basin Rim Trail, heading in the direction of Mount Royce, leads to a fantastic viewpoint at the top of a precarious cliff. The meaning of the name, Basin Rim, will come in a revelatory burst, as you scan down and out from a curve of precipitous slopes to Basin Pond, Horseshoe Pond, and portions of Kezar Lake, miles away and far below in the gentle hills of Maine.

To complete the triangle, return to Rim Junction and branch onto the Basin Trail at signs that point 2.2 miles back to the Wild River Campground. A rocky descent soon reacquaints hikers with the pleasures of Blue Brook. A lopsided stretch of this intriguing stream tumbles along a seam on the low side of a canted ledge, while peaceful pools invite a pause. The final Blue Brook moment comes just below a steplike cascade, where the trail crosses the stream to conclude the hike with a 0.7-mile damp-woods amble back to the trailhead.

PILOT RANGE

Combine the timberland of the North Country with the peaks of the Presidentials, and the mixture may resemble the northern outpost of the White Mountain National Forest that hovers west of the city of Berlin. Separated from the rest of the federal preserve by the Jefferson Highlands and U.S. Highway 2, this transition zone of moderate peaks and hidden ponds is attuned to a human scale. The pared-down summits and manageable distances of the Pilot and Pliny Ranges make for delightful hiking in an unsung portion of the state.

It takes an unusual tourist to forgo the Presidential Peaks and drive another hour north to access this unheralded country. If you find anyone on these trails, it's likely to be a local hiker, or someone long familiar with the beauty of these parts. Trails to the region's two 4,000-foot summits are notable exceptions. Peak baggers frequently climb Mount Cabot and Mount Waumbeck, the highest summits in their respective ranges. Hikers with less lofty interests should be grateful to these popular mountains for distracting the bulk of visitors from some of the best backpacking territory in the state. Spend a few days on the Kilkenny Ridge Trail near Rogers Ledge and Unknown Pond, and you'll rapidly discover the wild heart of this wonderful region.

94 Rogers Ledge and Unknown Pond

General description:	A perfect weekend backpack in the shadow of the Pilot Range.
General location:	About 8 miles west of the city of Berlin.
Length:	13.0 miles, including the detour to Rogers Ledge.
Difficulty:	Moderate.
Elevation gain:	1,800 feet.
Special attractions:	White Mountain views from Rogers Ledge, the beauty of Unknown Pond, and miles of solitude.
Maps:	USGS Stark and West Milan quads; USGS Pliny Range 7.5 x 15.
For more information:	Androscoggin Ranger Station, 300 Glen Road, Gorham, NH 03581-1399, (603) 466-2713.

Key points:

0.2	Right turn near flagpole.
4.2	Junction, Mill Brook Trail and Kilkenny Ridge Trail.
4.3	Campsite spur in direction of Rogers Ledge.
4.8	Rogers Ledge via detour.
4.7	Kilback Pond.
5.9	Top of ridge.

Rogers Ledge and Unknown Pond

6.3 Unknown Pond.
9.1 Views of Cabot, Terrace, and Weeks.
9.6 York Pond Road.

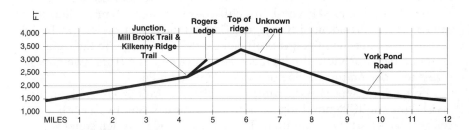

Finding the trailhead: Follow New Hampshire Route 16 north all the way to Berlin. In the middle of town, turn left onto Route 110 as it curves in front of the Berlin City Bank. You're on the right track if you soon pass the police station, but stay alert for small highway and truck route signs that mark the next left turn. A little more than 7 miles from downtown Berlin on Route 110, look for a large sign for the Berlin Fish Hatchery on the left. Paved York Pond Road leads 4.9 miles to the fish hatchery gate, which is closed after 4 P.M. until 8 A.M. the next day. To avoid hassles, I park in the area provided just outside the gate.

The hike: When people hear you're writing a hiking guide, they'll often ask for inside information. Just a tip about some sylvan spot more wild than a wilderness area, with inspiring views but no difficult climbs, a pristine place where they can hike and backpack among lots of wildlife and very few other humans. I've been tempted to laugh, slap them on the back and say, "Come on! Those days are gone," but someone told me about such a hike, and I'm bound to pass it along. We just hope you don't all go there.

Strong hikers can complete this trek within a single day, but with campsites located near both Rogers Ledge and Unknown Pond, this route is custom-made to be savored over a leisurely weekend. From the gate, proceed along York Pond Road into the heart of the hatchery grounds, past a pond and what appear to be several greenhouses used for growing fish. At a paved intersection near a flagpole, turn right just before a small bridge and head toward a large stone building a couple hundred yards up the road. Trail signs direct you to the left of the building, along a dirt driveway, and subsequently onto the Mill Brook Trail. The trail enters the woods just beyond a small pump house and before a tiny dam.

Lilies and blueberries pave the way through hardwood forest on an uphill track that maintains a respectful distance from a prototypical babbling brook. The trail becomes damp in a marshy clearing where it traces a smaller stream and shows by its character that it receives minimal use, except perhaps by moose. Eventually, the path departs the water and climbs up and over a bank. The trail bounces along for at least another mile, flattening in a gorgeous white-birch forest before descending easily through moose marshes to meet Kilkenny Ridge.

One of the major attractions of this hike requires a short detour. From the trail junction on Kilkenny Ridge, turn right (northeast) on the Kilkenny Ridge Trail, which passes a spur to an established campsite in less than 0.1 mile. It soon begins a steady 0.6-mile ascent to the top of Rogers Ledge. The last yards of this route briskly climb to a cliff-edge outlook with marvelous panoramas of the Presidential Range, the Carter Range, and the city of Berlin just above and beyond the low profile of docile Deer Ridge. To the right and closer at hand, the view also includes The Bulge and The Horn, two notable peaks that rise on the far side of hidden Unknown Pond.

Retrace your steps past the campsite back to the Mill Brook Trail junction and follow the Kilkenny Ridge Trail as it continues southwest with a real sense of backcountry exploration. This footpath leads through stony woods, buzzing marshes, and over mossy brooks in the most tantalizing part of the hike. Kilback Pond, part lake, part marsh, is one of those wonderfully quiet

Remote Unknown Pond.

settings that naturalists dream about, where you can take the time to squish off the trail, view wildlife, or scan the top of the distant ridge.

Beyond Kilback Pond, the Kilkenny Ridge Trail rises through airy glades of birch, crests the ridge, and drops down 0.4 mile to Unknown Pond. Several well-used sites confirm that this wild body of water is an idyllic camping spot. Those with sufficient time will find that treks on local paths subject the nearby summits to the investigation they deserve.

The Unknown Pond Trail diverges just yards above the shore. Turn left (southeast) for a path that skirts the end of the pond and returns 3.3 miles to York Pond Road. This rapid descent from the ridgetop pond catches glimpses of Presidential Peaks before converging with Unknown Pond Brook. After assuming the easy course of a logging grade, the trail spans the brook, a large tributary, and finally the brook again in a crossing that could easily drench your feet. There are views of Mounts Cabot, Terrace, and Weeks from a grassy clearing about half a mile before the trail rejoins a dirt extension of York Pond Road. Turn left (east) for an entertaining, 2-mile woodland walk that curls around York Pond and returns to the hatchery gate.

95 Mount Starr King/ Mount Waumbeck

General description: A comfortable day hike to a summit with views of the Jefferson Highlands and northern Presidential Peaks.

General location: About 18 miles west of Gorham, near the village of Jefferson.

Length: 6.4 miles round trip.

Difficulty: Moderate.

Elevation gain: 2,500 feet.

Special attractions: Mountain and valley views, with abundant wildflowers and colorful foliage in season.

Maps: USGS Pliny Range 7.5 x 15.

For more information: Androscoggin Ranger Station, 300 Glen Road, Gorham, NH 03581-1399, (603) 466-2713.

Key points:

  0.5 Right turn after springhouse.
  2.1 Spring by side of trail.
  2.5 Summit, Mount Starr King.
  3.2 Summit, Mount Waumbeck.

Finding the trailhead: From the intersection of U.S. Highways 3 and 302 at the traffic lights in Twin Mountain, follow US 3 for 2 miles north and turn right onto Route 115. This highway leads 9.5 miles farther north where it ends at US 2. Turn left (west) on US 2 for 3.6 miles and look for a gravel road marked with a large sign for the Starr King Trail, which enters on the right (north) directly across from the Waumbeck Resort golf course. Keep left at any forks in this gravel road, and look for the parking area and trailhead within 0.3 mile. (From the opposite direction, the turn off of US 2 is about two-tenths of a mile east of the junction with Route 115A in the center of Jefferson village.)

The hike: Compelling views of the Jefferson Highlands, broad pastures flanking the Israel River, and the distant Mount Washington Range still earn Mount Starr King too little respect, passed over by peak baggers in favor of Mount Waumbeck's slightly greater height. A likely candidate for an early-season wildflower walk or dazzling fall-foliage hike, the popular Starr King Trail curls to both summits of these Pliny Range neighbors, tracking an especially forgiving route to a 4,000-foot White Mountain peak.

    The trail departs on an overgrown road that is closed to vehicles beyond the parking area, swings left into the woods after 100 yards, and quickly finds the old grade of a second logging road several paces farther northwest. The straightforward walk saunters along a sun-dappled forest floor, gradually rising up the side hill of Mount Starr King's southwestern slope. A

324

Mount Starr King/Mount Waumbeck

stream keeps the trail company for a time as it passes the circled stones of an old springhouse. But the sounds of water fade after 0.5 mile where the trail turns sharply right, and resumes its moderate climb in closer contact with the underbrush. About two-thirds of the way to the top, look for blowdowns that open partial views over a broad ravine separating you from the crescent formed by Starr King's lesser peaks.

This trail should lurch sharply uphill, but it never really does, even after it passes a refreshing spring 0.4 mile before Starr King's summit. Disappointment may be your initial reaction upon reaching the very top and discovering that the survey medallion at the peak is rimmed by bothersome trees. Be patient! Views emerge only a few steps ahead on top of a slanting ledge and at another, larger site where a fireplace ruin recalls an earlier day. From either location you'll find vistas of the fertile valley that separates the Pliny Range from the hazy mass of Presidential Peaks that dominate the southern view.

It's a 0.7-mile walk from Mount Starr King to Mount Waumbeck on a trail that dips easily into a col and gains another 100 feet as it ascends the other side. Hike it for pleasure, to say that you've been there, or to add to your list a 4,000-foot mountain that barely attains the height. Don't hike it for the limited view.

The North Country

Physical features may delineate the narrow end of northern New Hampshire, but they fail to depict a territory best defined by a state of mind. People in the North Country speak, only partially in jest, about living "north of the notch" and refer to trips below the White Mountains like journeys to a foreign clime. Their lighthearted language strikes very close to the truth.

The territory north of White Mountain National Forest and south of the Canadian border remains a region of logging, hunting, and fishing, with an economy and orientation quite separate from the rest of the state. Far removed from megalopolis, the fortunes of this woodland area rise and fall with the health of the paper mills and the seasonal influx of tourists.

Few roads penetrate these vast boreal forests, but superb recreation is found along the Androscoggin and Connecticut Rivers, and all around the wilderness lakes that top their watersheds. In spite of the North Country's size, trails are few in number, yet the serenity of the Fourth Connecticut Lake or the stark beauty of Dixville Notch are readily accessible to hikers who travel in the region. At Scotland Brook and Philips Brook, you'll find quiet walks along with slices of history, while the view from the top of Sugarloaf Mountain quickly dispels the notion that the North Country doesn't generously share in New Hampshire's alpine endowment.

96 Table Rock, Dixville Notch

General description:	A two-hour round trip to a stunning perch overlooking Dixville Notch.
General location:	About 45 highway miles north of Berlin in the heart of the North Country.
Length:	2.0 miles round trip.
Difficulty:	Moderate.
Elevation gain:	800 feet.
Special attractions:	Without question the scariest, most spectacular overlook of any New Hampshire notch.
Maps:	USGS Dixville Notch quad; also trail guide published by The Balsams Grand Resort Hotel.
For more information:	The Balsams, Dixville Notch, NH 03576, (603) 255-3400.

Key points:

    0.9   Top of ridge.
    1.0   Table Rock.

Finding the trailhead: The Table Rock Trailhead is on the south side of New

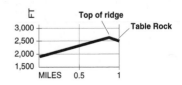

Table Rock, Dixville Notch

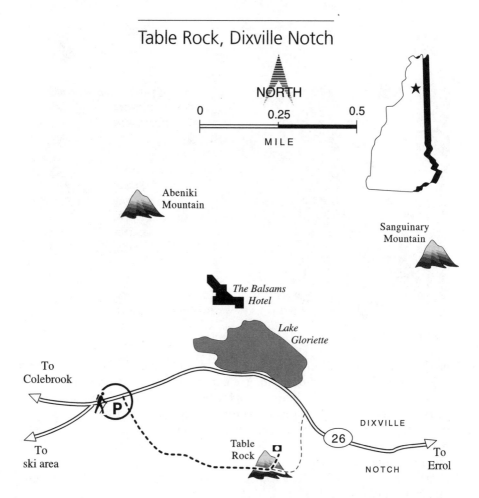

Hampshire Route 26 at the western end of Dixville Notch. A broad, grassy area immediately off the highway 0.15 mile east of the entrance to The Balsams Wilderness Ski Area will accommodate parking. Look for directions to Table Rock or a sign with the letter D.

The hike: Jagged, vertical, narrow, and compact, the distinctive appeal of Dixville Notch is unlikely to be confused with the expansive beauty of any other New Hampshire mountain pass. In this locale, the highway is barely able to squeeze up and through the curving 2-mile gap between Gloriette and Sanguinary Mountains. Formed by bare, vertical facets of jutting, stratified rock, the south wall of the notch in particular is far removed from typical New England scenery. Leading to the tip of one of the chiseled promontories that tower over the highway, this outing very seriously is not for those with children in tow, or anyone squeamish about heights.

The Balsams Hotel owns much of the property west of Dixville Notch and provides a trail guide for a number of hikes in the immediate area. The sign at the trailhead with the letter D corresponds to the listing in the hotel's guide. The hike begins reasonably enough as the trail rises above the highway

327

The Table Rock view of Dixville Notch, not for the faint of heart.

in short, steep bursts interspersed with an occasional wet spot. Later, it angles away from the road in a long, steep, steady climb running east to the top of the ridge that roughly parallels the notch. The grade eventually eases as the route swings back toward the highway, turns left at a signed trail junction, and descends sharply to the base of what looks like a short, rocky path. An alternate trail provides another means of access that is firmly NOT recommended, as it seems to drop over the edge to the right and ends in the heart of the notch. To reach your destination, proceed straight ahead and climb up about 20 feet.

Striding out onto Table Rock, it quickly becomes apparent that the trail is bound for the point of a narrow, 800-foot-high column of rock that extends 100 feet beyond the face of the cliff. Perhaps 20 feet across at its widest spot, the promontory narrows to less than 10 at its waist, and certainly does not exceed 4 feet in width by the time it reaches the tip. I readily admit that I did not actually walk to the point, although I did sort of crawl around and lie close to whatever felt solid.

The view from Table Rock is breathtaking. To the west, a resort hotel sits like a dollhouse behind Lake Gloriette with rolling alpine scenery extending to the far horizon. To the east, mountain masses frame the ribbon of highway that curves through the notch and disappears beneath your feet. Below, tall fir trees appear to extend only inches up the base of the cliff, and at your back you'll find scant comfort in the tops of more columns of rock. It all adds up to a precarious sense of being caught on the edge of the air. Sorry, but I really can't describe what's below you if you look straight down.

97 Fourth Connecticut Lake

General description: A short, international walk to the headwaters of the Connecticut River. Plan on one and a half hours round trip.

General location: At the northern terminus of U.S. Highway 3 on the Canadian border.

Length: A little over 1 mile round trip.

Difficulty: Moderate.

Elevation gain: 400 feet.

Special attractions: The headwaters of the Connecticut River, an international boundary, and possible wildlife viewing.

Maps: Maps available from the U.S. Customs Office at the trailhead; or USGS Second Connecticut Lake and Prospect Hill quads.

For more information: The Nature Conservancy, 2 1/2 Beacon Street, Suite 6, Concord, NH 03301, (603) 224-5853.

Key points:
- 0.2   End of steepest climb.
- 0.5   Left turn away from border.
- 0.6   Fourth Connecticut Lake.

Finding the trailhead: Travel north on U.S. Highway 3 to the Canadian border. Don't drive into Canada, but park across the highway from the U.S. Customs Office where you're obligated to check in. The people at customs maintain a hiker's register and assist with maps and regional information that may include hints on where the last moose was sighted. The trailhead is near a commemorative marker just behind U.S. Customs.

Fourth Conneticut Lake, gentle source of the Connecticut River.

Fourth Connecticut Lake

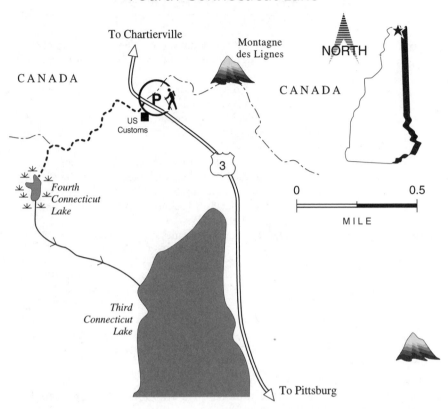

The hike: There aren't many New Hampshire hikes farther north than this one. The trail to the Fourth Connecticut Lake follows the erratic course of the United States/Canada border, a boundary established by the same 1842 treaty that squelched the local Indian Stream Republic, the ultimate attempt at Yankee independence. The logic that inscribed this irregular line along a watershed boundary is lost on hikers today, as the route weaves up and around rocky woodlands to the source of the Connecticut River.

No one could miss this unusual trail that's encased in a 35-yard security swath cleared through a fir-tree forest. Cutting has opened impressive views to neighboring mountains in Maine, New Hampshire, and Quebec and encouraged a profusion of wildflowers that make the most of the abundant sunlight. Moose and deer also leave their tracks along the length of this convenient corridor, as it meanders over a host of survey markers that periodically dot the trail. You'll definitely enhance your credentials as an international hiker as you repeatedly enter and leave the country on this short but adventurous route.

Within sight of the customs station, the first 0.2 mile of the walk is very steep and rough before the trail turns sharply left (southwest) and climbs moderately for the bulk of the journey to a boundary that marks the corner of Nature Conservancy land. As the grade levels, the path soon leads to a side trail on the left that descends a wooded slope about 300 yards to the lake. To find the turn, look for a Nature Conservancy sign, a directory sign to the "4th Conn Lake," and a rudimentary path presently blazed with blue tape. The hike continues to be more rugged than might be expected. During my visit, I encountered a number of blowdowns on this final segment of trail, but recent clearing may make your journey easier.

Fourth Connecticut Lake is a grandiose name for a small pond, but you'll not be disappointed by this remote pool encircled with marshes and countless acres of forest. At the end of the trail, the transition from woodland path to flowering fen is very abrupt indeed as you step off the edge of an evergreen-covered bank onto spongy peatland soil. Be careful to avoid the floating mat of delicate vegetation that surrounds the pond as you search for wildlife, investigate water-loving plants scattered throughout the bog, and gain a new perspective on this pristine habitat in the vast boreal woods. The memories you collect will be durable. Months later, crossing the mighty Connecticut River as it flows through southern New England, tranquil memories still take me back to this peaceful spot that gives the river birth.

98 Nash Stream, Sugarloaf Mountain Trail

General description: An afternoon's hike to a mountain peak with sweeping views of the Nash Stream watershed.
General location: About 20 miles northwest of Berlin midway between Groveton and Stark.
Length: 3.4 miles round trip.
Difficulty: Moderate.
Elevation gain: 2,100 feet.
Special attractions: A comprehensive overview of the Nash Stream Valley and wilderness vistas from one of the North Country's highest peaks.
Maps: USGS Percy Peaks quad.
For more information: New Hampshire Department of Resources and Economic Development, Division of Parks and Recreation, Trails Bureau, P.O. Box 1856, Concord, NH 03302, (603) 271-3254.

Key points:
0.1 Junction of snowmobile trails.
1.3 Cabin site.
1.7 Summit, Sugarloaf Mountain.

Finding the trailhead: The irregular arch of New Hampshire Route 110 runs generally east to west between Berlin and Groveton. Turn north from

Nash Stream, Sugarloaf Mountain Trail

Deserted cabins

Sugarloaf Mountain

Sugarloaf Mountain Trail

Brook

Cabin

P

NORTH

Nash Stream Road

Nash Stream

0   0.5   1

MILE

To Emerson Road and NH 110

this highway onto Emerson Road, 4.1 miles west of Stark, or 2.6 miles east of Groveton. This paved local road runs northeast toward the prominent Percy Peaks. After 2.1 miles, turn left onto the dirt Nash Stream Road that leads to a metal gate and sign at the entrance to the Nash Stream Forest. Stay on the

dirt road that parallels Nash Stream by bearing left at an intersection 4.5 miles past the gate, and cross the stream on a wooden bridge 3.1 miles later. The trailhead is on the left, about 100 yards past the bridge, adjacent to a cabin driveway.

The hike: Remember leveraged buyouts, corporate spinoffs, and divestitures? Nash Stream Forest is one positive result of those excessive boardroom activities. In the 1980s atmosphere of rapidly escalating real-estate values, vast tracts of wood-pulp forest in Maine and New Hampshire suddenly went on the auction block as expendable corporate surplus. Fortuitously, with the aid of the USDA Forest Service, the State of New Hampshire was able to salvage the immense Nash Stream tract and preserve for its traditional uses virtually the entire watershed of the Nash Stream Valley.

A visit to Nash Stream is reminiscent of travels to the Great North Woods of Maine that continue to be managed for wood pulp production and recreation. There's a certain bareness in the look of the gravel roads, the heavy thickets along the stony streams, and the many acres of sprout wood recovering from clear-cuts in the recent past. In spite of it all, this broad, flat valley exudes an enduring wildness in its bogs, brooks, and thousands of acres of uninhabited timberland. It's an area that's quickly mending itself for future generations.

One of the first improvements in this new state forest was the refurbishment of portions of the Sugarloaf Mountain Trail, saving it from oblivion after removal of the summit fire tower. The trail begins by heading up the driveway of a hunting cabin, passing through the front lawn, crossing a brook, and ducking past a metal gate. Enter the woods and bear right in the direction of Stratford Bog at a junction of snowmobile trails. What follows is a direct assault of the mountain's east slope along the persistently steep pitch of an old jeep road. The upward march continues stolidly straight ahead until reaching the site of an abandoned fire-warden cabin. Here the jeep road ends, views begin to open, and signs of moose and deer become increasingly abundant.

Having reached the cabin site, you've accomplished about 75 percent of the climb and expended as much as 90 percent of the total effort required. The hike becomes much more pleasurable as the trail enters a newly cleared swath and quickly attains the top of the ridge that radiates from the summit. The small, bare peak is easily reached by a pleasant walk that circles left following the crest of the ridge among fir, low spruce, and occasionally the sounds of moose that crash through the brush ahead.

Summit views look back to the bulging Percy Peaks at the opposite end of the valley and the Pilot Range that intervenes between you and the Presidential Peaks. Hikers who believe that the North Country world is flat will be surprised by this rugged region and enthralled with a first-hand inspection of Nash Stream's magnificent watershed. Lying below, cupped in the elongated sweep of encircling mountains, are the twists and turns of the road that traces the stream, numerous pale marshes, geometric patches of old logging cuts, and the random scarcity of evergreens that pepper the hardwood forest.

The walk back down the jeep path will reveal what kind of shape your knees are in and give you a chance to reflect on the special beauty of this wild corporate surplus.

99 Phillips Brook Backcountry Recreation Area

General description:	A northern-woodlands backpack trip to a comfortable hilltop shelter.
General location:	About 15 miles northwest of Berlin.
Length:	8.6 miles round trip.
Difficulty:	Moderate.
Elevation gain:	1,220 feet.
Special attractions:	Backcountry comfort, wildlife, and views of the Presidential Range.
Maps:	Maps and trail information are available at Paris Base; also USGS Dummer Ponds quad.
For more information:	Phillips Brook, P.O. Box 1076, Conway, NH 03818, 1-800-TRAILS-8 (872-4578).

Key points:

1.3 Junction, Big Bend Trail.
2.3 Junction, Long Mountain Col Trail.
3.2 Spur to Roberts Brook.
4.3 Long Mountain Yurt.

Finding the trailhead: From the junction of U.S. Highway 3 and New Hampshire Route 110 in Groveton, drive east on Route 110 for 6.7 miles to the village of Stark and its notable covered bridge. Continue east on Route 110 and turn left onto Paris Road 4.4 miles beyond Stark village. Cross a one-lane bridge over the Upper Ammonoosuc River, pass straight through a four-way intersection, and follow Paris Road when it bears right 2.1 miles from the highway. The Paris Base office of the Phillips Brook Backcountry Recreation Area is on the right 1.3 miles beyond the fork in the road.

The hike: Hike the trails at Phillips Brook, and you join an experiment. Operated on land leased from the International Paper Company, Timberland Trails, Inc. is the first business in the eastern United States to try to earn a profit by offering backcountry lodging on privately owned land. Spread across more than 24,000 acres of unspoiled watershed, several modern yurts and a classic waterfront lodge are connected by miles of multi-use trails that loop through a dense forest that still produces hardwood timber. Hikers, bikers, cross-country skiers, snowshoe plodders, and dog sled teams are welcome to use the trails. The only fee that is charged is for overnight use of accommodations.

The catch, of course, is that anyone who hikes these woodland trails will probably want to stay. East of Nash Stream State Forest (see Hike 98) and north of the White Mountains, the Phillips Brook Backcountry Recreation Area is pocked with small ponds and tracked by abundant streams. The low

Phillips Brook Backcountry Recreation Area

ridges and small summits of this boreal forest region are perfect for backcountry rambles and provide excellent cover for abundant wildlife. Along with views of the Presidential Peaks from the deck of a cozy yurt, I spotted a moose and four bears just as I was driving to the trailhead.

Stop at the office at Paris Base whether you're staying overnight or not. Numerous trails branch off the 10-mile gravel road that connects Paris Base with a gracious two-story log lodge on the shore of Phillips Pond. You can skim the heights of Dummer Ridge, climb to a fire tower, or track a secluded stream on routes that lead past well-equipped yurts overlooking a mountain or pond. The friendly staff at Paris Base will be happy to explain your options, supply you with local maps, and provide valuable information on current trail conditions.

After a quick briefing (and a detour to a waterfall just a few strides from the base), I chose the Roberts Brook Trail that swings southwest on easy terrain and climbs to a yurt with priceless views near the top of Long Mountain. From Paris Base, drive 3.2 miles north to the Jodrey Brook, Long Mountain, and Roberts Brook Trailheads at what looks like a fork in the road. Turn left and cross the brook. Just be sure to park well off the traveled portion of these active gravel lanes and far away from the one-lane bridge that still carries logging trucks.

Beginning on a rise just a few yards beyond the one-lane bridge, the Roberts Brook Trail turns south on a four-wheel-drive track, a high-speed hiking corridor that slices through dense woodlands and parallels Phillips Brook. Flagged with yellow blazes, the trail oscillates up and down over gently rolling terrain, turns west away from the stream, and passes the Big Bend Trail that enters on the left after 1.3 miles.

Long Mountain rises in the middle distance as the narrowing track passes the Long Mountain Col Trail that veers off to the right near the halfway point of the outbound hike. I was ambushed by a flock of partridge that exploded from a small knoll just before the trail sagged down to span a wooden bridge across an unnamed stream, climbed a long gradual hill, and descended the other side. Ignore an unused road that branches to the left and discovers Roberts Brook. Turn right, instead, at the base of the long hill, follow the trail with yellow flags, and begin the climb of Long Mountain Ridge that rises dead ahead.

No longer resembling a road, the path stumbles through a dry streambed that edges onto the trail and then follows a swath of beaten-down grass as it passes Loggers Rock and swings up to Coyote Knob. Continuing steeply uphill for another 0.5 mile, the trail finally breaks out into a large, ragged clearing about 200 yards below the crest of the ridge. Look to your left and work your way through low brush and stubble toward the round canvas yurt that waits near the upper corner of the far side of the clearing.

Phillips Brook's modern version of a nomad's hut offers fine, four-season shelter. Inside the spacious canvas yurt, six bunks with sleeping pads, a

The Long Mountain Yurt with Presidential views.

dining table with wooden chairs, pots, pans, plates, and utensils are warmed by a wood-burning stove. You'll even find gas lights, a jug of water, and a gas stove for cooking. But the best part of the Long Mountain Yurt is just outside the door. Peaceful and sunny on a south-facing slope, a deck with wooden benches surveys an alpine scene that should convince you to stay. While you nibble a snack or work on a tan, a breathtaking panorama of the full Presidential Range hovers above the trees. Relaxing in total comfort, you can spot New Hampshire's highest peaks in the center of your field of vision, flanked to the east by the rounded mounds of the Carter and Mahoosuc Mountains and flanked to the west by Mount Waumbek and the nearby Pilot Range.

100 Scotland Brook

General description:	A short nature walk through the fields and forests of beautiful Sugar Hill.
General location:	About 12 miles south of Littleton and 10 miles west of Franconia Notch.
Length:	1.75 miles.
Difficulty:	Easy.
Elevation gain:	100 feet.
Special attractions:	Diverse habitats with large inventories of wildflowers, ferns, birds, and wildlife.
Maps:	USGS Sugar Hill quad; a trail guide is also available from a mailbox at the trailhead or from the address below.
For more information:	The Audubon Society of New Hampshire, 3 Silk Farm Road, Concord, NH 03301-8200, (603) 224-9909.

Key points:

0.6   Edge of marsh, start of Birches Loop.
0.9   Second crossing of stone wall.
1.15   Return to edge of marsh.
1.75   Return to trailhead.

Finding the trailhead: Take U.S. Highway 302 west from its intersection with Interstate 93 at exit 42. After about 7 miles turn left onto New Hampshire Route 117, continue southeast for 4.9 miles, and turn sharply right onto Pearl Lake Road in the town of Sugar Hill. This local road passes several lovely homes in gorgeous alpine meadows that are reason enough for the journey to Scotland Brook. After 4 miles, Pearl Lake Road turns sharply left around the lake and reaches a T intersection with a dirt road about 2 miles farther along. Turn left onto the dirt road. The trailhead is on the right, just past the old Scotland School.

Scotland Brook

To Sugar Hill

Pond Hill

Pearl Lake

NORTH

0   0.25   0.5

MILE

Pearl Lake Road

To Landaff

Jim Noyes Hill Road

Scotland Brook

Scotland School (private)

P

The hike: The Scotland Brook Wildlife Sanctuary lies amid rolling hilltops and scattered peaks in the western foothills of the White Mountains. Two hundred years ago, Scotch and Irish settlers cleared this undulating land, creating pastures and high mountain meadows with a European feel that continues to exist today. By now the forest has nullified most of their efforts, but the history of settlement, reclamation, and reforestation can still be read by those who visit the area.

Given this history, it's fitting that the trail at Scotland Brook begins in a field of sprout wood that is rapidly reclaiming an area cut in the continuing struggle to hold back the forest. Today, though, clearing is not to support sheep or cattle, but to preserve a diversity of habitats within the sanctuary. Evidently, the strategy works. Moose, bears, deer, bobcats, porcupines, skunks, a wide array of birds, ten types of orchids, and fourteen varieties of ferns can be counted within the mix.

From a cleared section near the parking area, the trail bears left parallel to the road and quickly becomes a grassy path through a field scattered with young spruce trees and poplar and maple saplings. At the first junction, the Scotland Brook Trail (straight ahead) forms a loop through a stand of evergreens, crosses the brook twice, and passes examples of most of the varieties of fern found within the sanctuary. Turn right, instead, following orange stripe markers and the main trail that continues to skirt the edge of the same clearing that you faced back at the trailhead. Circling this sprout-wood field, the boggy path encounters patchwork evidence of the history of this land, passing immature hardwoods, rusting fence, and parcels of pasture pine.

After 0.3 mile or so, the ground rises enough to dry out your boots but descends in another 0.3 mile to meet a beaver pond/marsh at the junction with the Birches Loop. The outlook near this junction provides a good opportunity to scan the marsh for beaver activity or to spot a few of the many bird species that frequent this wetland environment.

Turn right in the direction of a low ridge to begin the Birches Loop, which completes the far end of the trail. The wooded course passes in and out of former sheep meadows, dips through a wet area, and finally climbs to cross a stone wall just below the top of the ridge. You're now on a woods road crossing private land that has been heavily logged for pine. Stay on the road as it follows a course parallel to the boundary wall.

The trail eventually re-crosses into the sanctuary at the end of the ridge, descends through a large grove of birch, and meets a more intricate stone wall that separates woodland from marsh. Skimming along the edge of the extensive wetlands, the Birches Loop returns to the junction near the overlook of the marsh. Take a second chance to scan for wildlife before continuing straight ahead and retracing your steps back to your car at the trailhead.

Appendix A

Forest Supervisor
White Mountain National Forest
719 Main Street
Laconia, NH 03246
603-528-8721

Ammonoosuc Ranger Station
660 Trudeau Road
Bethlehem, NH 03574
603-869-2626

Androscoggin Ranger Station
300 Glen Road
Gorham, NH 03581-1399
603-466-2713

Evans Notch Ranger Station
18 Mayville Road
Bethel, ME 04217-4400
207-824-2134

Pemigewasset Ranger Station
RR #3, Box 15, Route 175
Plymouth, NH 03264
603-536-1315

Saco Ranger Station
33 Kancamagus Highway
Conway, NH 03818
603-447-2166

Appendix B

TRAIL RATINGS AND EQUIPMENT

On walks rated "easy" within this guide, stout footwear is the only special equipment you'll need for safe enjoyment of your hike. These trails are generally short and gentle. Little of serious consequence is likely to result should a sprained ankle or sudden squall make hiking uncomfortable. Still, a rain jacket/ windbreaker and small water bottle are not much to carry, and there are times on even these routes when insect repellent would also be welcome.

Hikes rated "moderate" cover a very wide spectrum. For all trails at this level, rain protection, drinking water, and seasonal bug dope are minimum requirements. As distances and elevation gains marginally increase, the list should naturally expand by adding a small day-pack holding lunch, trail snacks, and a light wool sweater as elementary preparation for comfortable hiking.

Be alert to the fact that many of the moderate hikes described in this guide cross over the line where such elementary preparation is no longer adequate. Misfortune can strike on a half-mile hike, but my personal rule of thumb is to carry a full complement of day-hiking gear when the round-trip distance exceeds 3 miles or the elevation gain nudges 1,200 feet. On unusually steep or isolated routes, I ignore this rule, and my pack always goes with me. Your walking speed, ability, and comfort level may differ, but experience tells me that beyond these limits, travel is too rugged or remote to risk being unprepared should the unexpected happen.

On extended day hikes throughout the state, and on all but the shortest roadside trails in the White Mountain Region, I know I'm prepared if my pack holds the following:

- ☐ Hooded rain jacket
- ☐ Rain pants
- ☐ Waterproof pack cover
- ☐ Wool sweater
- ☐ Fleece jacket (optional in mid-summer outside the Presidential Peaks)
- ☐ Extra T-shirt
- ☐ Light long-sleeved shirt
- ☐ Wool hat
- ☐ Wool mittens
- ☐ Lunch (or enough trail snack to make a meal if necessary)

- ☐ Map
- ☐ Guidebook
- ☐ Compass
- ☐ Multi-function knife
- ☐ Two 1-quart plastic water bottles
- ☐ Toilet paper
- ☐ Insect repellent
- ☐ Waterproof matches
- ☐ Small flashlight
- ☐ First-aid kit

The first-aid kit need not be elaborate. Mine is strictly homemade: a small, waterproof, plastic box that houses a collection of bandages from small to large, butterfly-type tape, gauze, antibacterial ointment, elastic bandage, personal medications, and aspirin (or acetaminophen for children). For good measure, I also throw in a feather-light, emergency thermal blanket, matches, candle, sunscreen, lip balm, and a first-aid chart for anyone who may not know what she or he is doing.

All of this equipment fits a moderate-sized pack and leaves plenty of room for binoculars, cameras, or other good stuff you may like to carry. It's also insurance that a wrong turn or sudden cold rain will amount to nothing more than a minor inconvenience.

Note the emphasis on wool in the list of standby clothing. It bears repeating that wool will help you stay warm, even when wet. Avoid cotton, most especially blue jeans, because it will not. If you need to cover up, choose wool or synthetics.

Note also the presence of map and compass as standard equipment for extended hikes. Most New Hampshire trails are clearly marked and well maintained. Still, trail signs can be lost or damaged, fog and bad weather may obscure your route, and the best of hikers can confuse their position. Even a minimal ability to orient yourself with map and compass can bail you out of these dicey situations.

Preparation also requires that you know the dangers of hiking alone. We all know we shouldn't, but sometimes aesthetics compel that we do. The dangers are real. The decision is yours. If you still choose to venture out by yourself, good preparation demands at a minimum that you follow a hiking plan and file it with someone who will know and care if you haven't turned up and are overdue.

Finally, don't get hung up in concerns with clothing and equipment and forget to prepare your body and mind. Safe hiking demands that you be mentally able to recognize your own physical limitations. Most of us would never consider balancing on the edge of a precipice, yet many people haul their exhausted bodies to the harsh environment of a mountain peak. The need for a margin of safety is the same. Exhaustion weakens the muscles and dulls the mind. It's also not a lot of fun. If you are not in good shape, skim through this guide and find any one of dozens of great walks through beautiful natural environments that are easily within your current abilities. You'll have more fun and before long be prepared for a day when your hiking horizons may grandly expand.

Index

Page numbers in *italic* type refer to photographs.
Page numbers in **bold** type refer to maps.

A

Adams, Mount *273, 279, 286, 288,* 289–93
Adirondack-style shelters 15
Air Line, Short Line, and King Ravine Trails hike, King Ravine 270–74, **271,** *273, 274*
Algonquin Trail hike, Sandwich Mountain 149–52, **150,** *151*
Alton Bay 120–22
Ammonoosuc Ravine Trail hike, Mount Washington 294–98, **295,** *296*
Andover 97–100
Andrew Brook Trail hike, Mount Sunapee 101–3, **102,** *103*
Appalachian Mountain Club huts 14–15
Arethusa Falls Trail hike 189–93, **190,** *191*
Artists Bluff *173*
Asquam Ridge Loop hike, Gorge Brook 165–67, **166**
Avalanche Falls *170*

B

Baldface Circle Trail hike 312–16, **313,** *316*
Baldface Shelter 315
Bald Mountain 57–60
Bartlett 189–93, 207–11
Bear Brook State Park, Catamount Trail hike 36–39, **37,** *38*
bears, black 8
Belknap Mountain, Red Trail hike 128–30, **129**
Berlin 204–7, 260–63, 284–88, 294–98, 298–302, 306–8, 309–12, 312–16, 320–23, 326–28, 331–33, 334–37
black bears 8
black flies 7
Black Mountain and Guinea Pond Trails hike 152–56, **153,** *155*
Blue Brook Shelter 319
Blue Job Mountain hike 18–21, **19,** *20*

Blue Job Tower *20*
Bondcliff and Gale River Trails hike 219–23, **220,** *222*
Boott Spur and Davis Path hike, Mount Washington 298–302, **299**
Boulder Field Trail hike, Pawtuckaway State Park 44–46, **45,** *46*
Bretton Woods 223–26, 260–63, 294–98
Brooks Trail hike, Urban Forestry Center 30–32, **31**
bugs 7–8
bunchberry *16*

C

Camp Rich 125
Cannon Mountain, Kinsman Ridge Trail hike 171–73, **172,** *173*
Caps Ridge Trail hike, Mount Jefferson 260–63, **261,** *263*
Cardigan, Mount
   Manning Trail hike **105,** 108–9
   West Ridge Trail hike 104–7, **105,** *107*
Carrigain, Mount, Signal Ridge Trail hike 193–95, **194,** *195*
Carrigain Notch *195*
Carter Lake *311*
Carter-Moriah Trail hike 306–8, **307**
Carter Notch *311*
Carter Range 303–19
Cascade Path hike 147–49, **148**
Catamount Trail hike, Bear Brook State Park 36–39, **37,** *38*
Champney Brook Trail hike, Mount Chocorua 234–36, **235**
Champney Falls 236
Cherry Mountain Trail hike 264–66, **265**
children, hiking with 12–13
Chocorua, Mount *9*
Champney Brook Trail hike 234–36, **235**
   Liberty Trail hike 110–13, **111,** *112*
Claremont 89–90, 94–97
Clay, Mount *198,* 289–93

Clinton, Mount 293
Cloudland Falls 177
Cold River Campground 319
Concord 33–35, 36–39, 79–82, 82–85,
    85–88, 89–90, 94–97, 97–100,
    101–3
Connecticut River 329–31
Conway 110–13, 136–38, 234–36,
    240–43, 243–44
Crag Camp *276, 277, 278,* 293
Crawford, Abel 198
Crawford, Ethan Allen 198
Crawford Depot *210*
Crawford House 198
Crawford Notch 189–215, 289–93,
    294–98
Crawford Path *269*
Crawford Path, Mizpah Spring Loop
    hike 196–200, **197,** *198, 199*
Cricenti-Philbrick Bog hike 90–93, **91,**
    92
Crotched Mountain hike 54–57, **55**

D
Dartmouth/Lake Sunapee Region 79–
    103
Davis Path, Rocky Branch, Isolation
    Trail Loop hike 204–7, **205**
Davis Path and Boott Spur hike, Mount
    Washington 298–302, **299**
deer ticks 8
DePierrefeu-Willard Pond Wildlife
    Sanctuary hike 57–60, **58,** *59*
Derry 39–41
Desolation Shelter 203, 232
Diana's Baths *256,* 257
Dicey's Mill Trail hike, Mount
    Passaconaway 122–25, **123**
Dickey and Welch Mountains hike
    158–61, **159,** *161*
disabilities, hikes for persons with 13–
    14
Dixville Notch, Table Rock hike 326–
    28, **327,** *328*
Dry River, Mount Isolation hike 207–
    11, **208,** *210*

E
Echo Lake *173*
Edmands, J. Rayner 278
Edmands Col, Lowe's Path, the Gray
    Knob Trail, and the Randolph Path
    hike **271,** 275–79, *276, 278, 279*
Edmands Path hike 267–70, **268,** *269*

Eisenhower, Mount *198,* 293
Ethan Pond Trail hike 216–19, **217**

F
families, hiking for 12–13
Firescrew *107,* 108–9
Fitzwilliam 74–76
flies, black 7
Flume, Mount/Mount Liberty, Liberty
    Spring Trail hike 177–80, **178,** *179*
Flume hike 168–71, **169,** *170*
Forest Protection Areas 9–10
Fourth Connecticut Lake hike *329,*
    329–31, **330**
Fox State Forest, Ridge Trail hike 79–
    82, **80**
Franconia Brook and Lincoln Brook
    Trails hike 227–30, **228**
Franconia Brook Campsites 227–28,
    232
Franconia Notch 168–88, 219–23,
    337–39
Franconia Notch Parkway *173*
Franconia Ridge 174–77, *179*
Franklin 108–9, 117–19
Franklin, Mount 293
Frost, Robert 40

G
Galehead Hut 221
Gale River and Bondcliff Trails hike
    219–23, **220,** *222*
garbage 8–9
"Garden for the Senses" 31
Giardia lamblia 8
Gilford 128–30
Glen 204–7, 216–19
Glencliff Trail hike 163–65, **164**
Goffstown 50–53
Gorge Brook, Asquam Ridge Loop hike
    165–67, **166**
Gorham 270–74, 275–79, 279–83,
    304–6, 306–8, 317–19, 324–25
Gray Knob cabin 277, 293
Gray Knob Trail, the Randolph Path,
    Edmands Col, and Lowe's Path
    hike **271,** 275–79, *276, 278, 279*
Great Bay Estuarine Reserve hike 21–
    24, *22,* **23**
Great Bay National Wildlife Refuge
    hike 25–27, **26**
Great Gulf *263*
Great Gulf Trail, Spaulding Lake hike
    284–88, **285,** *286, 288*

Greeley Ponds and Mount Osceola hike 143–47, **144,** *146*
Greenfield 54–57
Greenleaf Hut 176
Groveton 331–33
Guay, Napoleon 40
Guinea and Black Mountain Pond Trails hike 152–56, **153,** *155*
Guyot Campsite 222

H
Hale, Mount, Zealand Loop hike 223–26, **224,** *226*
Halfway Brook *116*
Hancock 57–60, 60–63
Hancock Notch Trail, Hancock Loop hike 237–40, **238**
Hanover 104–7
Harris Center for Conservation Education, Harriskat Trail hike 60–63, **61**
Hay, John M. 84
Hebron Marsh and Paradise Point hike 117–19, **118**
Hermit Lake Shelter 301–2
Hiker Shuttle 15
Hillsborough 79–82
Holderness 126–28, 130–33
huts 14–15
Hyla Brook Nature/Poetry Trail hike 39–41, **40**
hypothermia 5, 7

I
Imp Trail Loop hike 304–6, **305**
Indian Head 186–88
Indian Stream Republic 330
insects 7–8
Isolation, Mount, Dry River hike 207–11, **208,** *210*
Isolation Trail Loop hike, Rocky Branch, Davis Path 204–7, **205**

J
Jackson-Webster Trail hike 213–15, **214**
Jefferson 264–66, 324–25
Jefferson, Mount *198,* 289–93
Jefferson, Mount, Caps Ridge Trail hike 260–63, **261,** *263*
Jim Liberty Cabin 113
John Hay National Wildlife Refuge hike 82–85, **83**

K
Kancamagus Highway 234–44
Kearsarge, Mount
    Rollins Trail hike 85–88, *86,* **87**
    Winslow Trail hike **87,** 89–90
Kearsarge, Mount, North, hike 248–51, **249,** *250*
Kearsarge North fire tower *250,* 251
Keene 54–57, 57–60, 60–63, 63–66, 66–68, 68–70, 71–73, 74–76, 79–82
Kilburn Loop hike, Pisgah State Park 71–73, **72,** *73*
King Ravine: The Air Line, Short Line, and King Ravine Trails hike 270–74, **271,** *273, 274*
Kinsman Peaks and Lonesome Lake hike 181–84, **182**
Kinsman Ridge Trail hike, Cannon Mountain 171–73, **172,** *173*

L
Laconia 114–17, 120–22, 128–30
Lafayette, Mount/Mount Lincoln Bridle Path Loop hike 174–77, **175**
Lafayette Campground 183
Lakes of the Clouds Hut *14,* 263, 291, *292, 293,* 298
Lakes Region 104–38
Lake Sunapee/Dartmouth Region 79–103
Lebanon 104–7
Liberty, Jim 112
Liberty, Mount/Mount Flume, Liberty Spring Trail hike 177–80, **178,** *179*
Liberty Cabin *9*
Liberty Spring Trail hike, Mount Liberty/Mount Flume 177–80, **178,** *179*
Liberty Trail hike, Mount Chocorua 110–13, **111,** *112*
lightning 7
Lincoln 165–67, 171–73, 227–30, 230–33, 237–40
Lincoln, Mount *179*
Lincoln, Mount/Mount Lafayette Bridle Path Loop hike 174–77, **175**
Lincoln Brook and Franconia Brook Trails hike 227–30, **228**
Lincoln Woods 230–33
Little Harbor 27–30

Littleton 171–73, 174–77, 337–39
Livermore Road hike, Mount
    Tripyramid 140–43, **141**
Log Cabin 277, 293
Lonesome Lake and Kinsman Peaks
    hike 181–84, **182**
Lonesome Lake Hut 183
Long Mountain Yurt *336*, 336–37
Loon Center at the Markus Wildlife
    Sanctuary hike 114–17, **115**, *116*
Lowe's Path, the Gray Knob Trail, the
    Randolph Path, and Edmands Col
    hike **271**, 275–79, *276, 278, 279*

M

Madison, Mount *273, 279, 288, 289*,
    289–93
Madison, Mount, Valley Way Trail hike
    279–83, **280**, *281, 282*
Madison Spring Hut *273, 274*, 281,
    282, 283, 291
Major, Mount, hike *120*, 120–22, **121**
Manchester 36–39, 39–41, 44–46, 47–
    49, 50–53, 54–57
Manning Trail hike, Mount Cardigan
    105, 108–9
Markus Wildlife Sanctuary Loon
    Center hike 114–17, **115**, *116*
Merrimack River 36–39
Merrimack Valley 33–53
Miller State Park 70
Mill Pond *96*
Mine Falls Park, Nashua River Trail
    hike 41–43, **42**
Mizpah Spring Hut 199, 210, 293
Mizpah Spring Loop hike, Crawford
    Path 196–200, **197**, *198, 199*
Monadnock, Mount *4*
    Pumpelly Trail hike 63–66, **64**
    White Cross Trail hike **64**, 66–68, *67*
Monadnock Region 54–78
Monadnock-Sunapee Greenway hike,
    Pillsbury State Park 94–97, **95**, *96*
Monroe, Mount *269*, 289–93, 293
Montalban Ridge 204–7
moose 8
Moosilauke, Mount *162*, 162–67
Moriah-Carter Trail hike 306–8, **307**
mosquitoes 7–8
Moultonborough 114–17
Mountain Pond Trail hike 251–54,
    252, *253*
Mount Washington Hotel *199*
Mud Pond Bog 81

N

Nancy Pond Trail hike 200–203, **201**,
    202, 203
Nash Stream, Sugarloaf Mountain Trail
    hike 331–33, **332**
Nashua 41–43, 63–66, 66–68, 68–70,
    76–78
Nashua River Trail hike, Mine Falls
    Park 41–43, **42**
Newbury 82–85, 101–3
Newfound Lake 108–9, 117–19
New London 90–93
Nineteen Mile Brook Trail hike 309–
    12, **310**, *311*
Norcross Pond *202*
North and South Doublehead, The Old
    Path, Ski Trail hike 245–48, **246**,
    247
North Baldface Mountain *316*
North Conway 196–200, 200–203,
    213–15, 245–59, 260–63, 267–70,
    284–88, 294–98, 298–302, 312–16
North Country 326–42
North Doublehead *247*
North Moat Mountain hike 254–59,
    255, *256, 258*
North Woodstock 165–67, 174–77,
    227–30, 230–33, 237–40
No-Trace camping 10, 11

O

Odiorne Point State Park hike 27–30,
    28, *29*
Old Man and Profile Lake hike 184–
    86, **185**, *186*
Old Path and Ski Trail hike, North and
    South Doublehead 245–48, **246**,
    247
Osceola, Mount, and Greeley Ponds
    hike 143–47, **144**, *146*
Owl Cliff *242*
Owl's Head Mountain 227–30

P

Pack Monadnock, Wapack Trail hike
    68–70, **69**
Paradise Point and Hebron Marsh hike
    117–19, **118**
parking fees 10
Passaconaway, Mount, Dicey's Mill
    Trail hike 122–25, **123**
Pawtuckaway State Park
    Boulder Field Trail hike 44–46, **45**, *46*
    South Mountain Loop hike 47–49, **48**

Peak House 112
Pease Air Force Base 25
Pemigewasset, Mount, hike 186–88, **187**
Pemigewasset River 168–71
Pemigewasset Traverse hike 230–33, **231**, *233*
Pemigewasset Wilderness and Zealand Notch *203*, 216–33
Pequawket, Mount 250
Perch 278, 293
Philbrick-Cricenti Bog hike 90–93, **91**, *92*
Phillips Brook Backcountry Recreation Area hike 334–37, **335**, *336*
physically challenged, hikes for the 13–14
Pillsbury State Park, Monadnock-Sunapee Greenway hike 94–97, **95**, *96*
Pilot Range 320–25
Pinkham Notch 284–88, 304–6, 309–12
Pisgah State Park, Kilburn Loop hike 71–73, **72**, *73*
plants 17
Plymouth 117–19, 122–25, 133–36, 140–43, 143–47, 147–49, 149–52, 152–56, 156–58, 158–61, 163–65, 177–80
Portsmouth 21–24, 25–27, 27–30, 30–32, 44–46, 47–49
Presidential Peaks 260–302, *303*
Presidential Range-Dry River Wilderness 207–11
Presidential Traverse hike 289–93, **290**, *292*, *293*
Profile Lake and Old Man hike 184–86, **185**, *186*
Pumpelly Trail hike, Mount Monadnock 63–66, **64**

R
Ragged Mountain hike 97–100, **98**
Randolph 289–93
Randolph Path, Edmands Col, Lowe's Path, and the Gray Knob Trail hike **271**, 275–79, *276*, *278*, *279*
Red Ridge *258*
rhododendron *12*
Rhododendron State Park hike *74*, 74–76, **75**
Ridge Trail hike, Fox State Forest 79–82, **80**

Ripley Falls 218
Robert Frost Farm 40
Rochester 18–21
Rocky Branch, Davis Path, Isolation Trail Loop hike 204–7, **205**
Rocky Branch Shelter No. 1 204
Rocky Branch Shelter No. 2 207
Rogers Ledge and Unknown Pond hike 320–23, **321**, *323*
Rollins State Park 85
Rollins Trail hike, Mount Kearsarge 85–88, *86*, **87**
Round Pond *46*
Rye 27–30

S
Sabbaday Falls hike 243–44, **244**
Sandwich Mountain, Algonquin Trail hike 149–52, **150**, *151*
Sandwich Range *2*, *151*
Sawyer Pond Trail hike 240–43, **241**, *242*
Scotland Brook hike 337–39, **338**
Scotland Brook Wildlife Sanctuary 338–39
Seacoast Region 18–32
Seacoast Science Center 28–29
Sheldrick Forest hike 76–78, **77**
shelters, Adirondack-style 15
Shoal Pond *233*
Short Line, King Ravine, and Air Line Trails hike, King Ravine 270–74, **271**, *273*, *274*
Signal Ridge Trail hike, Mount Carrigain 193–95, **194**, *195*
Silk Farm Wildlife Sanctuary hike 33–35, **34**
Ski Trail and The Old Path hike, North and South Doublehead 245–48, **246**, *247*
Solitude, Lake *103*
South and North Doublehead, The Old Path, Ski Trail hike 245–48, **246**, *247*
South Mountain Loop hike, Pawtuckaway State Park 47–49, **48**
Spaulding Lake hike, Great Gulf Trail 284–88, **285**, *286*, *288*
Squam Lake 130–33, *132*
Squam Lakes Natural Science Center hike 126–28, **127**
Stark 331–33
Star Lake *281*, *289*

Starr King, Mount/Mount Waumbeck
hike 324–25, **325**
Stinson Lake 133–36
Strafford 18–21
Sugarloaf Mountain Trail hike, Nash
Stream 331–33, **332**
Sunapee, Lake 82–85, 101–3
Sunapee, Mount, Andrew Brook Trail
hike 101–3, **102**, *103*

T
Table Rock, Dixville Notch hike 326–
28, **327**, *328*
Tamworth 136–38
Tecumseh, Mount, hike 156–58, **157**
tent platforms 15
13 Falls 229
Thoreau Falls 219, 233
Three Ponds Trail hike 133–36, **134**
thunderstorms 7
ticks, deer 8
Timberland Trails, Inc. 334
trash 8–9
trees 17
Tripyramid, Mount, Livermore Road
hike 140–43, **141**
Twin Mountain 189–93, 196–200,
200–203, 207–11, 211–13, 213–15,
216–19, 219–23, 223–26, 264–66,
267–70

U
Uncanoonuc, North Peak hike 50–53,
51, *52*
Unknown Pond and Rogers Ledge hike
320–23, **321**, *323*
Upper Greeley Pond *146*
Urban Forestry Center, Brooks Trail
hike 30–32, **31**

V
Valley of the Giants 78
Valley Way Trail hike, Mount Madison
279–83, **280**, *281, 282*

W
Wapack Trail hike, Pack Monadnock
68–70, **69**
Warner 85–88
Washington, Mount *112, 198, 263,*
289–93
Ammonoosuc Ravine Trail hike
294–98, **295**, *296*
Boott Spur and Davis Path hike
298–302, **299**

Waterville Valley 139–61
Waumbeck, Mount/Mount Starr King
hike 324–25, **325**
weather 5, 7
Webster-Jackson Trail hike 213–15,
214
Welch and Dickey Mountains hike
158–61, **159**, *161*
Welch Mountain *161*
West Ossipee 136–38
West Rattlesnake hike 130–33, **131**,
132
West Ridge Trail hike, Mount Cardigan
104–7, **105**, *107*
White Cross Trail hike, Mount
Monadnock **64**, 66–68, *67*
White Lake State Park hike 136–38,
137
White Mountains
Carter Range 303–19
Crawford Notch 189–215
Franconia Notch 168–88
Kancamagus Highway 234–44
Mount Moosilauke 162–67
North Conway 245–59
Pemigewasset Wilderness 216–33
Pilot Range 320–25
Presidential Peaks 260–302
Waterville Valley 139–61
Zealand Notch 216–33
Wilderness Areas 9
wildlife 8, 15, 17
Wild River Campground 319
Wild River hike 317–19, **318**
Willard, Mount, hike 211–13, **212**
Willard Pond-DePierrefeu Wildlife
Sanctuary hike 57–60, **58**, *59*
Wilmot 89–90
Winnipesaukee, Lake 114–17, *120,*
120–22
Winslow, John A. 89
Winslow State Park 89
Winslow Trail hike, Mount Kearsarge
87, 89–90
Wonalancet 122–25

Z
Zealand Falls 226
Zealand Hut 222, 226
Zealand Loop hike, Mount Hale 223–
26, **224**, *226*
Zealand Notch and Pemigewasset
Wilderness 216–33

About the Author

Larry Pletcher first acquired a taste for backcountry hiking during weekend escapes to the Sierra Nevada while a student in California. Returning east in 1973, the mountains, forests, and quality of life in the Granite State made New Hampshire his home of choice, where Larry combined a professional career with outdoor photography, freelance writing, and avid exploration. Whether bagging New Hampshire's forty-eight 4,000-foot peaks, rambling through the woods near his home in Warner, hiking with children to White Mountain huts, or canoeing with his family, Larry amassed innumerable miles of backcountry travel throughout New England and eastern Canada. After twenty-five years of New Hampshire hiking, camping, canoeing, and climbing, the author was delighted to revisit the trails in this guide and recount them in these pages as old, familiar friends.

American
Hiking
Society

American Hiking Society is the only national nonprofit organization dedicated to establishing, protecting and maintaining foot trails in America.

Establishing...

American Hiking Society establishes hiking trails with the AHS National Trails Endowment, providing grants for grassroots organizations to purchase trail lands, construct and maintain trails, and preserve hiking trails' scenic values. The AHS affiliate club program, called the Congress of Hiking Organizations, brings trail clubs together to share information, collaborate on public policy, and advocate legislation and policies that protect hiking trails.

Protecting...

American Hiking Society protects hiking trails through highly focused public policy efforts in the nation's capital. AHS affects federal legislation, shapes public lands policy, collaborates with grassroots trail organizations, and partners with federal land managers to protect the hiking experience. Members become active with letter-writing campaigns and by attending the annual AHS Trails Advocacy Week.

Maintaining...

American Hiking Society maintains hiking trails by sending volunteers to national parks, forests and recreation lands; organizing volunteer teams to help affiliated hiking clubs; and publishing national volunteer directories. AHS members get involved, get dirty and get inspired by participating in AHS programs like National Trails Day, America's largest celebration of the outdoors; and Volunteer Vacations—week-long work trips to beautiful, wild places.

Join American Hiking Society...

Be a part of the organization dedicated to protecting and preserving the nation's footpaths, our footpaths, the ones in our backyards and our backcountry. Visit American Hiking Society's website or call to find out more about membership. When you join, Falcon Publishing will send you a FREE guide as a special thank you for contributing to the efforts of American Hiking Society.

American Hiking Society
1422 Fenwick Lane
Silver Spring, MD 20910
OR CALL: (888) 766-HIKE ext. 1
OR VISIT: www.americanhiking.org